WIN MORE, TRADE BETTER - A Practical Guide to Trading and Investing

Andy Hai Dinh

Published by Andy Hai Dinh, 2025.

WIN MORE, TRADE BETTER - A PRACTICAL GUIDE TO TRADING AND INVESTING

First edition. March 9, 2025.

ISBN: 979-8230501367

Written by Andy Hai Dinh.

Also by Andy Hai Dinh

ACRYLIC AND DIPPING POWDER - Product Knowledge and Applications
The Nail technician's Career Guide
A Beginner's Guide to Trading - Stock and Forex Technical Analysis
WIN MORE, TRADE BETTER - A Practical Guide to Trading and Investing

Watch for more at https://pensight.com/x/lona.

Table of Contents

WIN MORE, TRADE BETTER - A Practical Guide to Trading and Investing....1

Dedication....2

Introduction....3

Chapter 1: Price Action Trading In A Nutshell....4

Chapter 2: Introduction To Trading....11

Chapter 3: How Markets Work....40

Chapter 4: Charting Essentials....69

Chapter 5: Indicators....101

Chapter 6: The Art Of Calculated Risk....134

Chapter 7: Chart Patterns Explained....168

Chapter 8: Best Losers Win....242

Chapter 9: Dopamine Battles....262

Chapter 10: Beginner Strategies....275

Chapter 11: Pro Strategies....295

Chapter 12: Guide To Trading Platforms....312

Chapter 13: Stocks 101....323

Chapter 14: Crypto....344

Chapter 15: Forex....352

Chapter 16: Commodities....364

Chapter 17: Taxes....375

WIN MORE, TRADE BETTER - A Practical Guide to Trading and Investing

Dedication

To my incredible children, Audrey and Neal -

May you always approach life with curiosity, resilience, and the confidence to pursue your dreams. Just as in trading and investing, may you embrace challenges as opportunities, learn from every experience, and never stop growing.

Everything I do is with you in mind, and this book is no exception. I hope it inspires you to think boldly, act wisely, and always believe in the power of perseverance.

With all my love,

Andy Hai Dinh

Introduction

This book is for those who prefer action over reading lengthy instruction manuals. After some years as a student of Technical Analysis and a part-time trader, I've felt a need to compile much of the must-know knowledge into a comprehensive guide for myself and for other people who want to learn about trading and investing.

Let's be real: you can't master trading and investing in just 10 minutes. Not enough to make life-changing money. But you can try to turn your first $1 into $10. With time and effort, you will be able to turn $1k into $10k, and eventually $10k into $100k. Believe it or not, it's the same process.

This book contains highly effective, yet simple and beginner-friendly strategies, used by both Wall Street professionals, as well as retail traders like you and I.

Chapter 1: Price Action Trading In A Nutshell

Lesson 1: What You'll Need

First, a candle chart with real-market data. It can be a trading simulator or a demo account with a trading platform. Up to you.

- Timeframe: 1-minute or 5-minute.
- Trading Volume indicator.
- Auto MA indicator in the simulator, or 9 SMA on any of your trading platforms.

Now let's briefly go over how trading works, and how exactly this strategy can be used to make a profit.

Lesson 2: How Money Is Made In Trading

At its core trading is a two-step process.

1. Buy an asset when you believe its price will rise.

1. Sell it when you expect it will fall.

In this strategy, you will use the **Moving Average (MA)** to find precise entry (**buy**) and exit (**sell**) points without any guesswork.

Lesson 3: Strategy Overview

Often, around 11 AM New York time, many assets begin to show significant trends on the 1 and 5-minute charts.

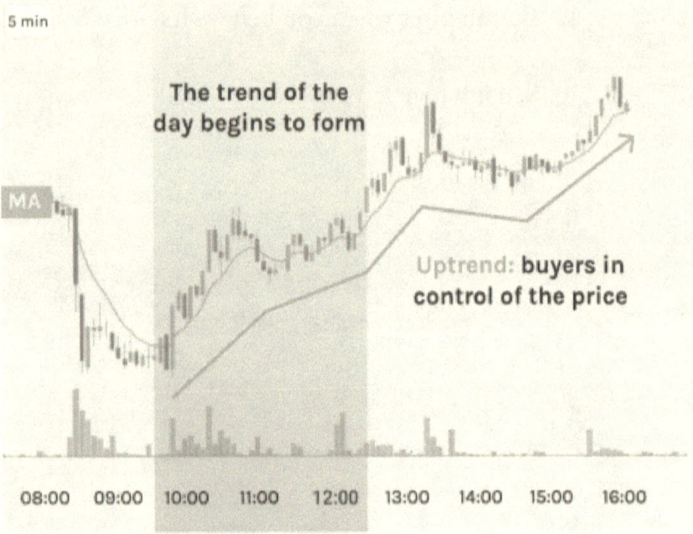

By definition, the MA is a visual line representing the average price over a specific time period.

But during these daily trends, the MA line can serve as a **support or resistance** line.

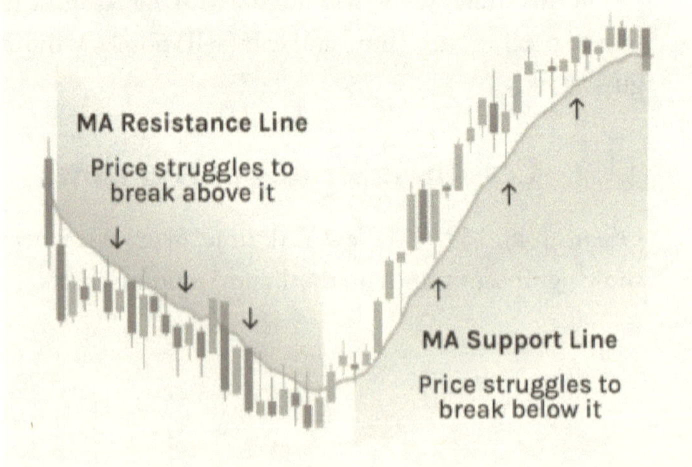

The Moving Average often acts as a barrier, preventing the price from rising above it. Conversely, when the price breaks above the Moving Average, it can act as support, preventing the price from falling below it.

The setup you'll look for is when the price breaks above the Moving Average and establishes it as a support level.

Lesson 4: Here's How You Can Trade This Price Action:

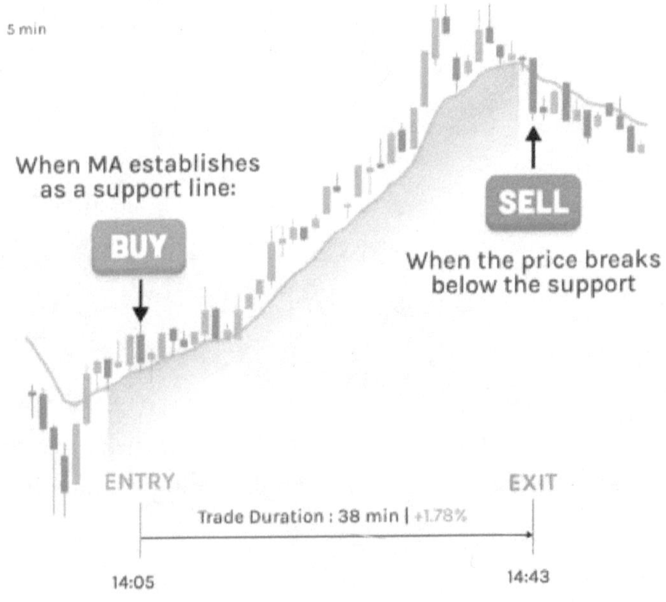

In essence, you buy when the price breaks above the support, ride the trend, and sell when the price breaks below the support.

Lesson 5: Avoiding False Breaks

False breaks often occur when prices appear to break through support or resistance levels only to reverse.

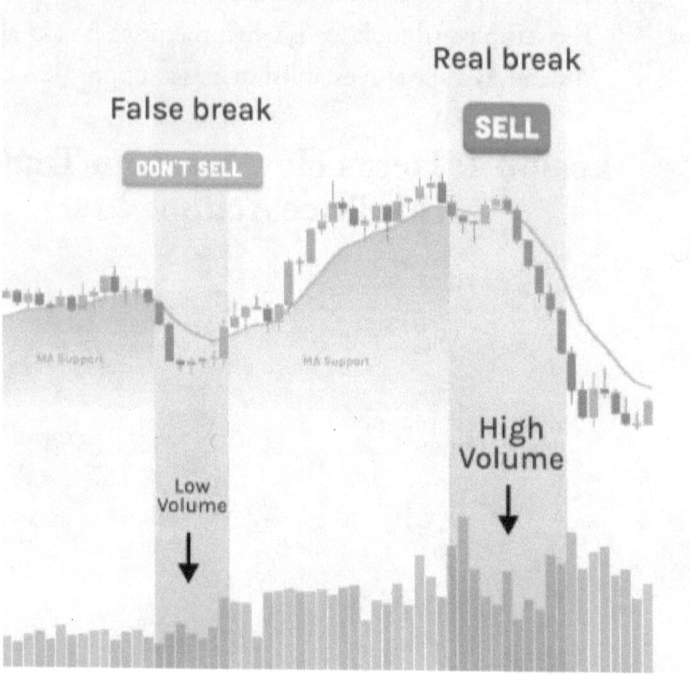

The volume indicator is crucial here; it helps identify the strength of a market move. High trading volumes during a break suggest it's genuine.

Lesson 6: Timing Is Key

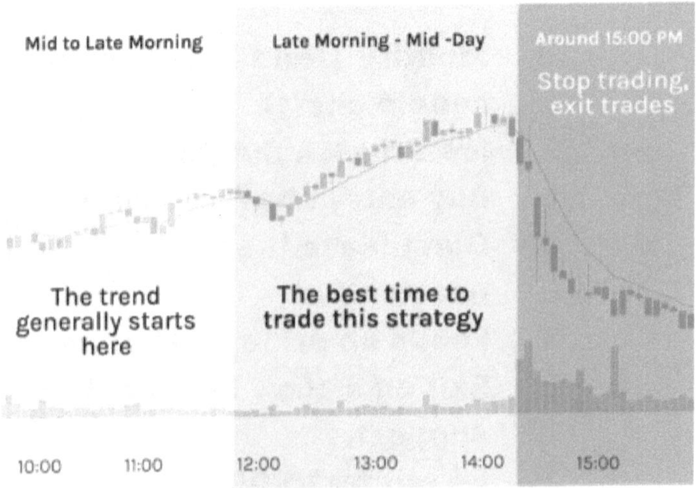

Trade between late morning and midday ET, when market activity and volatility are typically lower.

Aim to exit the markets by 3 PM ET, as this is when professional traders and firms start adjusting their positions before the market closes, potentially leading to wild, unpredictable price swings.

Lesson 7: Stick to the plan

1. **Identify Trend (1 or 5-min candle chart)**
2. **Identify MA Support**
3. **Buy entry above the support**
4. **Don't leave the trade unattended.**
5. **Focus on price and volume.**
6. **Exit on a clear break below support.**
7. **Be out by 15:00 ET**

This is a fast-paced strategy. To improve your odds of success, **focus on trading just one asset at a time.**

As you progress further in my book, you will learn additional tricks and tips to enhance this strategy, your skills, and your chances of success. Good luck!

Chapter 2: Introduction To Trading

Lesson 1: You're Already Trading

Many successful traders started exactly where you are right now-wondering if trading is just for Wall Street pros, or if regular people can actually make it work?

The Big Myth

Truth is, you don't need to be special or have some unfair advantage to be a trader. You've been trading your whole life-whether you know it or not.

- You trade time for money when you work.
- You trade that money for essentials like food and bills that keep you going.

- And maybe you trade salad over candy to **invest** in your future health.

Every day, you make decisions that involve trading one thing for another. Just like traders do:

The difference now is, you're going to learn how to trade in markets where **the stakes are higher and the rewards are greater**.

Let's start with a simple example that will change your whole understanding of how this works.

Lesson 2: How Trading Works

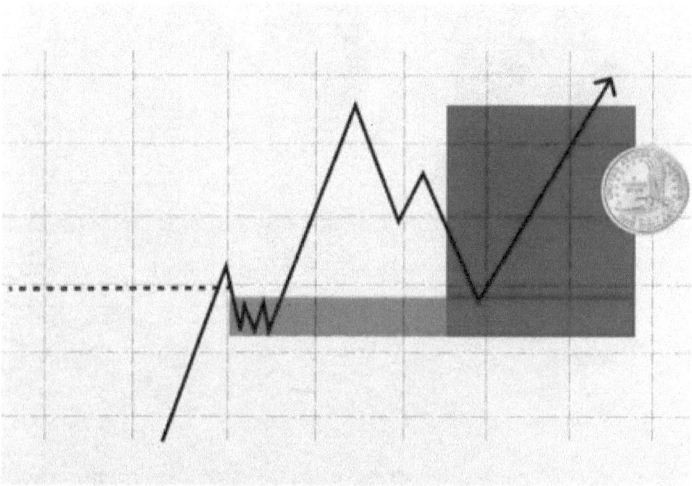

Trading is a skill. Just like learning a language, playing golf, or improving your saving habits.

The core idea in trading is to buy something at a lower price and sell it at a higher price to make a profit.

Real example of trading

1. **You buy** a ticket to Taylor Swift for $70 months before the concert.

As the event gets closer, the demand increases. "Swifties" really want those tickets, but seats are limited. There's a fixed amount of tickets available.

2. On the concert day, **you sell** it for $1,000 to a fan who just "has to be there".

You bought the ticket for $70, and sold it for $1000 later on. **Your profit is $930.**

Now, imagine you anticipated this high demand and bought 10 tickets instead. That's a potential profit of $9,300 - serious money.

$$(\$1000 - \$70) \times 10$$

$$=$$

$$\$9,300$$

But here's the catch:

What if the concert gets canceled? What if Taylor Swift announces a second show, and now there are more tickets available? Your profit potential just became uncertain...

This is where trading gets real. The concept is simple but the execution is full risks and uncertainties.

Which is why the key to long-term success is **risk and money management.**

Play defense before offense

Before you set your expectations on making big bucks, a more realistic first goal is simply not to lose the bucks you have.

Here's a little secret: **everybody loses.**

The Best Traders have a win rate of around 60%. Yes, that means 40% of time they get it wrong. If we plot this data on a calendar, it means about 13 losing days in a month.

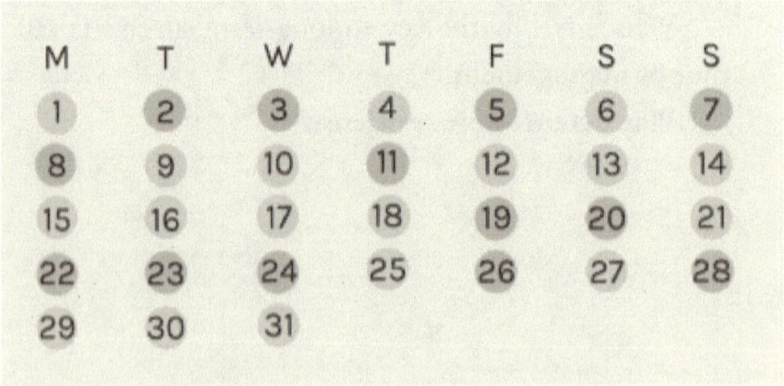

But the key is to **not lose foolishly**:

When you lose, lose small. And when you win, win a bit more than you lost. Don't worry - I'll teach you how to do that shortly.

Next up: what can you trade and why?

Lesson 3: What To Trade? Stocks, Crypto?

ASSET CLASS	STOCKS	CRYPTO	FOREX	COMMODITIES
HOURS	8:00 -16:00	24/7	24/5	9:00 - 17:00
MARKET SIZE	Large	Small, Growing Fast	Largest	Large
LIQUIDITY	High, (Top stocks)	High (Top 5 assets)	Highest	Moderate
AVG. DAILY PRICE CHANGE*	1.33%	4%	0-1%	1-2%
LEVERAGE**	Up to 5X	Up to 100X	Up to 100X	Up to 20x

*Yearly Data/Divided by day **Varies By Trading Platform/Country

In trading, four asset classes dominate: **Stocks, Crypto, Forex, and Commodities.**

Most of the trading happens in these, but each demands its own strategy.

Take, Bitcoin and Gold. Both are valuable assets, but the way you manage risk with Bitcoin is very different from how you handle a commodity like gold. Here's a theoretical trade example:

BUY	AMOUNT	LEVERAGE	VOLATILITY	PROFIT
	$1000	x100 ($1000x100 = $100,000)	4%	$4,000
	$1000	x20 ($1000x20 = $20,000)	1%	$200

Bitcoin's higher volatility and leverage makes its profit potential much bigger. But volatility also makes it far more riskier.

Whereas gold, a more stable commodity, tends to fluctuate less. Each requires a different approach to risk management.

Therefore: **The best traders specialize.**

Instead of trading everything, aim to learn 1-2 markets inside and out. Then you'll be able exploit inefficiencies and make money. Here's a brief summary of each asset class:

Stocks: Shares of companies

- **Market Hours:** 9:30 AM to 4:00 PM EST for U.S. stocks. The action is intense but follows a predictable rhythm.

• **Volatility:** Mostly stable, but earnings reports and news can shake things up.

• **Liquidity:** High for popular stocks, less for relatively unknown companies.

Crypto: 24/7 volatility

• **Market Hours:** 24/7 no breaks, no mercy. You'll need a plan to manage trades around the clock.

• **Volatility:** Extreme. If a 15% swing in a day scares you, stay out.

• **Liquidity:** High for majors like Bitcoin, but altcoins can dry up fast.

Forex: Currency vs currency

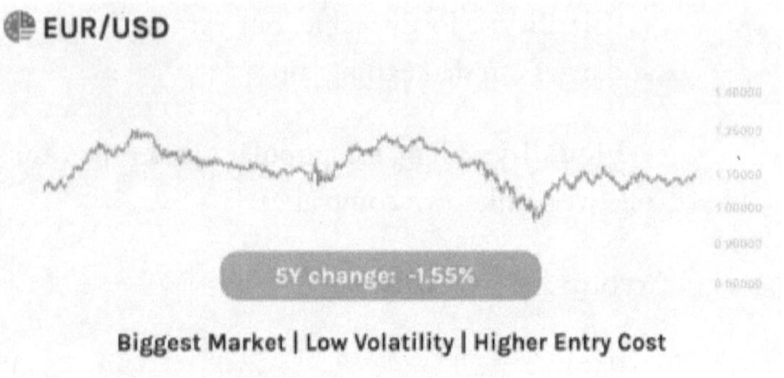

- **Market Hours:** Open 24 hours, Sunday 5PM(EST) - Friday 5PM(EST).

- **Volatility:** Low but central bank decisions and monthly economic reports increase it.

- **Liquidity:** Very high for major pairs.

Commodities: Natural resources

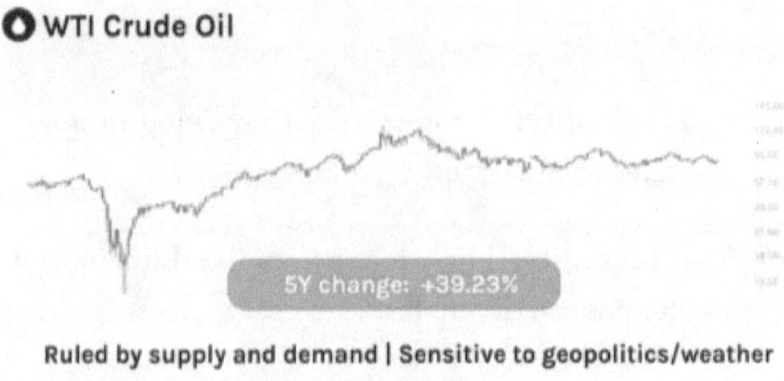

- **Market Hours:** Highly dependent on the commodity. Generally 24/5.

- **Volatility:** Unpredictable. Supply chain issues, geopolitical tensions, and weather events can send prices soaring or crashing.

- **Liquidity:** Varies. Gold and oil? No problem. But trade something like coffee, and you might find yourself waiting for moves.

So, what should you trade?

Trading runs by market, not your schedule. If you're in Australia and want to day trade U.S. stocks, your market hours will be 2 AM to 10 AM local time. In short - not possible.

Also, not all assets are available in every country, and some brokers don't even offer access to certain markets.

Build and practice your strategies around assets you can actively trade, considering both timing and region.

Check the Top Brokers section to learn what assets trading platforms offer in your region, before we dig deeper into analysis, and specific strategies.

You'll learn assets in-depth in chapters 11-14. Next up, how much can you make?

Lesson 4: How Much Can You Make?

You can make serious money trading - there's no denying that. **But most don't.**

The top traders, much like top lawyers, doctors, or any high-level professional, earn millions each year.

But here's where things get skewed: nobody expects to become a world-class surgeon in a few months, yet many think trading is different.

Since you can start trading from your phone, with no formal training or barriers, it feels easy - like success should come quickly. Unfortunately, it's rarely the case for most.

In this book, I've put together the absolute best blend of knowledge, experience, and strategies to get you started, and I'm confident it'll help you move faster.

But here's the catch, **most people skip the "work" part.**

Don't expect miracles in a week. It might not sound flashy, but our results show that committed traders typically see gains of 0.5% to 1% per day.

Your actual earnings will depend on your account size:

Account Size	Daily Gain (0.5%)	Monthly Gain (20 Trading Days)
$100	$0.50	$10
$500	$2.50	$50.00
$10,000	$50	$1.000.00
$100,000	$500	$10,000.00

*excluding trading fees

If you came here expecting to turn $100 into $100,000 by the end of the week, this can feel pretty discouraging. This is why the vast majority quit before truly trying.

Is it easy to make money?

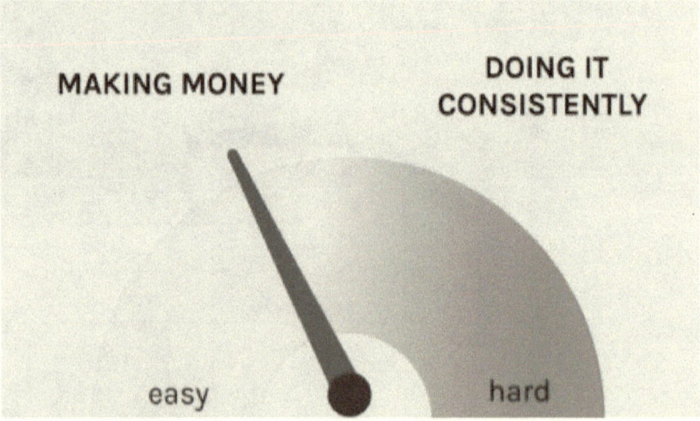

You know the basics: **buy when prices will rise, sell when they'll fall**. Simple.

The real challenge is being consistent. Just like hitting the gym once is easy, but sticking with a routine for a year isn't.

Results will always depend on your effort and market conditions, but my book equips you with tools and insights to help you make more informed decisions in the markets.

... **if you are, consistent, disciplined, and practice regularly**.

That said, not everyone wants the grind of active trading. In the next lesson, we'll break down two other strategies with different levels of effort and reward.

Lesson 5: Trade, Invest, Or Copy?

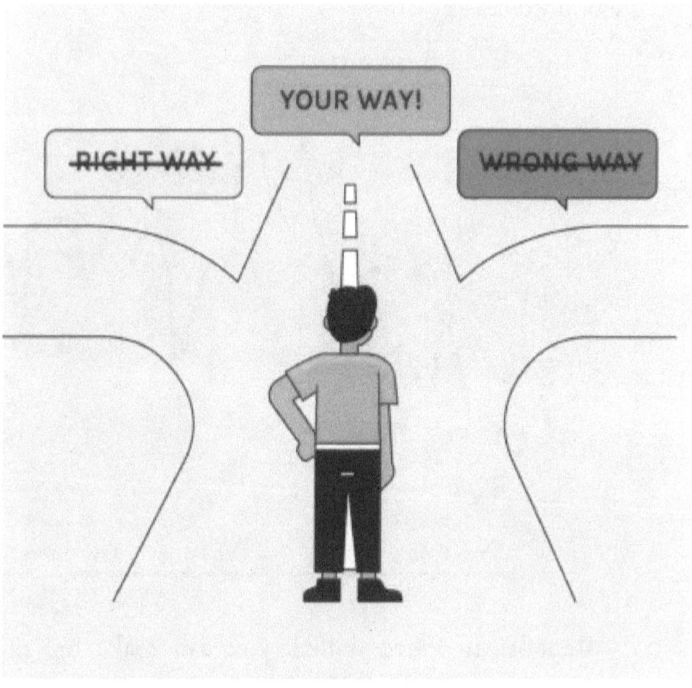

There are three key ways to profit in the markets, and your choice depends on three factors:

- How much time can you devote?
- Your starting capital
- Your personality and lifestyle

This overview will help you consider which might be the best for you.

1. Trading: High risk = high reward

Trading is about seizing short-term opportunities in the market. It's fast, intense, and unforgiving to the uncommited.

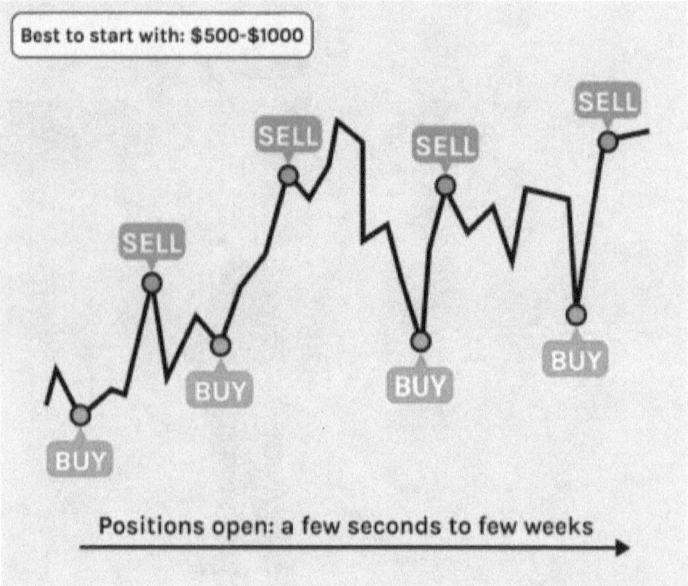

Benefit: If you're skilled, you can make big money quickly. Trading is skill that outshines any other market approach.

Downside: If you want to trade for a living, it's a full-time commitment, especially when starting. Discipline and emotional control are non-negotiable.

2. Investing: Slow but reliable

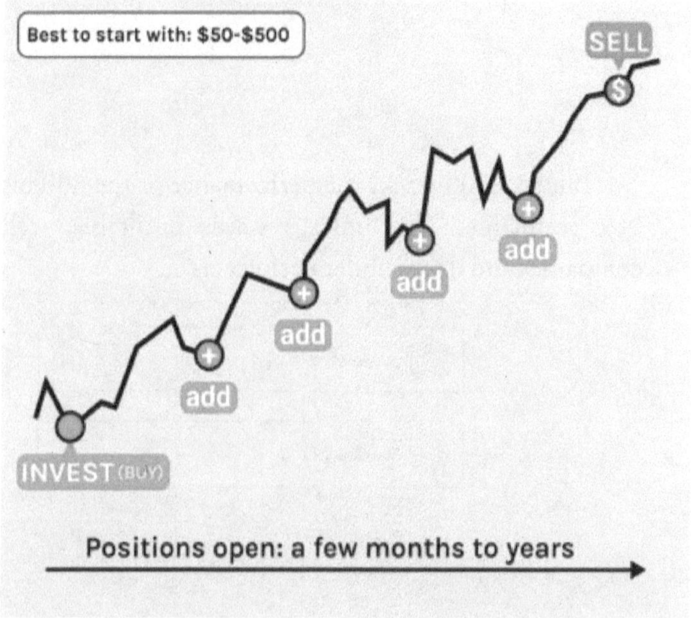

Benefit: Less anxiety as you're not glued to the screen all day. With the right strategy using compound interest, $1K today could turn into $1M in 30 years.

Downside: Patience is crucial. Don't expect fast returns - this takes time.

Example: Regular investing in ETFS

For 80% of people, a simple solution is to buy an S&P500 ETF regularly, also known as dollar-cost-averaging (DCA).

The S&P500 tracks the performance of the 500 biggest U.S. companies. The index rewards profitable, well-run companies and drops under performers.

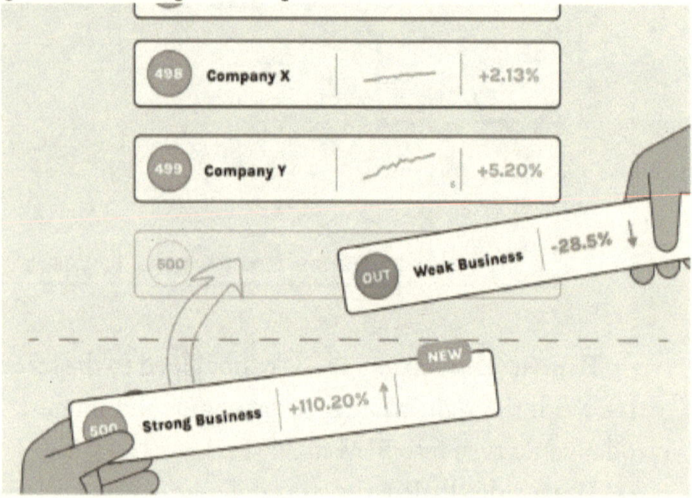

This has his driven returns upward, with the ETF averaging 10% annually over the past 30 years. If this trend holds, here's what your future could look like starting today.

Invest In ETF:	From Paycheck:	20 Years Later:
5%($50)	$1000	$34,307
10%($150)	$1500	$102,922
25%($750)	$3000	$514,612
50%($3000)	$6000	$2,058,448

This strategy is ideal for those who want to prioritize their career and family while gradually building financial security with lower risk.

3. Copy Trading: For busy people

What if you could hand your money to a professional trader and say: "**Turn this into more money**"?

Well, actually you can. And you can start copying with as low as $200.

How it works

1. Pick a copy trading platform such as **eToro** and a trader with solid past performance.

1. Decide your amount and copy. If they make 10%, you make 10%.

1. All of their trades are automatically copied to your account.

This method requires no market expertise - they handle trading while you learn from them in real time.

Where's the catch?

Copy trading **doesn't guarantee profits**, and **losses are possible**. However, like ETFs, there's a mechanism that encourages winning more and losing less.

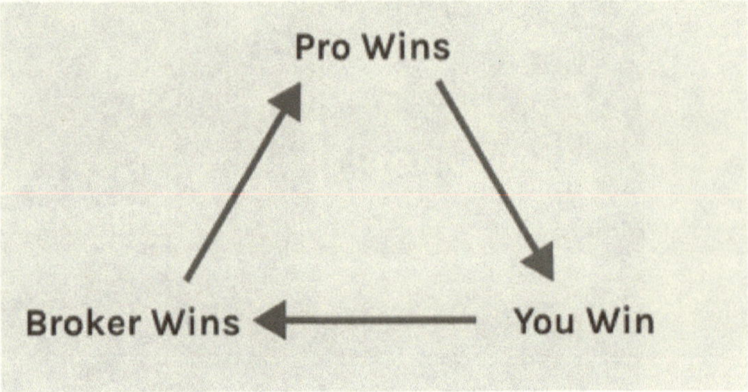

Brokers reward top traders with bonuses for attracting copiers. Better performance equals more rewards. Brokers benefit from increased trading activity, so everyone wins.

Plus, the pro is trading their own money - not yours. **They're in it to make a profit!**

(I'll guide you to pick proven and trusted traders later in the course).

The Bottom Line

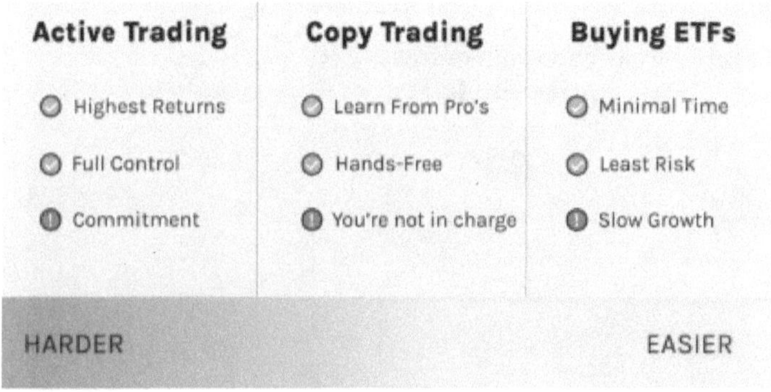

You don't need to decide right now— start by exploring your options!

Many traders reinvest their profits in ETF's, and investors often use copy trading for short-term gains without sacrificing time.

I'll cover each method and its strategies later in the book.

For now, let's continue with trading specifics!

Lesson 6: Four Steps To Your First Trade

Did you know commercial pilots log about **100 hours in flight simulators** before flying a real plane? Similarly in trading - confidence comes from hands-on experience.

Research shows: students who practice simulated trading grasp market dynamics better.

Please use a trading simulator with real-time market data, just like any trading platform. This lesson will guide you through making your first simulator trade.

Basics of a trade

#1 - What to trade

Since your market knowledge is still limited at this point, your best bet is to trade a single asset you have most information on.

#2 - Trade Size

In trading, a common rule is to open a position with no more than 2-4% of your account size. Here's an example:

- $500: $10 - $20 per trade
- $1000: $20 - $40 per trade

- $10,000: $200- $400 per trade

#3 - Leverage

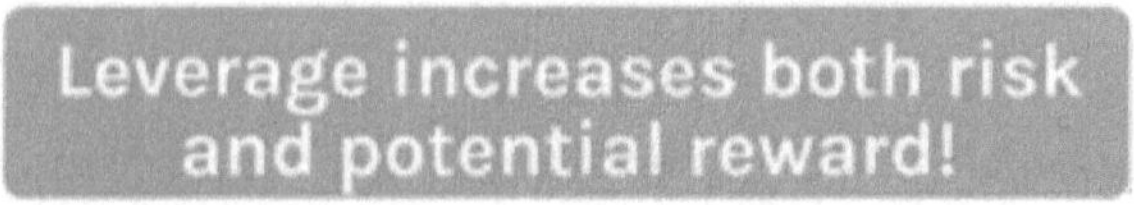

Leverage allows you to borrow funds from a broker, letting you trade with more capital than you have. Using a trading simulator will show you how leverage can quickly impact your account, before risking real money.

Here's the math behind profit and loss with 1x(no leverage) vs 10x leverage:

Position size	Leverage	True Size	1% price move (P / L)	10% price move (P / L)
$400	1x	$400	+ $4 / - $4	+ $40 / - $40
$400	10x	$4000	+ $40 / - $40	+ $400 / - $400

Leverage amplifies your position size. A 10% price move with 10x leverage can double your profit - or wipe out your entire position if it moves against you.

That's why solid risk management is crucial when using leverage.

#4 - Risk Management

Risk management is about setting strict rules to minimize losses. A key rule is to never risk more than 1% of your total account on any single trade. Example ($10,000 simulator account):

- Your position size is 4% - $400.
- Your max acceptable loss is 1% - $100.

You achieve this with a stop-loss order, which automatically closes your trade if the market moves against you.

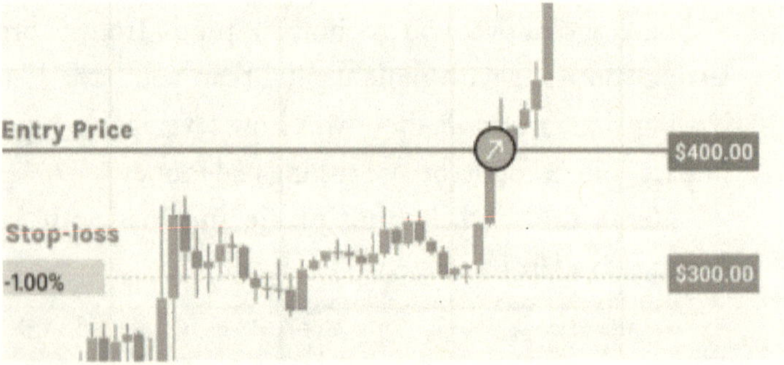

Scenario: You're buying 1 share of stock worth for $400. You're risking 1% of your account, which is $100. (1% of $10,000)

- **Buy price:** $400 per share
- **Stop-loss:** $300 (caps your loss at -1%)

To further refine your strategy, you pair this with a take-profit order. This allows you to aim for a 3:1

reward-to-risk ratio. So, for every $1 you risk, you aim to make $3.

In this setup, even if you're wrong 7 times out of 10, you can still be profitable over time. But remember, 3:1 is just one approach. We'll refresh this knowledge and explore other ratios, stop-loss strategies, and risk management techniques in more detail in later chapters.

Main Takeaway

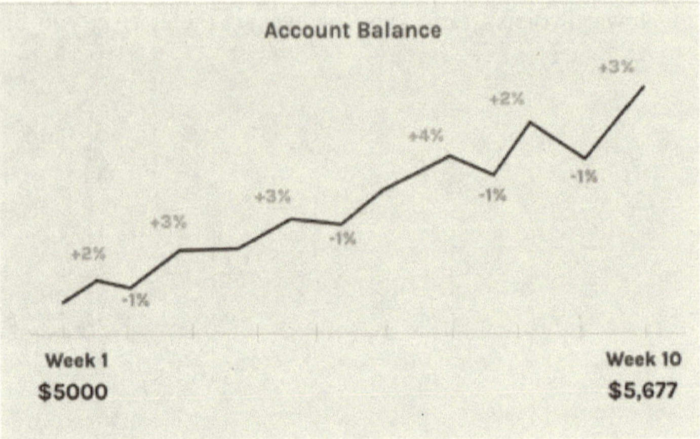

Before diving into the simulator, keep this in mind: trading isn't about winning every single trade.

It's a step-by-step process of making the best trading decisions possible, while risking as little as possible.

Next up, I'll reveal a big challenge many new traders face during this process.

Lesson 7: The Big Problem

There is just one difference between a multimillionaire trader and you:

HAVING THE RIGHT INFORMATION

But in 2025, finding information is easier than ever. There is an overabundance of it:

- Hundreds of books on strategy
- Dozens of apps copying our formula

- Thousands of fake gurus on social media selling their "secret" methods

- Tens of thousands of courses

So, why isn't every trader a millionaire in a few months? Sure, avoiding the work is one pitfall. But there's a bigger problem, even for those who do put in the effort.

The info tsunami

Most motivated beginners fall into the same trap: they're serious, focused, and willing to put in the work. They dive in, study hard, and - boom - hit a wall.

It's called **Information overload.**

Suddenly, every decision feels impossible, and trading - where split-second choices matter - turns into a mental maze.

The more you learn, the more you drown in confusion about what to do. What strategy? What time frame? Which asset? When?

6+ years of success/failure

Since being a newbie in the trading craft in 2019 until now, I've had the opportunity to gain a full spectrum of experience, from making mistakes and falling into traps to making correct decisions and more consistently making profit.

Consequently, this has given me key insights:

- Why some win while others lose.

- Why less is more in trading.

• What kills trading success.

• How you can progress fast with less information and simple actions.

Here's one I shared earlier, about the need to specialize in specific assets.

Did you know that on average the best traders trade just 3 assets or less?

Less assets to analyze = less overload.

You'll learn more about this in the "5 asset rule" lesson. Here's the main takeaway.

Less is always more!

New traders often think more is better - more strategies, more indicators, more money, more trades. They look for the next 'secret' that will magically unlock success.

But here's a truth I gotta tell you:

More is a distraction. It kills profitability.

If at any point you feel overwhelmed and uncertain, stick to:

1 Asset. 1 Time Frame. 1 Strategy.

Every trade already has a 50/50 shot - prices go up or down, and you have one decision - to buy or sell. The more you complicate it, the more you risk falling into information overload.

Each lesson in this book is written with one goal: to help you **win more and lose less.**

What comes next is a streamlined section that simplifies the markets, so you can start making the right decisions with the right information and zero complexity.

Now, let's get started. See you in Chapter 3.

Chapter 3: How Markets Work

Lesson 1: Market Basics

"Financial Markets" are places where you can buy and sell various types of money-related assets from around the world. Each type of asset falls into a distinct class:

- **Forex:** Currencies like EUR and USD
- **Stocks:** Shares of companies
- **Commodities:** Raw resources like oil
- **Crypto:** Digital currencies like Bitcoin
- **ETFs:** Funds that hold many assets.

Each asset class has specific times when you can trade them.

When Can You Trade?

Despite different opening times and a few other nuances among them, all assets traded in financial markets operate on one common principle:

Every trade involves a buyer and a seller. The buyer exchanges cash for an asset, while the seller trades their asset for cash.

The role of a broker

To trade assets like stocks or currencies, you need a broker, which is usually the trading platform you decide to use.

Its task is to connect buyers and sellers and ensure their trades go safely and smoothly. For this the broker charges a small fee called the bid-ask spread.

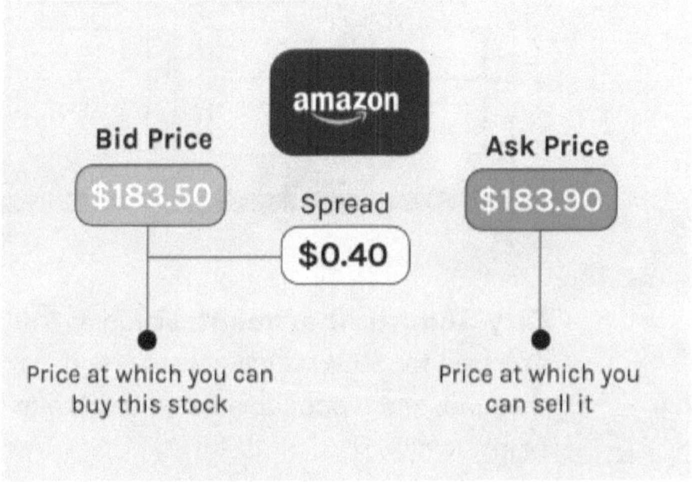

The bid price will almost always be lower than the ask price. If it weren't, traders could easily make a profit by buying an asset and selling it right away at a higher price, pocketing the difference.

Why do some assets have big spreads?

The cost you pay in spreads is mainly influenced by two factors:

1. Liquidity: This is about how quickly you can buy or sell an asset without impacting its price significantly. High liquidity means the asset is traded often and by many, resulting in a lower spread.

Real-Life Liquidity Example

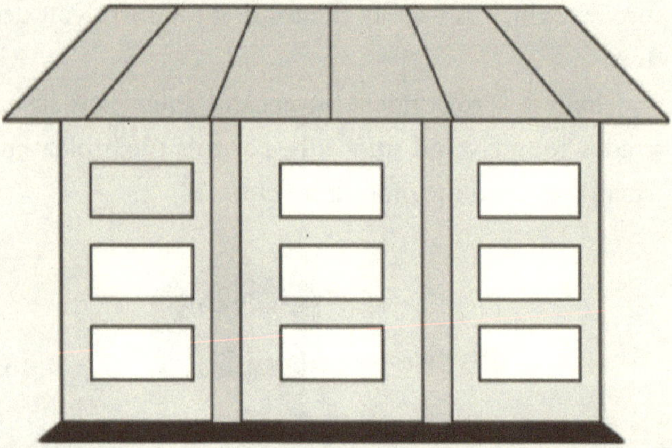

City Suburb Apartment: Listed at $100k and sold for $95k within a week. High demand, and a popular area contribute to high liquidity.

Tropical Island Villa: Originally priced at $10 million but sold for $3 million after several years on the market. Limited demand, remote location, and less potential buyers means lower liquidity.

2. Volatility: Refers to how quickly an asset's price can change. Generally, more volatile assets are riskier and have higher spreads.

For example, Bitcoin might see a 10% price change in a single day, while EUR/USD might take weeks for a similar shift, resulting in lower spreads for Bitcoin, and much lower for EUR/USD.

Main Takeaway

Financial markets give you the chance to earn profits from fluctuations in asset prices. However, every trade involves a cost known as the bid-ask spread. This is the fee you pay when entering or exiting a position, so don't be surprised when a new trade you open makes a small loss.

Up next, we'll delve into the key differences between buying and selling.

Lesson 2: Buy Or Sell?

The market can be split into two groups: buyers and sellers. Both have the same objective - to make money, but the strategies and methods are different.

In this lesson, we'll explore what each group does and how they achieve their goal.

Buyers "go long"

Going long means buying an asset because you expect its value to go up. If you're optimistic about an asset's future, you go long on it.

Explanation: You buy the asset at $100 and sell it when the price rises to $125. Your profit is 25% minus the spread.

Case Study: $8,000 to $5.7B

In August 2020, a relatively unknown crypto "Shiba Inu" launched. It was priced incredibly low, just $0:000000000189.

One trader capitalized on this, purchasing 70 trillion coins for $8,000. A year later, this investment skyrocketed to $5.7 billion, marking a 7,000,000% increase and earning the title **"greatest long trade of all time."**

Similar opportunities continue to happen in highly speculative and risky crypto assets.

But what if traders believe the price will fall?

Sellers "go short"

Short-selling involves selling an asset and making a profit when price falls. You do this when you're pessimistic about the specific asset.

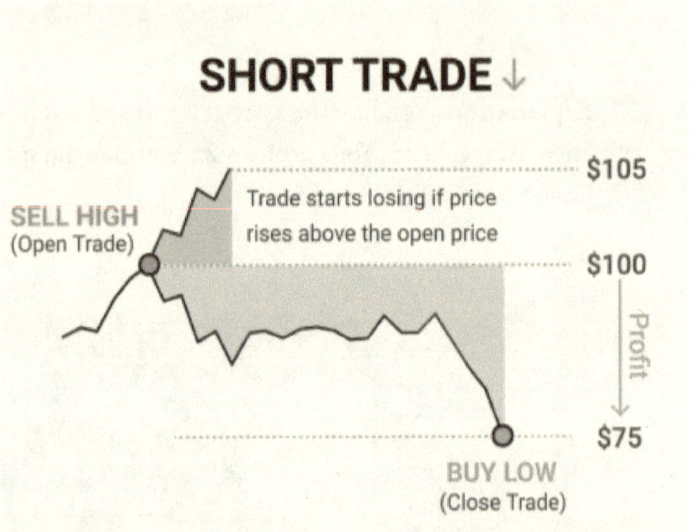

Explanation: You short-sell the asset at $100 and close the trade when the price falls to $75 pocketing around 25% profit, minus the spread.

Beginners usually scratch their heads at this point: **"How can I sell something I don't own in the first place?"**

Selling vs shorting

Selling an asset implies you have owned it at some point and are seeking to close your long trade. In contrast, short-selling entails borrowing an asset to sell it, with the intent of repurchasing it later at a lower price.

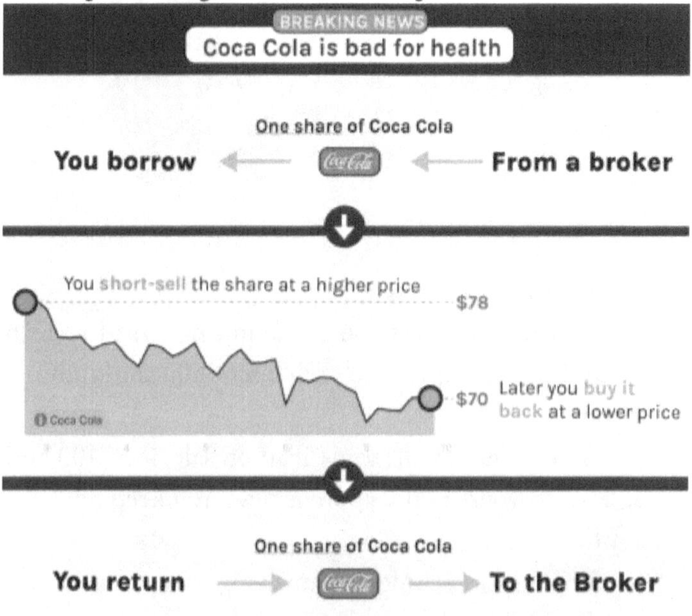

Explanation: You borrow a share of Coca-Cola and short-sell it for $78. This $78 isn't your profit yet, because you still have to return the share. If Coca-Cola's stock price drops to $70, you buy the share back and return it, keeping the $8 difference as your profit. All of this happens automatically.

I don't understand yet

Here is another example:

Your friend lends you his brand new iPad to help you study. But you immediately sell it for $600 and study on your phone.

Later, you buy the same iPad on sale, for $400 and give it back to your friend, good as new. You keep $200 as your profit.

That's short-selling in a nutshell.

P.S Be a good friend, don't try this at home.

One thing to remember

Going long has a limited loss potential - the worst-case scenario is the asset's value drops to zero.

However, shorting carries the theoretical risk of **infinite loss** because asset prices have no upper limit.

It's crucial to choose a **regulated broker** which offers "**negative balance protection**" to avoid this risk. And then there is risk management as well.

I will cover both in detail, later on.

Lesson 3: What Moves Prices?

Price fluctuations are essential for trading; without them, there would be no profit opportunities and markets would stall.

This lesson will explain the key forces driving these fluctuations, giving you a new perspective on what you see in the charts.

Traders make prices

The markets are governed by a powerful, unseen force: the economic law of supply and demand. It determines what the price of an asset is.

Specifically, it's the interaction between **demand (buyers)** and **supply (sellers)**:

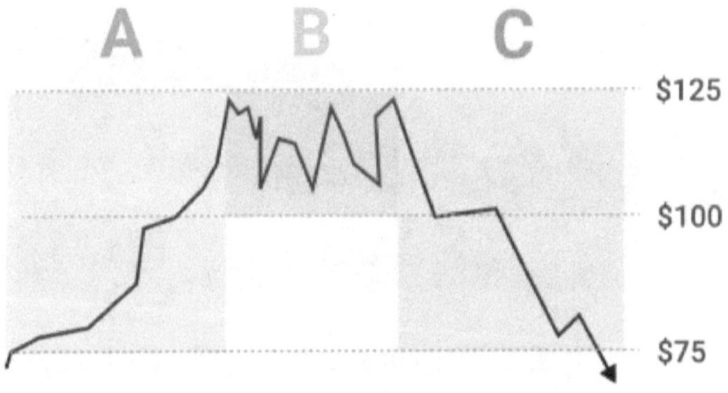

- **A - Price Rises:** Occurs when demand exceeds supply. Buyers are willing to pay more, allowing sellers to raise their prices.

• **B - Price is Stable:** Happens when supply equals demand. The balance keeps prices relatively steady.

• **C - Price Falls:** When supply exceeds demand. Sellers lower prices to attract buyers.

Supply and demand in oil

Oil producers (the supply side) sell to oil buyers (the demand side).

Oil is crucial for various sectors and its price plays a significant role in shaping global economic conditions. Producers, such as OPEC, can adjust supply to influence prices and manage profits, while demand remains relatively static due to global dependence.

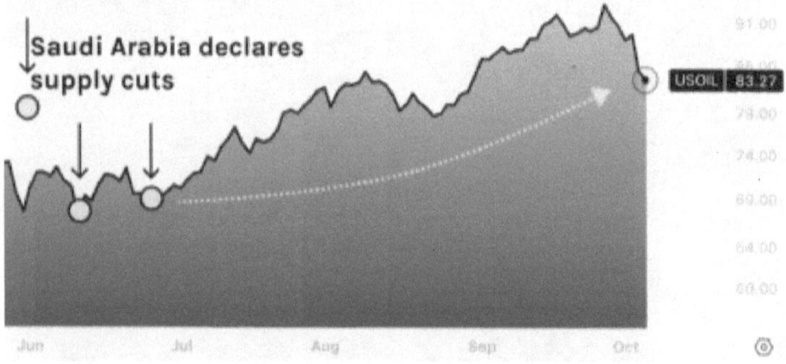

In 2023, OPEC cut the daily oil supply by 1.2 million barrels-about 1% of global demand. Combined with a surge in demand post-Covid, this reduction caused a 30% increase in oil prices over ten months.

Traders who understood the supply and demand profited from this move.

How it actually works

Supply and demand plays out in real-time through the "order book" - a digital list of buy and sell orders.

In trading, there's two main order types:

- **Market Order:** Execute immediately at the best available price.

- **Limit Order:** Execute only at a specified price.

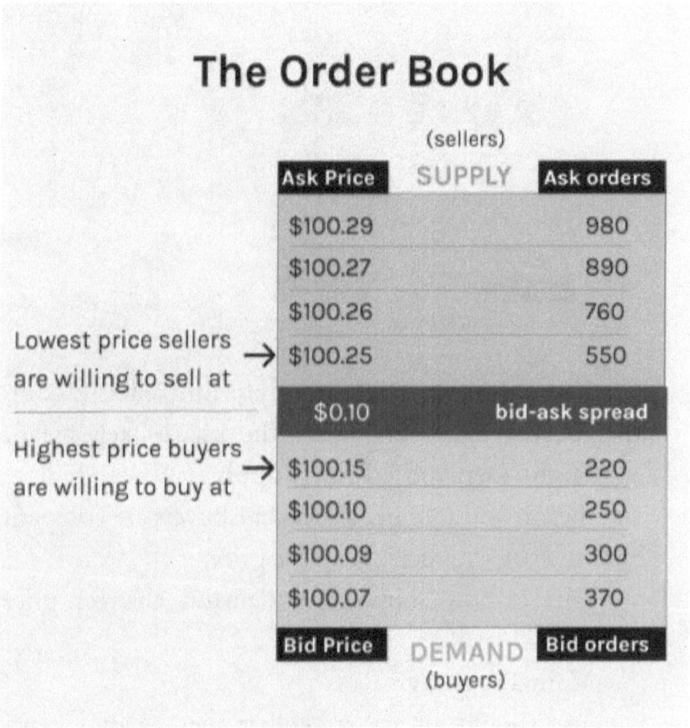

When a market order is placed, it matches the highest bid for sellers and the lowest ask for buyers.

The price of an asset is the last price at which buy and sell orders matched.

For instance, if you're selling 10 shares of a stock and the highest bid covers 5 shares at $100.15 each, those are sold first, with the remainder potentially selling at a slightly lower bid, such as $100.10.

Behind the chart

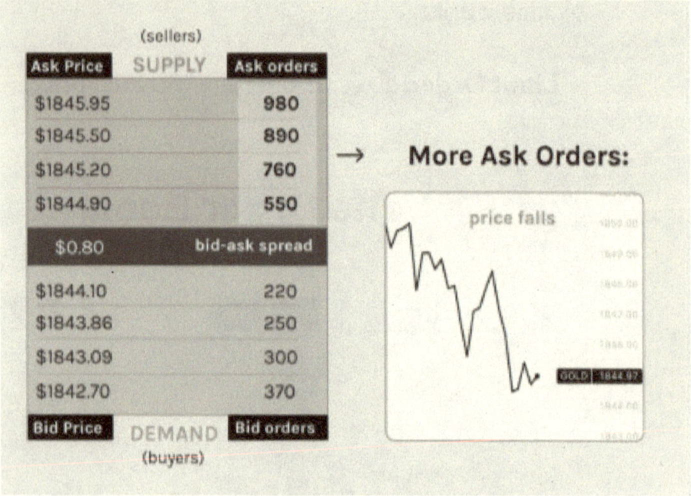

Low Demand, High Supply: More sellers (ask orders) than buyers (bid orders) means the price is likely to fall.

High Demand, Low Supply: When bid orders significantly outnumber ask orders, buyers are competing to get the asset, thus driving up the price.

This is how supply and demand changes prices in practice.

Main Takeaway

You should always remember that beyond news and events, supply and demand is what dictates the price.

These dynamics apply universally, from financial markets to everyday commodities like food, and products you use.

Next up, let's look at periods of high demand and low demand, and what do they mean for you.

Lesson 4: Market Cycles

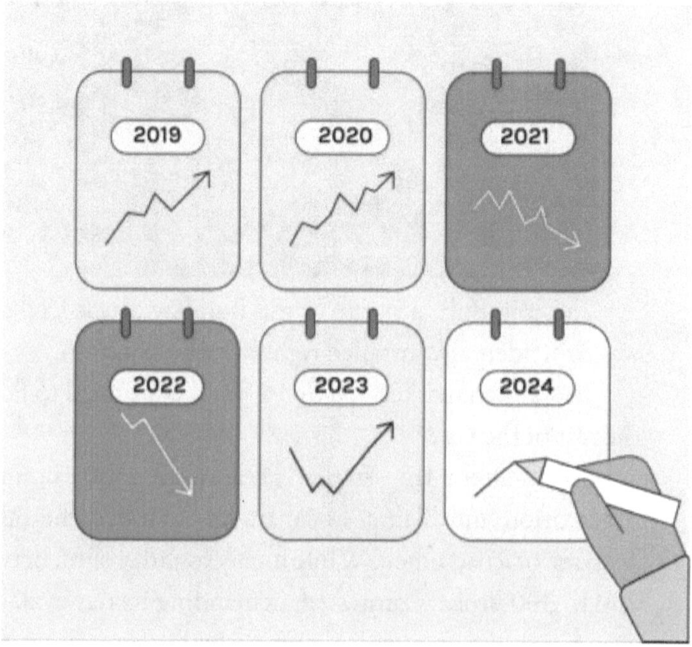

Supply and demand are shaped by hard data like inflation and economic indicators, as well as equally powerful intangible forces such as trader and investor beliefs and sentiments.

This lesson delves into how these factors collectively drive the long market cycles of optimism and pessimism.

Fun Fact: Irrational Beliefs

The 'Big Bull', a statue at the Bombay Stock Exchange, was coincidentally installed right before a big crash.

The Indian markets fell by 14% and continued to fall for the rest of the year.

Soon after, the statue became a focal point of superstition and blame. Local traders branded the bull as 'panvati' or a bad omen. While it may sound absurd, between 200 to 300 brokers protested, demanding its removal. They even consulted an astrologer who advised reinstalling it at a better time to reverse the bad fortune. **That's belief.**

We'll start the cycle with a period of optimism, growth and active public participation in the markets.

Phase one - Bull market

In a bull market, prices rise as investors, traders, and the public are optimistic about the future expecting the good times to last.

The high demand is often coupled with strong economic conditions and low unemployment. This encourages buying assets which then drives prices higher.

Greed also plays a big role as everyone aims to make as much money as possible while the bullish period lasts.

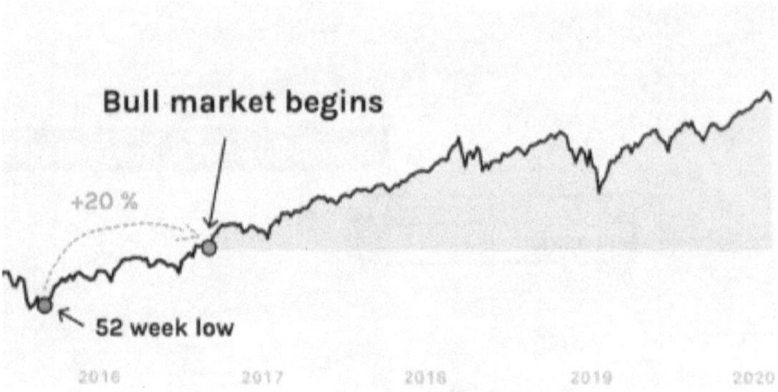

By definition: a bull market starts when an assets price rises by at least 20% from their 52-week low price.

Unfortunately, good times rarely last forever.

Phase two - catalyst and transition

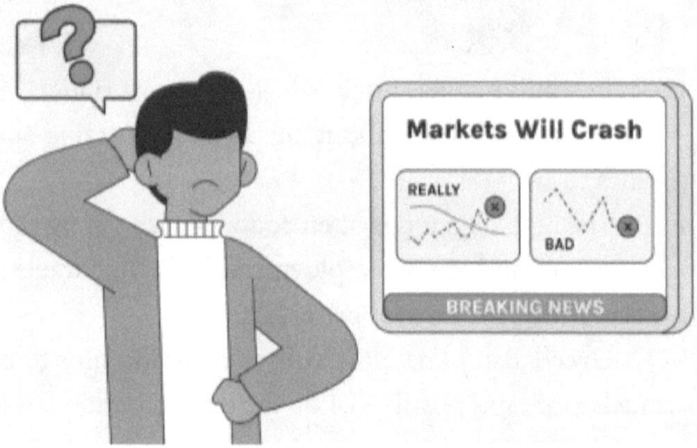

Inevitably, a catalyst appears. It's often something that makes people worried about the future, and their money.

For example bad economic data, ecological disasters, geopolitical instability, or global health crises:

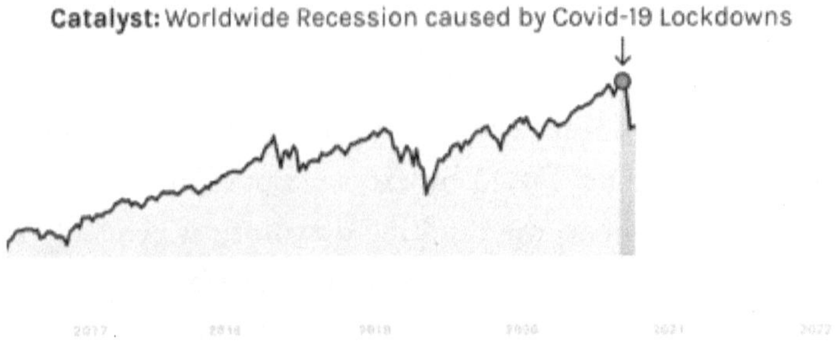

This worry starts a chain reaction. People sell their investments to avoid potential losses, but this in turn causes prices to fall further.

Optimism shifts to pessimism and doubt, often leading to a market correction.

What is a market correction?

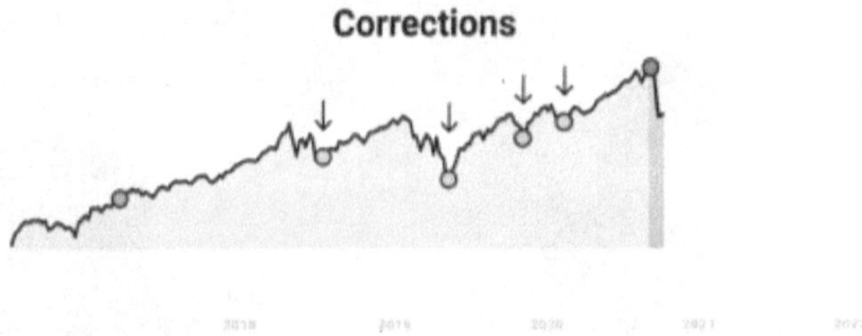

A market correction is a like a 'pit stop' for the markets-during strong bull runs, prices sometimes dip by around 10 - 15%.

Usually lasting less than two months, these corrections often happen when investors decide to 'lock in' some profits by selling.

This brief downturn can actually be healthy, setting the stage for more sustainable growth without the risks associated with **market bubbles**.

Bubbles occur when asset prices inflate far beyond their intrinsic value, fueled by excessive optimism. When such a bubble bursts, the resulting downturn is generally much more severe than a simple market correction.

In severe cases, this shift can completely change the market trend.

Phase three - bear market

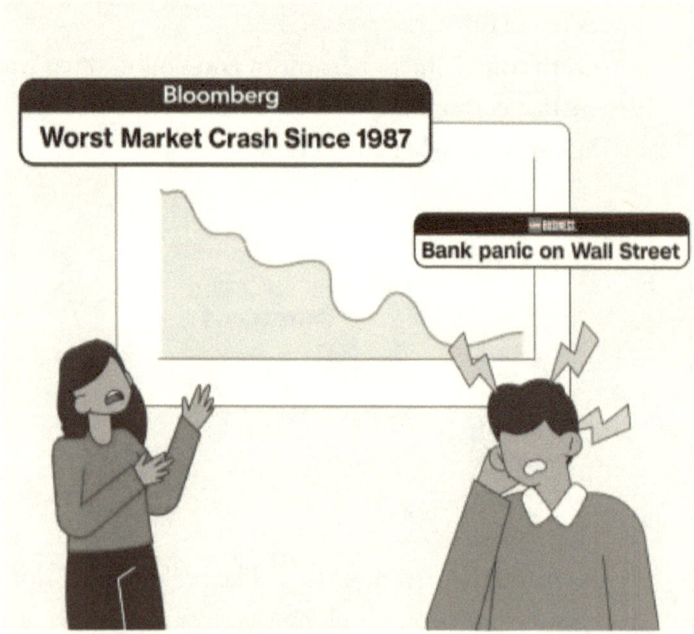

With a strong enough catalyst, investor beliefs pivot dramatically - the optimism and greed that once powered the bull market is replaced by pessimism, uncertainty and a cascade of selling.

It's officially a bear market when there's at least a 20% dip in asset prices.

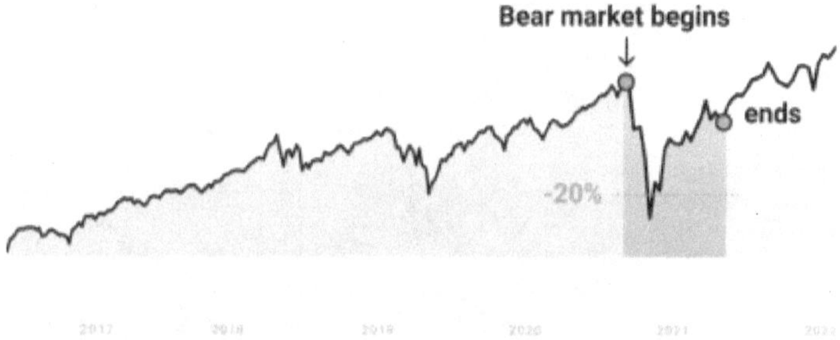

Luckily bear markets are typically much shorter in duration. The average:

- **Bull market - 6.6 years, 339% returns**
- **Bear market - 1.3 years, 36% loss**

Which is more profitable?

Actually, with the right strategy, both bull and bear markets present opportunities for profit. Active traders can profit from rising and falling markets alike.

Long-term investors typically rely on rising prices but can also benefit from bear markets by **'buying the dip'** - purchasing assets at lower prices for greater gains upon recovery.

We'll delve into these strategies later in the course. Now, let's take a deep dive into market trends.

Lesson 5: Surfing Market Trends

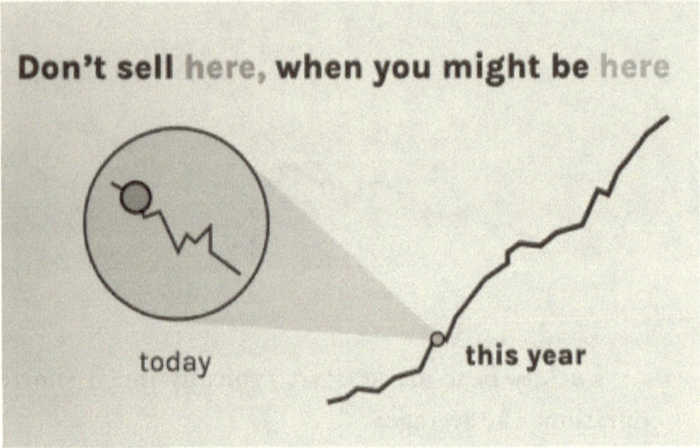

In this lesson we'll go over what are trends, how they form and how you can use them to find trading opportunities.

A trend is simply the direction the price is going over time. But there are few extra bits if you want to trade them successfully.

Case Study: S&P 500 Bull market from 2009 to 2020

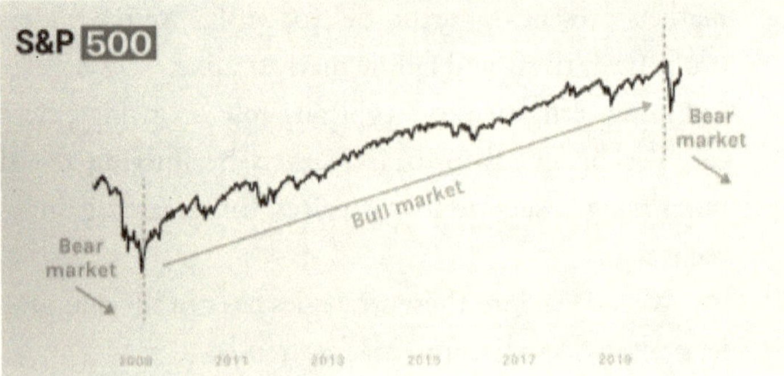

- Length: 132 months
- S&P 500 Return: 400.5%

- Maximum Drawdown: -19.8%.

The bull market that began in March 2009 is the second-longest bull market in the history of the S&P 500. It started as a recovery rally from the 2008 financial crisis and was later fueled by unprecedented fiscal support from the Federal Reserve.

During this time: **the S&P 500 was in strong primary uptrend.** Had you invested at the start and rode this trend until the next bear market, you would have made over 400% in one trade.

What defines a trend?

Uptrend: Characterized by higher highs (HH) and higher lows (HL).

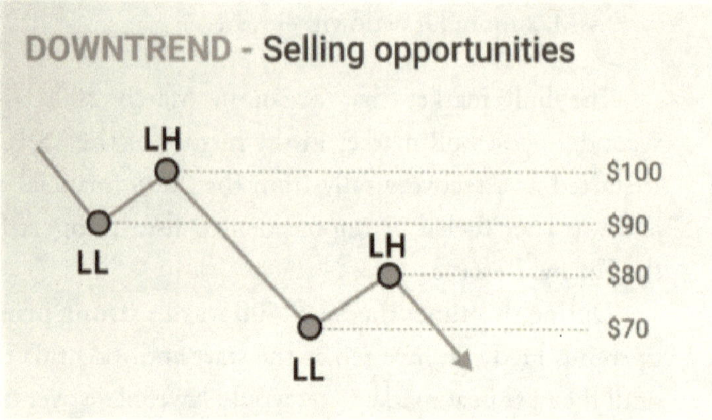

Downtrend: Defined by lower highs (LH) and lower lows (LL).

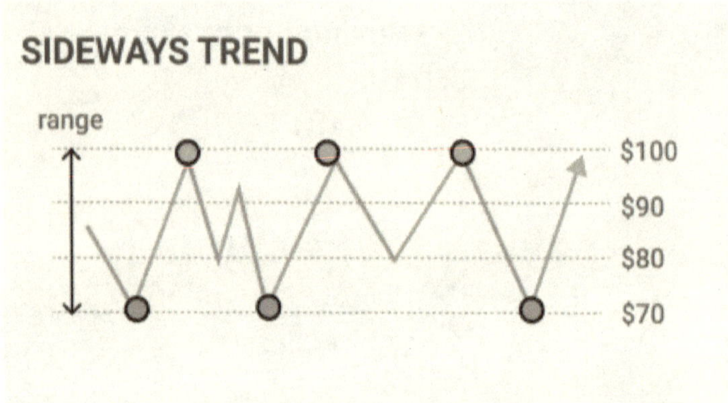

Sideways Trend: Price trades within a range, reflecting a balanced market, often as the market recalibrates after a substantial price movement.

When the price eventually breaks a range like this, the move can be very significant.

Trend Hierarchy

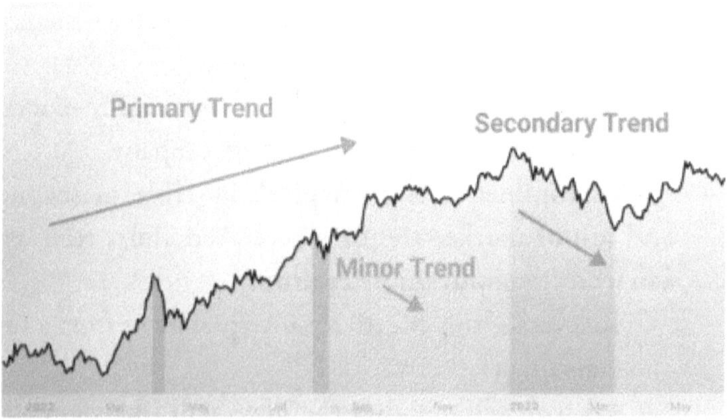

Primary Trends: Overarching trends that last over a year, defining the long-term market direction as bullish or bearish.

Secondary Trends: Last weeks to months and act as corrections to the primary trend. (Opportunity to take counter positions).

Minor Trends: These short-lived fluctuations last less than three weeks. (Opportunity to trade short term moves).

Trend prediction with news

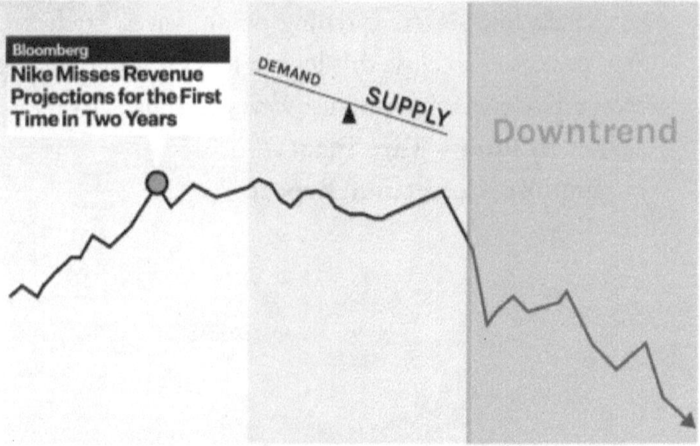

News serves as a powerful catalyst in financial markets by impacting supply and demand dynamics.

For instance, negative news can temporarily reduce the stock price of a fundamentally strong company.

This influence is particularly notable in secondary and minor market trends where even short-term issues can lead to significant price drops.

To leverage this effectively, interpret news from a supply and demand perspective.

Ask yourself whether the news will likely encourage selling or boost demand?

Brief introduction to waves

Much like surfers catching ocean waves, traders catch market waves. To close this lesson, let's explore two primary wave types in trading: impulse waves and corrective waves, as defined by **Elliott Wave Theory**.

Impulse. Correction. Repeat.

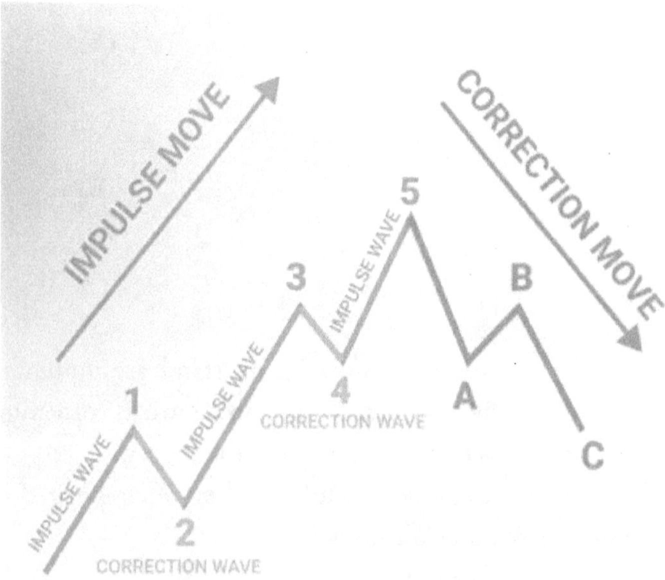

Impulse waves propel the market in the direction of the prevailing trend, while corrective waves counter this movement.

These wave patterns exist across various timeframes.

So what to do with this information?

Not every market trend strictly follows Elliott Wave Theory. If you try to force it on the chart without sufficient skill, you will lose.

Yet, the theory effectively shows the zigzag nature of market trends.

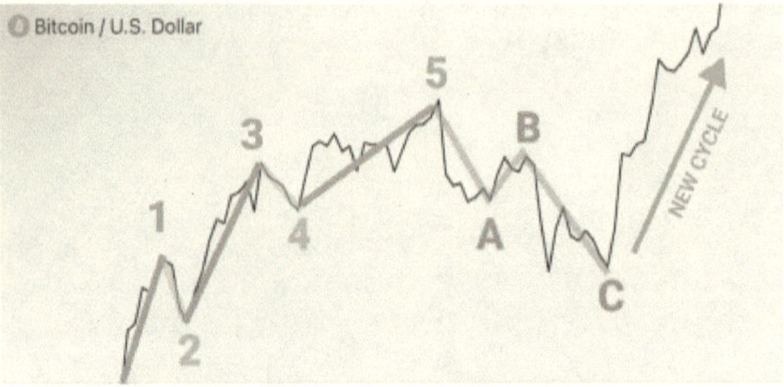

The optimal entry points in any trend, are at points 2, 4, A, and C in the wave structure - also known as corrections or reversals - this is true even beyond the theory.

As one cycle concludes, another often begins, often resuming the previous trend.

Main Takeaways

- **Understand Trend Types:** Recognize if the market is in an uptrend, downtrend, or a sideways trend.

- **Identify Wave Patterns:** Look for impulse and corrective waves within these trends.

- **Enter trades at Corrective Waves:** Use corrective waves as your entry points, aligning with the direction of the primary trend.

We will build upon the concepts of this chapter later on, when we craft your strategy.

It's time to take an exam.

1. What is the predominant emotion during bull markets?

- Uncertainty
- Greed/Optimism
- Fear

1. All assets can be traded 24/7?

- True
- False

1. What is the fundamental force behind price changes?

- Buyers and sellers
- Supply and demand
- News

Answer:

1. Greed/Optimism

1. False

1. Supply and demand

Chapter 4: Charting Essentials

Lesson 1: Market's Treasure Map

Most trading losses can be reduced to one costly mistake, which is:

"buying and selling at the wrong time"

The most common reason for this is a simple but a deadly sin in trading:

Ignoring the chart before opening a trade.

Look at the chart as a treasure map, guiding you toward strategic buy and sell points without guesswork. Let's explore...

Charting versus flying blind

Observe two former novices, Alex and Mikaela, as they trade the same asset using different approaches.

#1 Alex's trade: Alex was the typical beginner, excited to become rich overnight but overlooking the basics.

He got a hot stock tip from a buddy who had apparently struck gold with AMD stock. Driven by **FOMO** (fear of missing out), Alex bought AMD too. Unfortunately at the worst possible time. He lost big.

#2 Mikaela's trade: Mikaela was a naturally cautious person, the kind who triple-checked her locked door. Her decision-making went as follows:

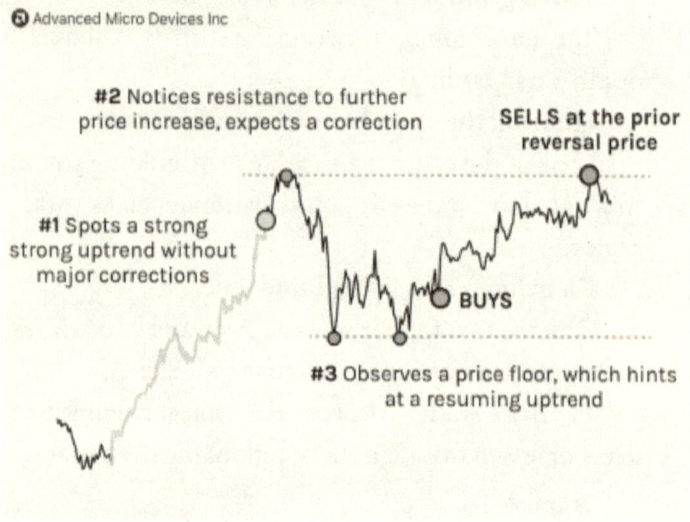

Armed with the very basics of chart analysis and good timing, in just a few weeks Mikaela closed a profitable trade.

Main Takeaway

Contrasting Alex and Mikaela proves the utility of even basic charting skills.

The following lessons will deepen your understanding of technical analysis-the art of deciphering trading charts for precise trade entries and exits.

But first, I have to **debunk a myth...**

Lesson 2: Is Technical Analysis Nonsense?

Can a few lines on a chart truly dictate your trading success? Skeptics often dismiss **technical analysis (TA)** as subjective and ineffective. While they have a point, their understanding falls short of grasping TA's influence on market trends. Let's dissect this.

The power of collective belief

Many traders often draw the same trend lines and recognize similar patterns in charts. **It's not random.**

When a sufficient number of traders act upon the same pattern, they create a self-fulfilling prophecy, causing a price reaction.

It's like a viral TikTok dance: one person starts, and soon everyone's in sync, making it a popular trend.

Quick facts:

- 83% of traders frequently use TA, according to a 2019 study.

- A 2017 research paper concluded that strategies based on TA outperform random strategies.

TA and market psychology

Trading isn't just about numbers; it's about reading what the market is thinking too.

When a lot of people believe something will happen in the market and act on it, prices move.

In our upcoming lessons, I'll show you how it works. I'll go over the most popular techniques, helping you be on the right side of the trade more often.

Let's start with charting basics and build from there.

Lesson 3: Simple But Effective Line Chart

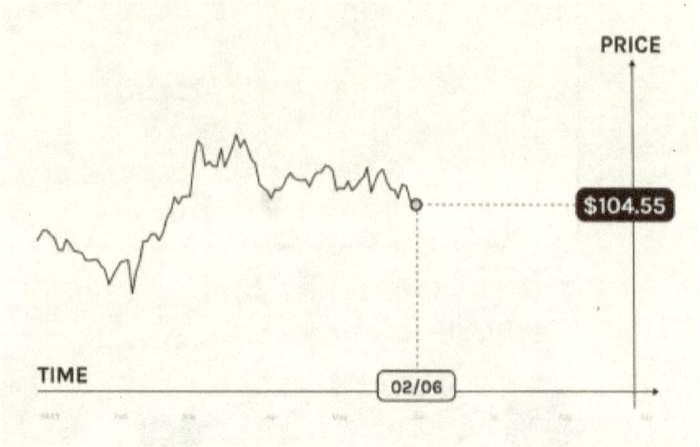

First off, what is a line chart? It's a series of data points connected by a line.

While that sounds simplistic, it's the very simplicity that makes line charts very effective for traders. According to a study by **Trading View** (a must-have platform that offers an intuitive charting, backtesting and trade automation), over 40% of traders use line charts, particularly when starting out.

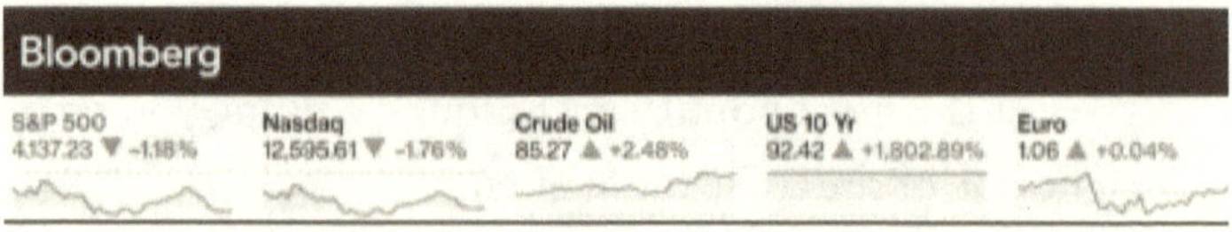

It's what you'll often see referenced in major financial news as well, giving you a quick glance at the current trend.

Line Chart vs Noise

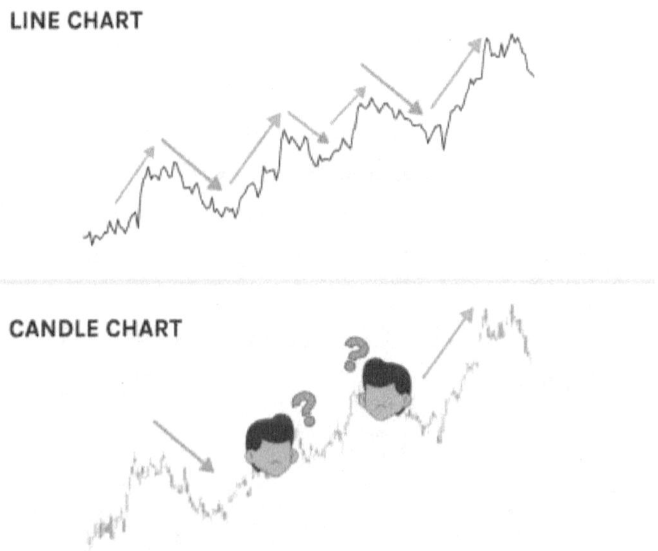

In trading, **'noise'** refers to distracting data that can divert focus from the core trend.

Because the line focuses on closing prices - **often deemed the most critical metric of the price** - they filter out this noise, giving you a quick snapshot of market direction.

For investing, you don't need much else, but even for medium-term styles like swing trading, a line chart can cut down analysis time by around 30%.

Two line charts = secret insights

Overlaying two line charts is an easy way to visually discern the relationship between different assets.

When both charts move in tandem-either up or down-it's a strong indicator of positive correlation. Conversely, if one line ascends while the other descends, you're likely observing a negative correlation. Which means you can go long on one asset and short on the other. If we simplify...

Case Study: Correlation between CAD/JPY and Crude Oil

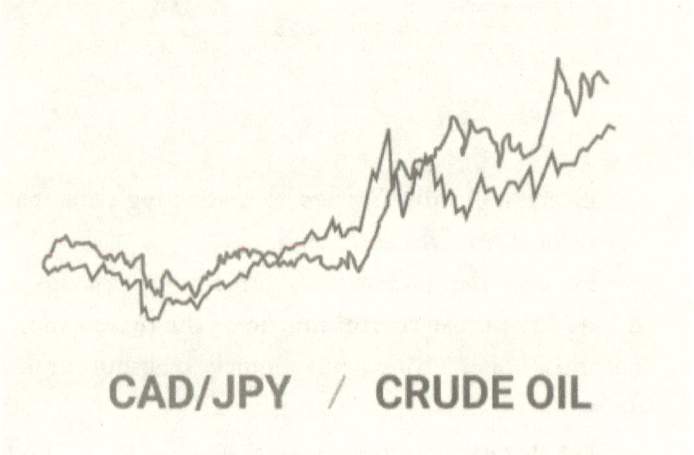

If you're watching the Canadian dollar and Japanese yen exchange rate, also keep an eye on oil prices. **Here's the rationale:**

- Rising oil prices bolster Canada's financial standing, fortifying the CAD.
- Japan, heavily reliant on oil imports, faces economic strains when oil prices rise, potentially

devaluing the yen. Thus, there is often a correlation between the price of oil and the CAD/JPY currency pair.

• When the price of oil goes up, the CAD/JPY tends to follow suit.

Let's take it up a notch

Depending on your approach to the markets, a line chart might be all you need.

Yet, to truly understand market psychology, you must learn to read a candle chart.

Lesson 4: Candlestick Chart

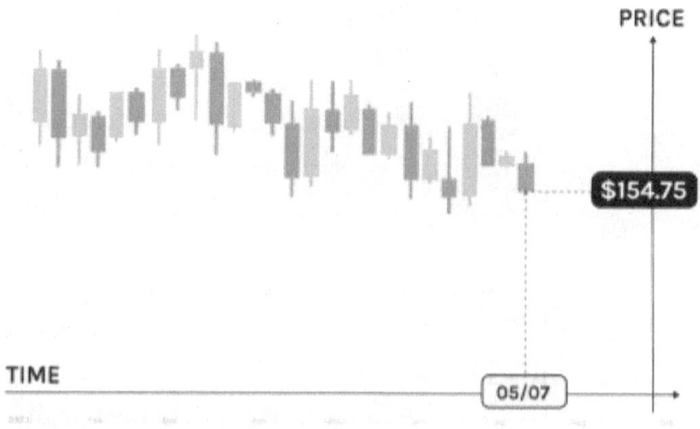

Candlestick charts add another layer of depth to your market analysis.

They're not essential for a beginner, but incredibly beneficial nonetheless as they reveal more than just trends and the price.

Candles give you insights into, emotion, volatility, reversal points, and the strength of buyers and sellers at any given moment.

The four part story

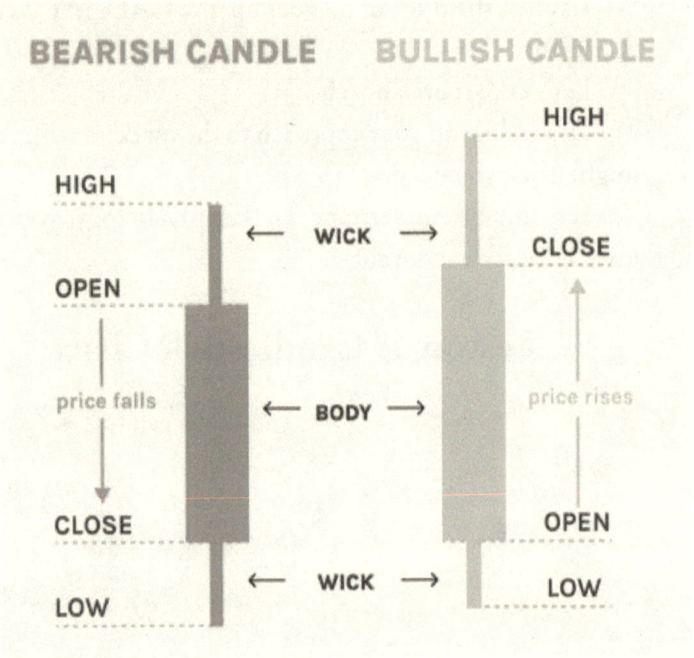

Each candlestick captures four key prices: Open, High, Low, and Close (OHLC), revealing the tug-of-war between buyers and sellers in a set timeframe.

Follow steps 1-6 to see how it works practically on the chart.

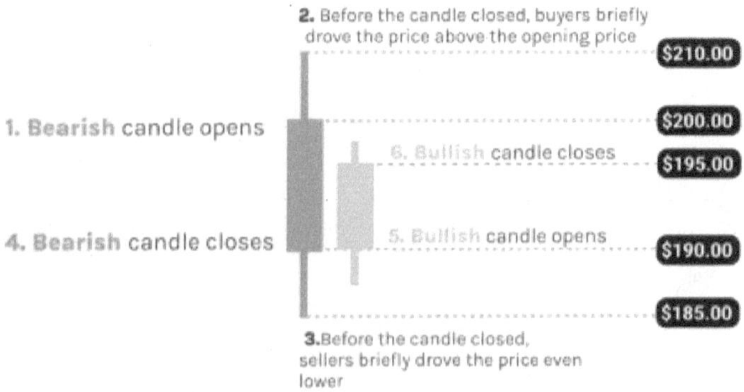

- Bearish candles open higher and close lower, signaling a price drop.

- Bullish candles open lower and close higher, indicating a price gain.

- Wicks mark the candles highs and lows, consistent in both types of candles.

Before I explain **time frames**, let's take one last look at how candles can show the strength of buy and sell sides.

The hidden signs behind different candles

The size of the wick compared to the body of the candlestick is really important. It can give you hints about how the price might move next. Take a close look at the following illustration.

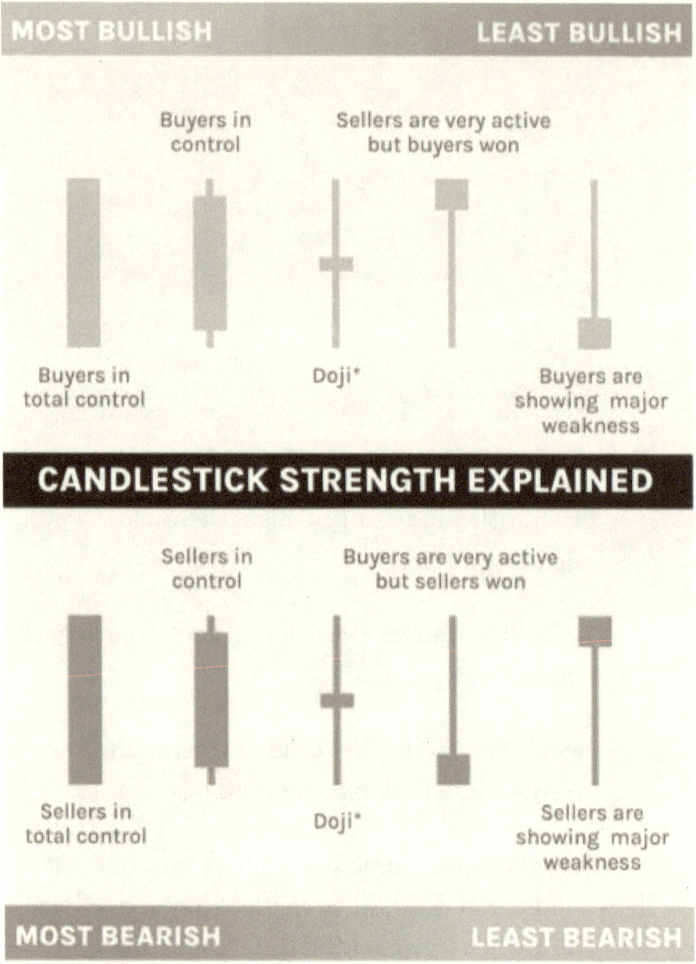

For example, a long wick and a small body on a candle suggest that the price was reversed during that period, indicating the strength of the opposing market force.

Subtle cues like these offer insights into the battle between buyers and sellers. **Lastly...**

A Doji candlestick is a sign that the market is uncertain, with neither buyers nor sellers taking a clear lead.

While Dojis alone shouldn't dominate your decision-making, their presence can be more telling when combined with other market indicators. In other words, Dojis become more insightful when used as part of a comprehensive trading strategy.

Next, we'll delve into the subject of **time frames** in chart analysis.

Lesson 5: Time Frames Explained

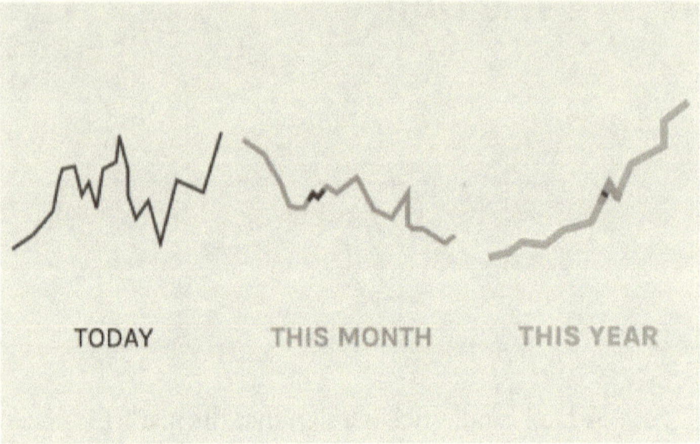

Time frames are like filters through which you view market movements. For example, you can look at how the price is moving minute by minute, or perhaps how it changes from week to week.

Price action trough different lenses

Consider time frames similar to a camera lens. Just like varying focal lengths (mm) bring out distinct details in a photograph, different time frames also offer different perspectives of the same thing.

- On a 1-hour chart, it looks like buyers are in full control.
- However, dial down to a 5-minute chart, and you'll see sellers also made significant attempts during this period.

Your choice of time frames should resonate with your trading strategy. The detailed data you see in shorter time frames may not be as relevant if you're a long-term investor, and vice versa. We'll unpack this shortly.

What does 'opening' and 'closing' mean?

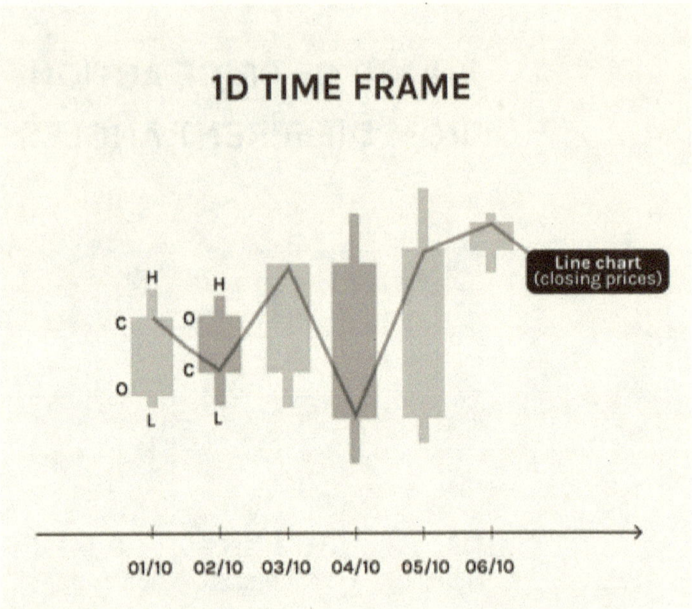

Your chosen time frame dictates when candles open and close. For instance, on a daily time frame, a new candle starts each day and closes by the end, representing that day's price action.

From this perspective, a candlestick is **a unit of time + price action.** This time frame selection then guides the extent of time and price data your candlestick chart displays.

How many timeframes to use?

When trading, choose 2-3 primary time frames to avoid information overload - the

"noise" we covered already.

- **Day Trading: 1min to 1h charts**
- **Swing Trading: 4h to 1d charts**
- **Investing: 1week to 1month charts**
- **Copy Trading: Pro traders decision.**

Over the coming lessons you will learn various technical analysis tools and strategies, so keep in mind:

Apply analysis only to the time frames that you plan to trade!

Next up - arguably the most important concept of chart analysis.

Lesson 6: Support And Resistance

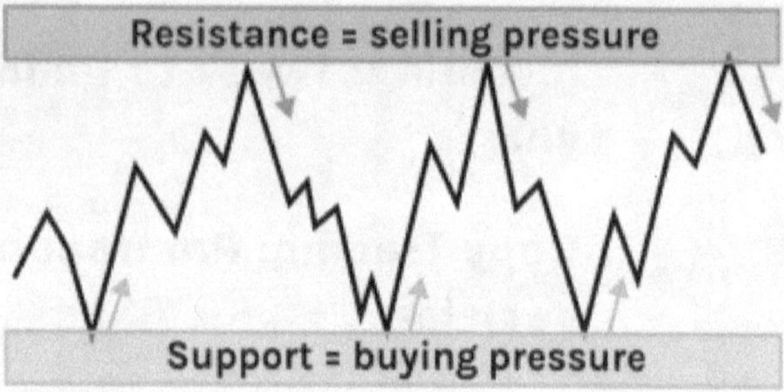

In this lesson, we dive into one of the most important concepts in technical analysis: support and resistance. These are levels or areas on the chart where the price failed to push pass in the past.

- When there are many **buyers (buy orders)** at a certain price, it creates a "support" level that stops the price from going lower.

- Similarly, high amount of **sellers (sell orders)** at a certain price forms a resistance level.

Subjectivity is a problem

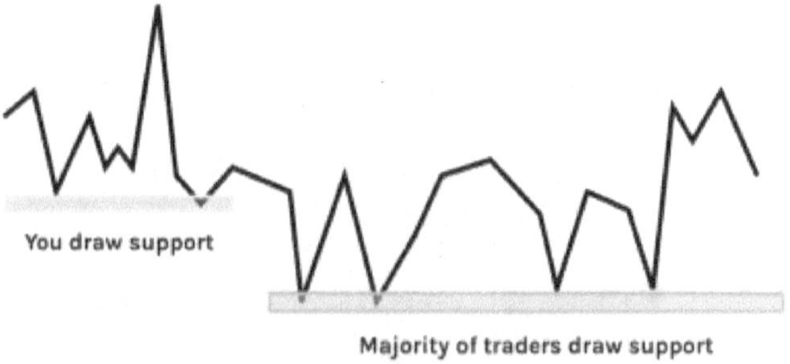

It's vital to mention individual interpretation plays a significant role; what appears as a 'support' to one may seem like mere noise to another. This subjectivity often leads traders to sketch arbitrary lines, perplexed when the price action doesn't pan out as expected.

We can fix it by following these steps to find the strongest levels.

Identification strategies

#1 Consider it as an area, not a clear line

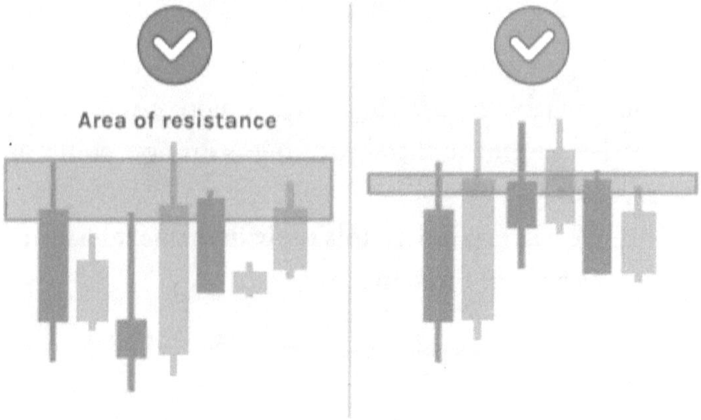

Market volatility necessitates thinking of support and resistance as zones, rather than rigid lines.

#2 Key levels are found on higher time frames

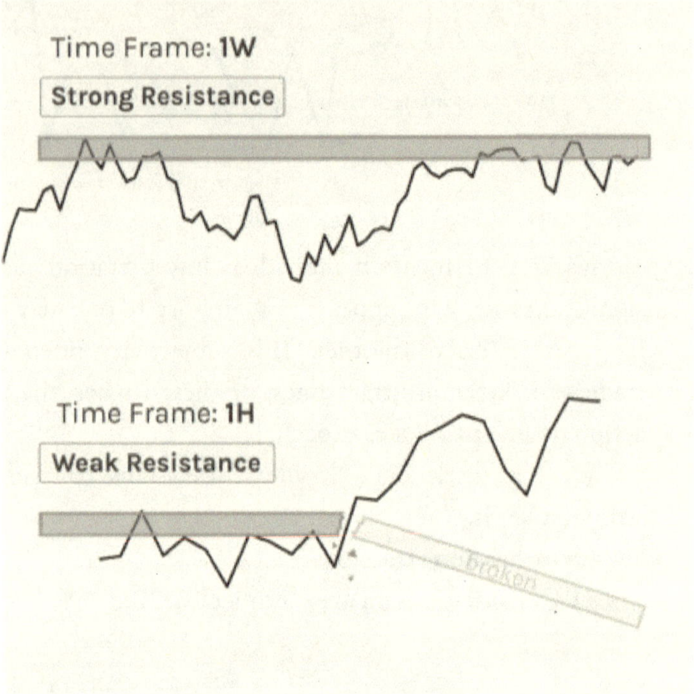

Higher time frames like the daily or weekly often offer more reliable levels. They cover a more extensive range of market sentiment, thereby serving as stronger points of price reversals.

We will expand on this topic in the next lesson!

#3 Rule of three touches

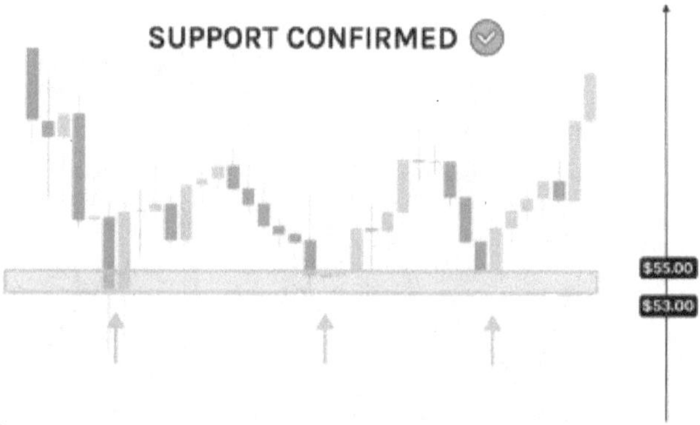

If the price bounces off a certain price area at least 3X, it's worth paying attention to.

In the example above, three reversals show sustained buying pressure at the area on the chart between $53-$55. This can then be considered a support zone.

Most popular S/R types

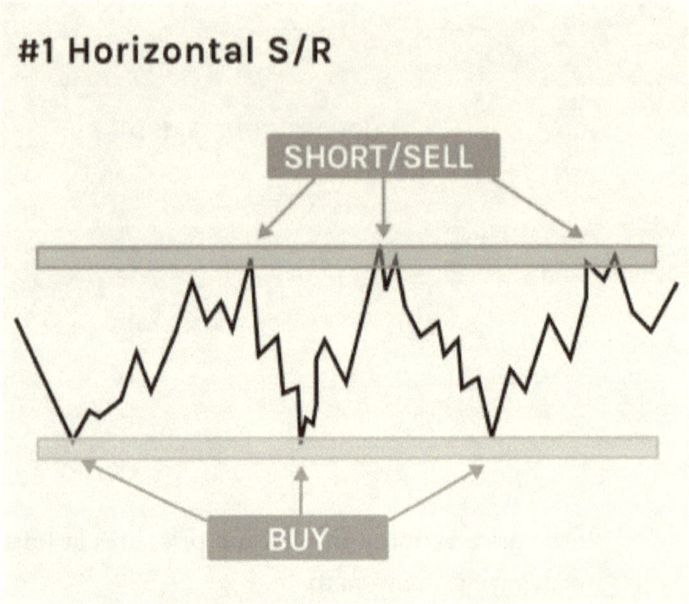

Horizontal levels serve as a foundational tool for analyzing the chart.

These can also manifest around significant numbers.

#2 Round number S/R

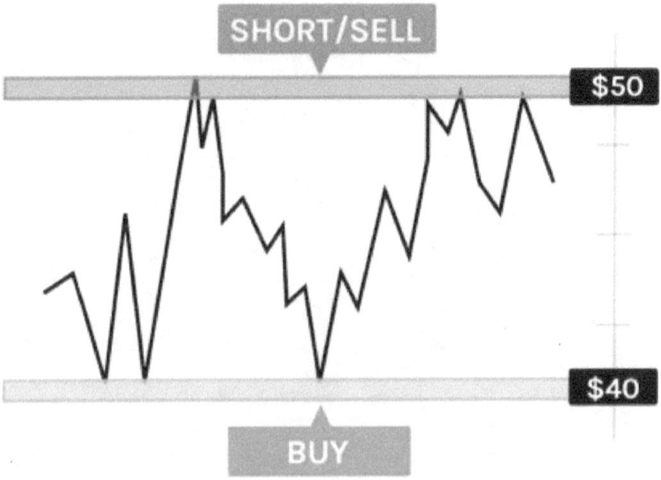

In trading, people pay more attention to round numbers like $25, $50, or $100, that's why you see more buying and selling happen at these prices. The surge in traders interest can turn these price points into S/R levels on the chart.

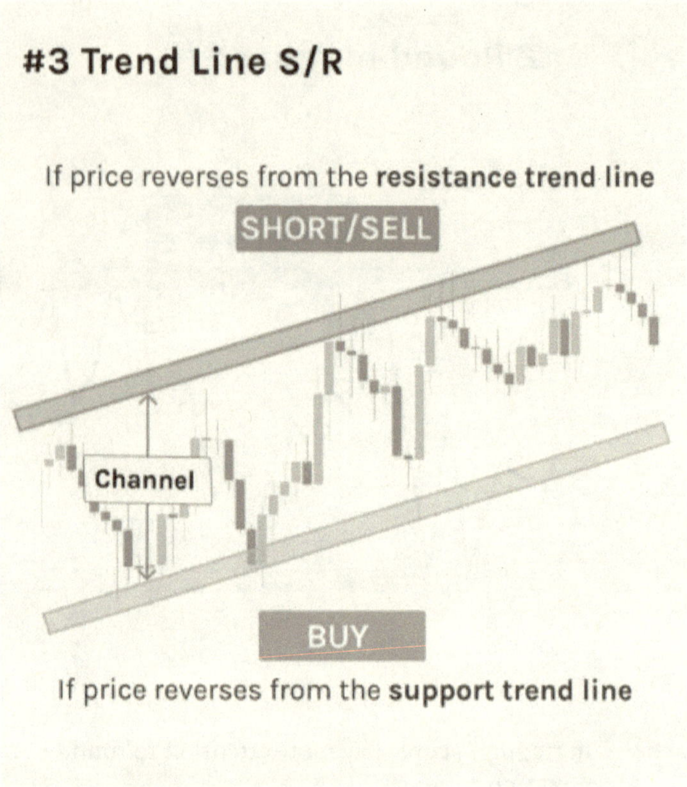

In a trending market, you'll usually see support or resistance levels guiding the price. Sometimes, you'll spot two trend lines creating a price channel. Trading within this channel is straightforward: Buy or short at one line and aim to exit at the other.

When a level finally breaks...

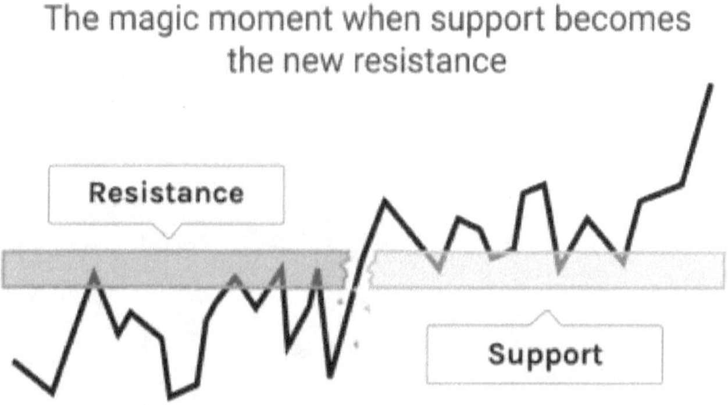

Support and resistance levels often flip roles. A level that previously acted as support can later serve as resistance, and vice versa. The breakouts themselves are often volatile moves that bring both risk and reward.

The bottom line

In closing, it's important to remember that while support and resistance levels offer valuable insights, they are based on past market data, which doesn't guarantee future performance.

However, this limitation isn't unique to S/R; it's a characteristic of most forms of technical analysis. In the next lesson, I'll introduce market structure. A concept that can significantly improve the probability of you buying and selling at the right time.

Lesson 7: Market Structure

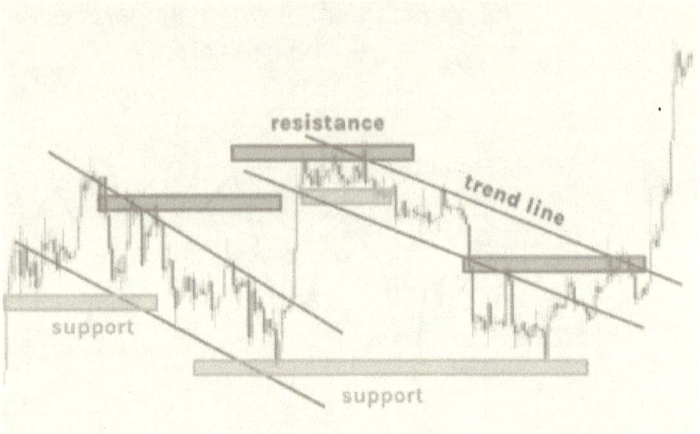

Great progress! Let's explore how you can create a blueprint based on your existing knowledge of charts. This will help you see and understand what is happening on the chart and where opportunities might lie.

What is market structure

Market structure refers to the visible elements on a chart that show what's happening in real time. These include highs and lows, support and resistance levels, and trends and other key areas of interest.

To make the best sense of these elements, understanding **market sentiment** is key.

BEARISH SENTIMENT

Sellers will actively try to break structure to the downside. Upside moves will be weaker.

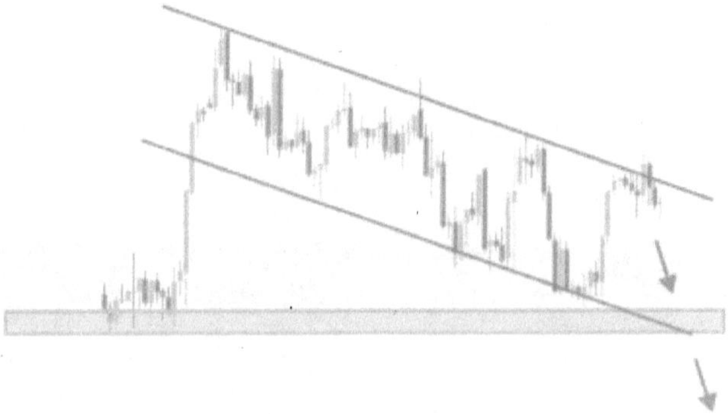

Sentiment reflects the general mood about an asset, as its influenced by news and the overall economy. By combining sentiment with chart analysis, you can effectively map out market structure.

It's best to start your analysis with a top-down approach:

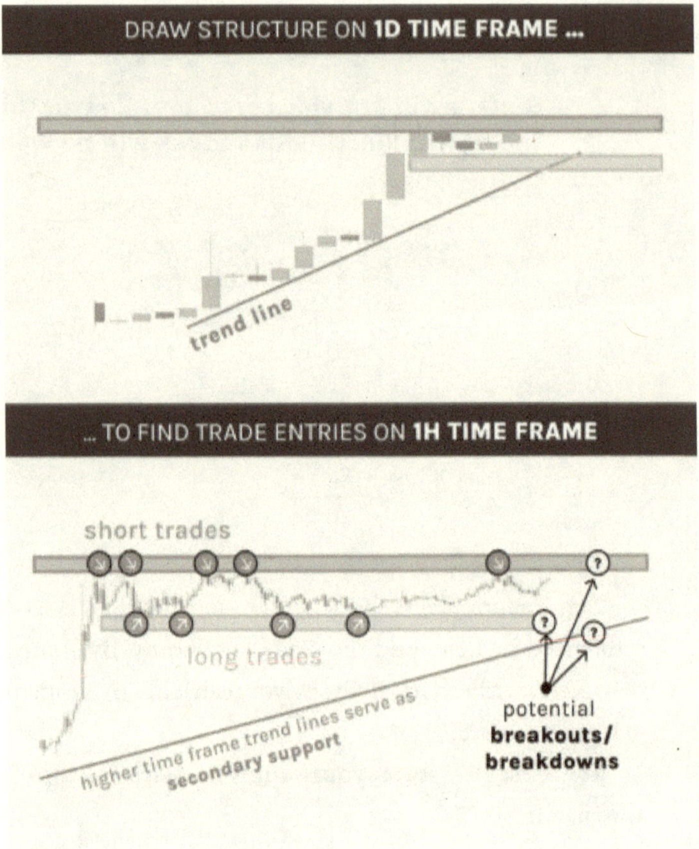

Top-down analysis begins with a **higher-timeframe chart (HTF)** where you identify:

- Trend lines and channels
- Support and resistance zones
- Chart patterns (**next lessons**)

The HTF serves as your guide for understanding market movements, while the lower timeframe helps you pinpoint precise trade entries.

Price action within market structure

Let's explore the key types of price movements within the structure you draw.

#1 Pullback/retracement

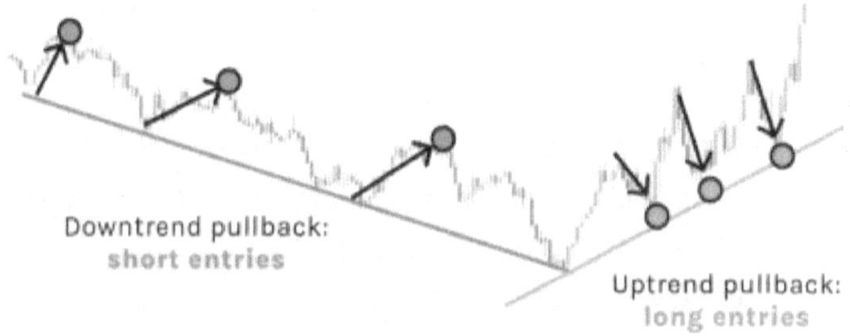

These are brief reversals in the trend where the price moves against the main direction, often creating opportunities to enter the trade at a better price.

#2 Breakdown/breakout

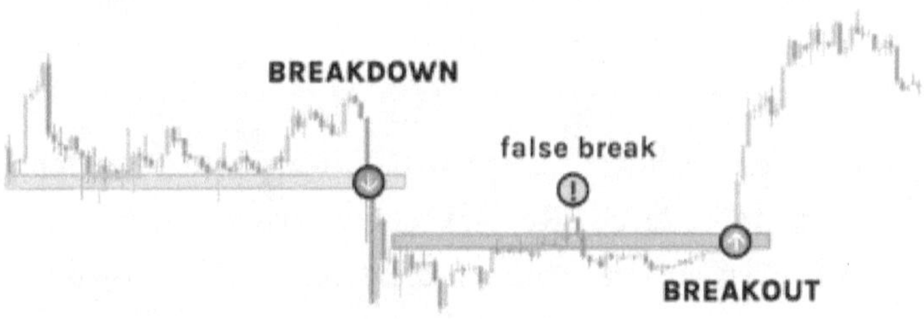

- A breakdown is a significant downward move below a key support area or trend line, indicating high selling pressure.

- A breakout is a strong upwards move out of a well-defined range or above an area of resistance.

Breakout is often used to describe both up and down moves.

- A false break is when either happens but the price quickly reverses back into it's previous range.

Beginners often lose big on false breaks because they fail to validate breakouts and breakdowns with other factors, like volume. **More on this soon!**

#2 Test / Retest

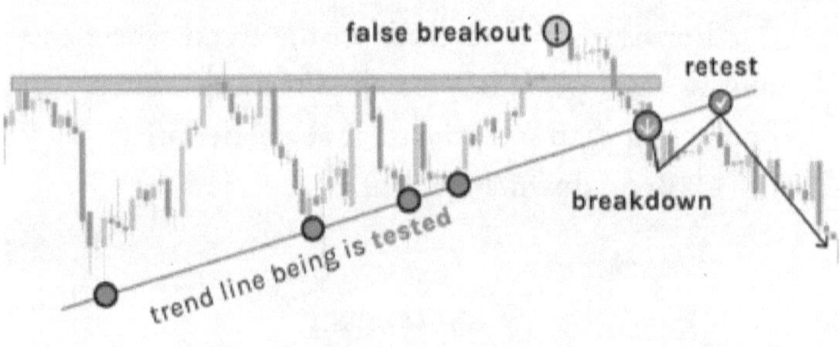

Tests validate market structure elements like trendlines or support levels. **Retests** happen when the price revisits a broken structure after a breakout or breakdown, usually confirming a new market direction.

The bottom line

I encourage you to apply what you've learned by identifying the structure on an actual trading chart. **Start chart watching!**

I must note that, some strategies are based on specific elements of market structure. For example:

- **Opening Prices:** Some strategies focus on the opening price of a day or month, which is critical as it sets the tone for that period's trading activity.

- **Highs and Lows of the Day:** Other strategies are focused on trading breakouts, which center around these daily extremes.

As you progress, you will begin to see what fits for you and what you don't need. Now let's talk indicators.

Exam - Charting Essentials

1. How does market psychology relate to TA?

- It renders TA useless as trading is purely rational

- Support and resistance gain meaning when traders believe and act on them.

- There is no correlation between psychology and Technical Analysis

1. What four key prices does each candlestick capture?

- Bid, Ask, Open and Close
- Open, Close, Volume and Change
- Open, High, Low, and Close

1. What is the purpose of using a different time frame in trading?

- To offer different perspectives of the same price action
- To change the trading strategy
- To display different currencies

Answer:

1. Support and resistance gain meaning when traders believe and act on them.

2. Open, High, Low, and Close
3. To offer different perspectives of the same price action

Chapter 5: Indicators

Lesson 1: Trading Volume

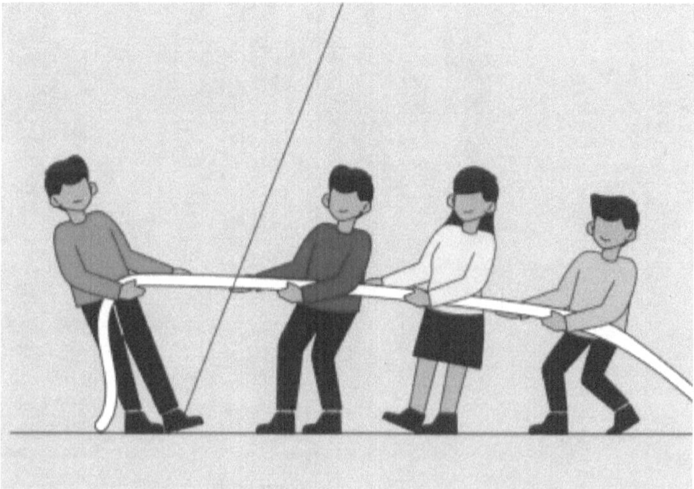

The secret of the volume indicator lies in its simplicity and the crucial insights it provides into the price action that cannot be found elsewhere.

This lesson will teach you how to use it to confirm whether price movements on the chart have strength and potential trade opportunities.

The Ultimate Indicator

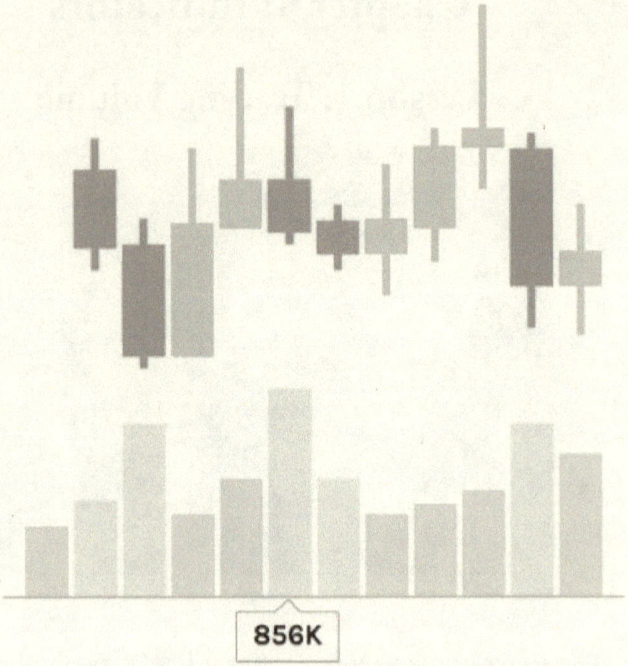

Volume indicates **the number of times** an asset was traded within a specified period.

Think of it this way: Which scenario creates a bigger buzz - **a small concert with an audience of 50 or a sold-out stadium packed with 10,000 enthusiastic fans?**

Similarly volume showcases the traders participation and activity during a price movement.

VOLUME BAR COLOR

If the matching candle is bearish the volume bar is coloured red

---

Conversely a bullish candle will have a green volume bar

Higher volume indicates commitment and confidence in a price move, and thus it's the best indicator for confirming:

- trend reversals
- chart patterns
- support and resistance breakouts

Let's go over a few examples.

A strong trend is typically accompanied by increasing or elevated volume, indicating the commitment of traders to the prevailing direction.

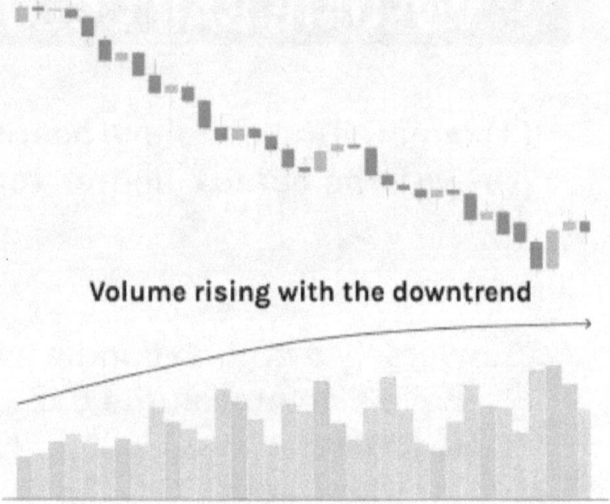

When the price is clearly trending but volume is decreasing, it is called a divergence and can be one of the first signs of an incoming trend reversal.

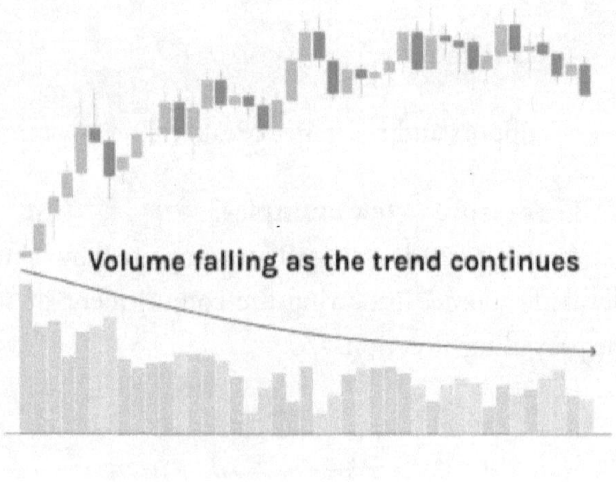

Confirm breakouts using volume

High trading volume during breakouts can indicate strong interest or conviction in the price move. Here's an example:

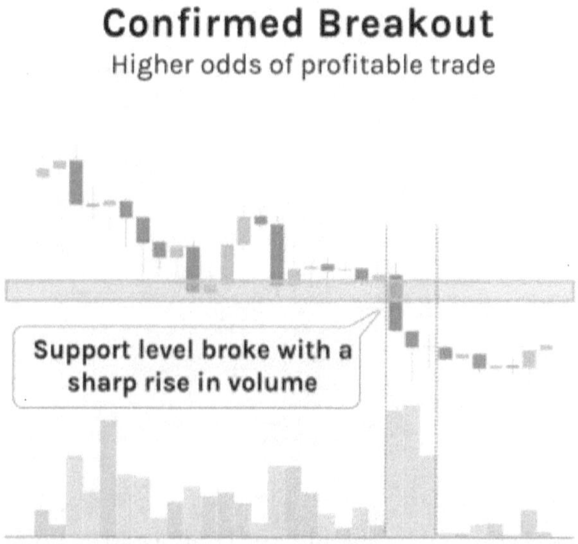

In contrast, low trading volume can indicate uncertainty or disinterest in the price move, and it's the #1 predictor for false breakouts.

Here's an example:

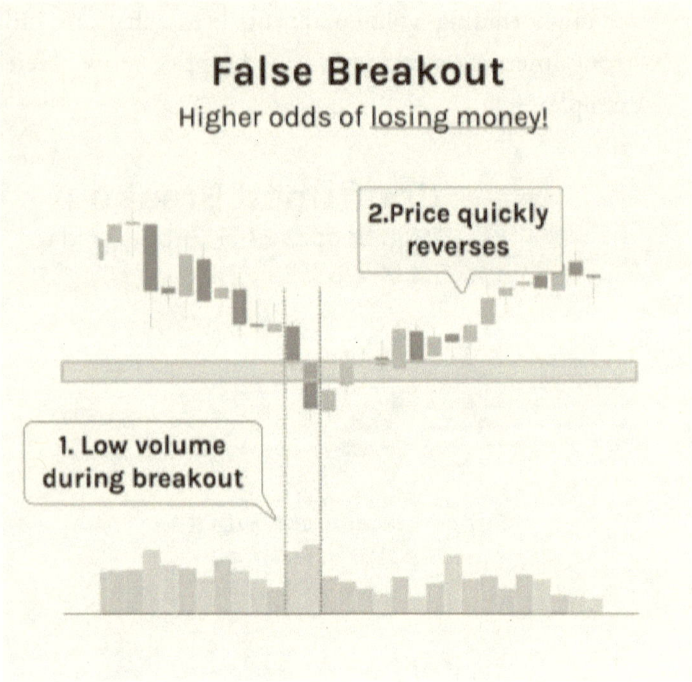

Acting on profitable breakouts is a key component of successful trading, and it can be achieved through various methods such as chart patterns, support and resistance levels, trend lines, and other technical structures.

By confirming breakouts with volume and trading only the most convincing price moves, you can greatly improve your success rate.

Lesson 2: Relative Strength Index

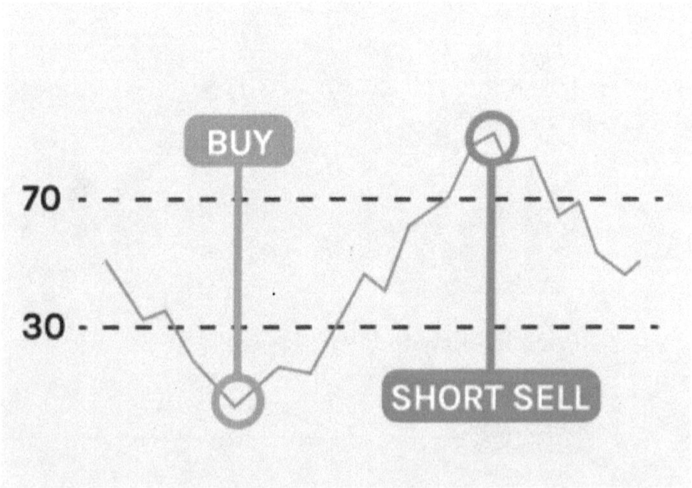

The **Relative Strength Index (RSI)** is a potent yet straightforward tool that aids in recognizing lucrative price reversals. It accomplishes this by indicating whether an asset is overvalued or undervalued, relying on recent price data for its assessment.

Predicting reversals with RSI

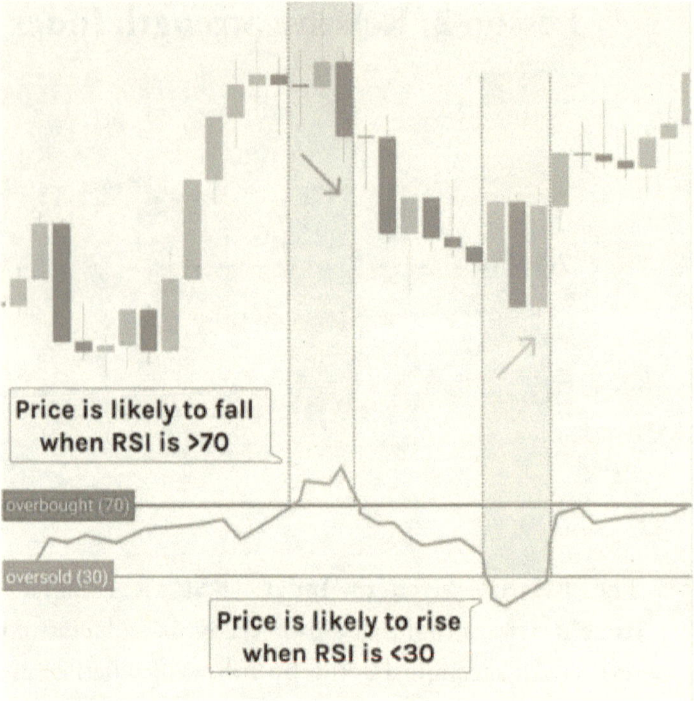

The RSI is an oscillator that spans from 0 to 100.

Typically, when the RSI indicator crosses 30, it suggests a bullish signal, while a crossing of 70 indicates a bearish signal.

However, during strong trends, the indicator can stay in overbought or oversold conditions for an extended period of time.

Like the volume indicator, it is commonly displayed as a graph beneath the chart, but there is a better way to show it.

Never miss the next trade

We can customize the RSI indicator to provide real-time readability and convenience.

In a simulator, you can set up the RSI so that it will seamlessly overlay on the chart, allowing you to observe the correlation between the current price and the indicator as it unfolds.

We put RSI right where the price action is

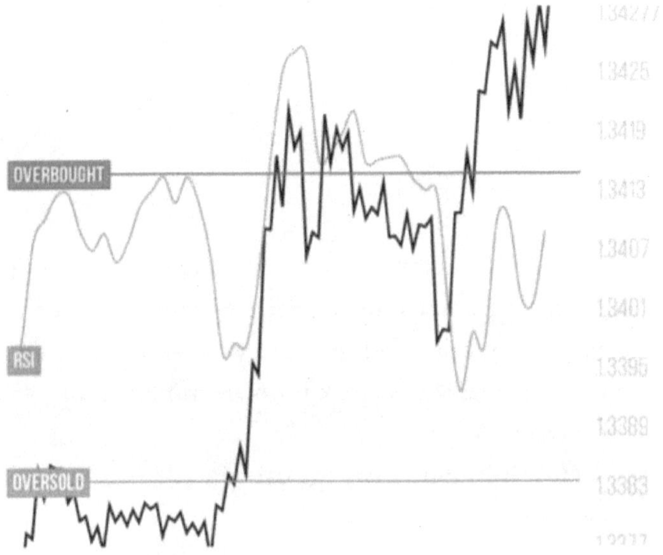

As you have learned, the RSI indicator alone does not guarantee success in trading. Its value lies in its role as a supplementary tool to validate potential price movements on the chart.

Lesson 3: Moving Average (MA)

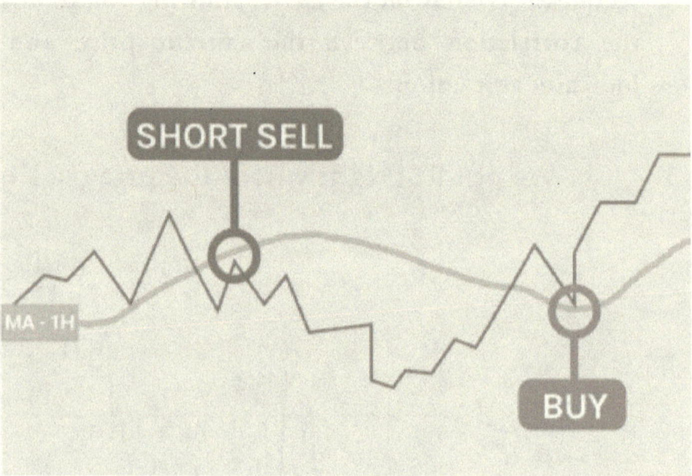

The MA indicator helps to filter out market noise, by showing the average price over a certain period of time. It creates a smooth trend line that you can use as a signal for opening trades. Let's break it down and learn how to use it effectively.

How is Moving Average calculated?

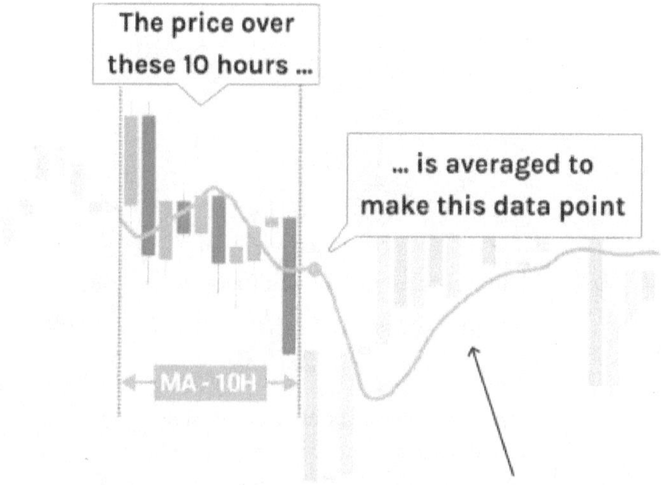

The process repeats continuously, creating a line of connected data points known as a "moving average."

Traders utilize a range of setups, some favour a 30-day period, while others opt for shorter intervals like 10-day or 5-day periods.

To address this diversity, we should use a longer MA period on a larger time frame to confirm a trend and the breakout before placing our entry order.

Find strong trends using a longer MA period (MA - 90D)

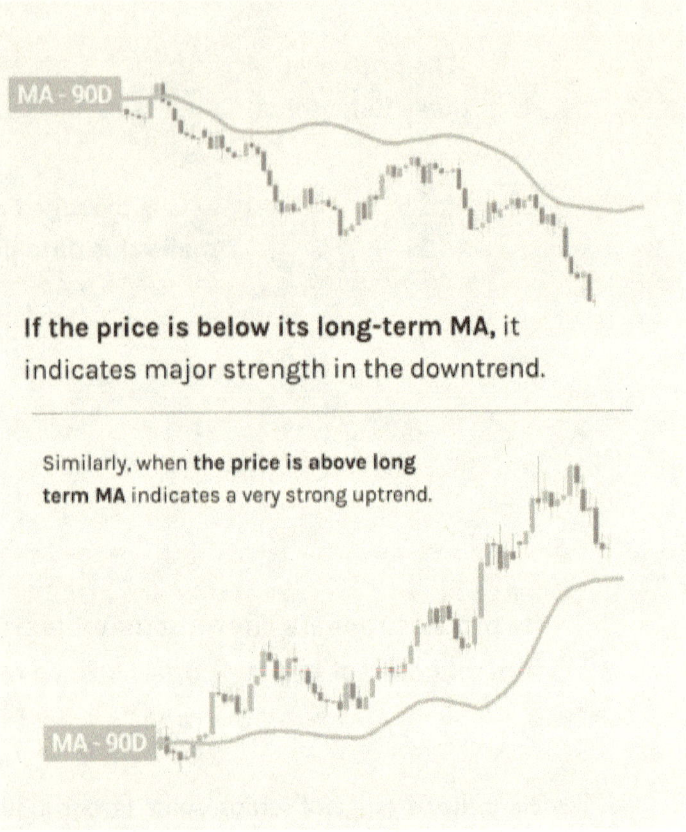

To avoid trading weak moves, consider using a long-term moving average (MA) on a larger timeframe. As mentioned earlier, the importance of these levels tends to amplify with higher timeframes.

Trading MA breakouts

A moving average (MA) breakout occurs when the price of an asset breaks above or below its moving average line. The longer the moving average period, the more significant the breakout and thus the trade opportunity.

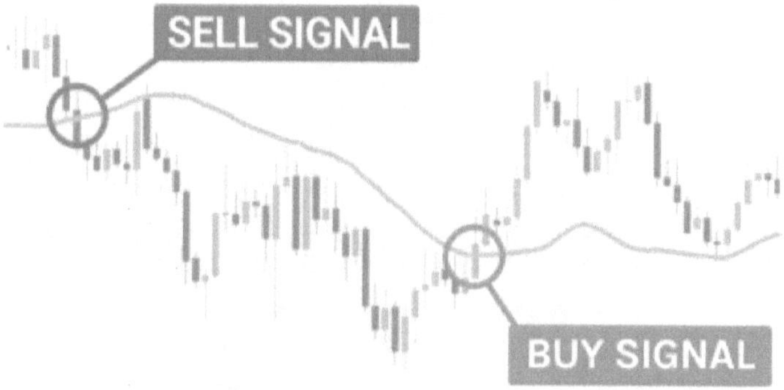

MA as support and resistance

The MA indicator can also act as as either a support or resistance level, which opens a whole other set of opportunities to go long or short when the price reverses from either level.

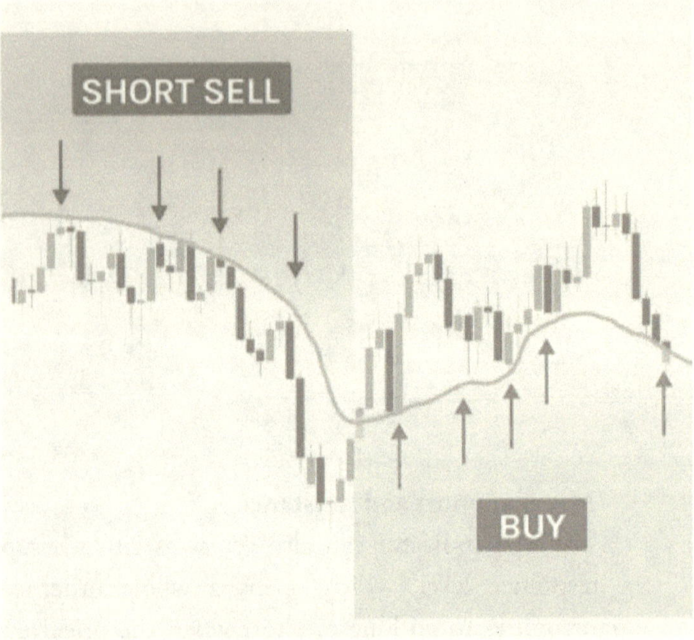

Similar to the standard support and resistance (S/R) levels, the MA levels can also flip, causing the previous support level to become the new resistance level. **To validate a successful breakout, you can use the volume indicator.**

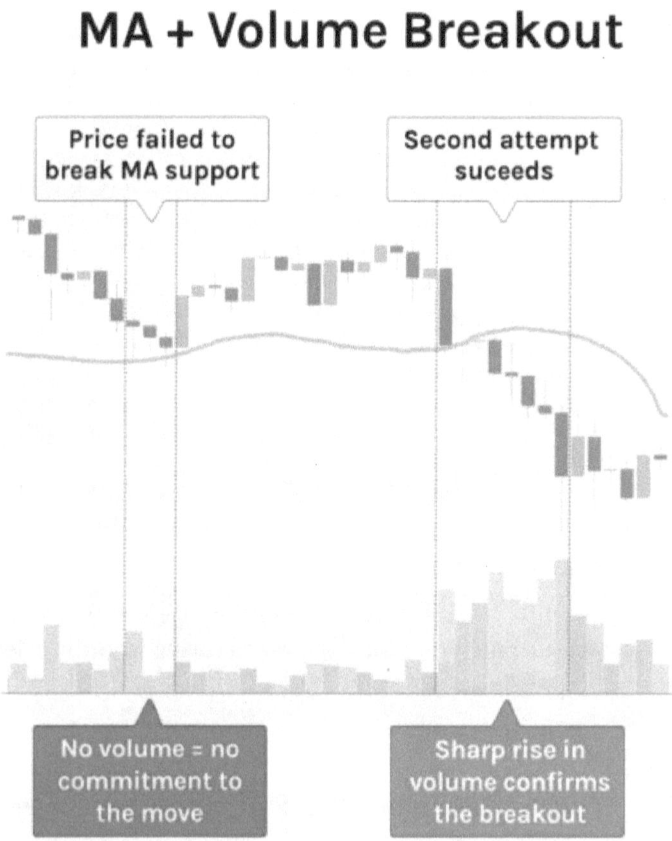

In the given example, the combination of two signals once again reinforces the movement, amplifying its strength.

Lesson 4: VWAP

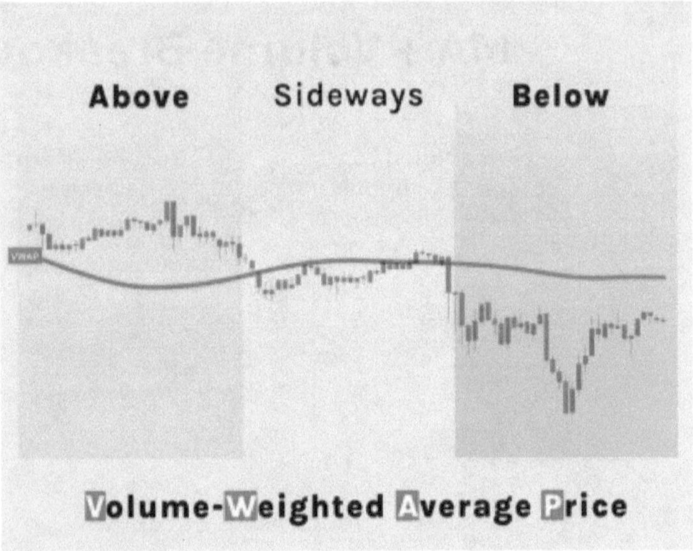

Simple Definition

VWAP is a moving-average-like indicator, showing an asset's average price for the day, factoring in both price and volume.

Why it matters

- Institutions use VWAP to execute large orders without disrupting price.

- Retail traders use it to identify trend direction, entries, and exits.

- It resets daily, making it ideal for intraday trading but not for swing trading, or long-term analysis.

How Institutions Use VWAP

Big players-hedge funds, mutual funds, and market makers - use VWAP as a benchmark for execution.

Their algorithms aim to buy below VWAP to get a better price without pushing the market up.

Next Time In Charts: If you see price hovering around VWAP with large volume, it could be institutions working an order.

How To Use This Indicator

#1 Support & Resistance Levels

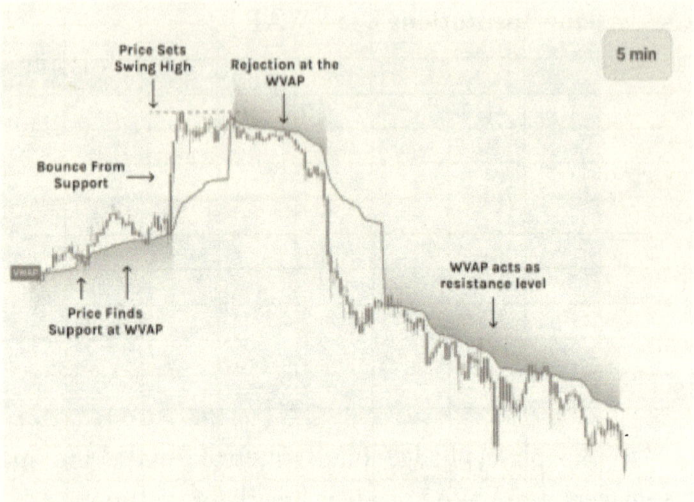

Support and resistance remain the key concepts in charting, and that applies to the VWAP line as well.

- **Above VWAP:** Acts as support (bullish bias).
- **Below VWAP:** Acts as resistance (bearish bias).

VWAP Slope = Trend Indicator:

- Rising VWAP = Uptrend confirmation.
- Flat VWAP = Consolidation, choppy market.
- Declining VWAP = Downtrend confirmation.

#2 Entries & Exits (VWAP As a Trade Filter)

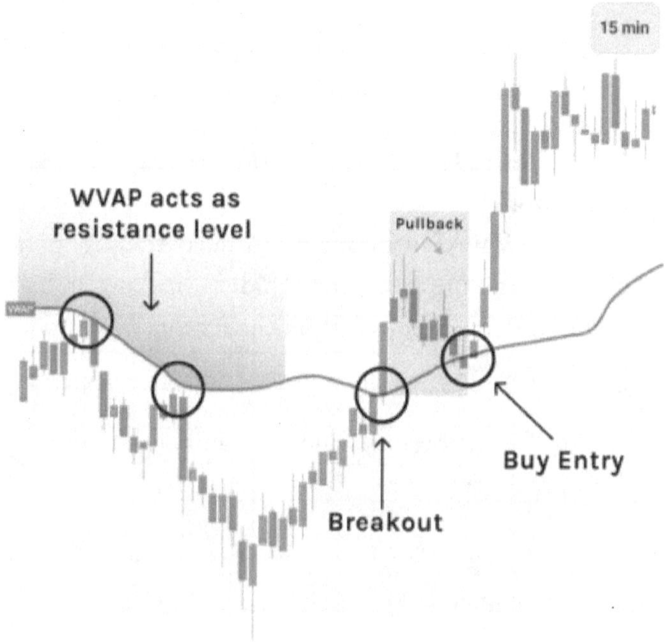

Entry Setups:

- Long entries: Buy pullbacks to VWAP with volume confirmation.

- Breakout trades: Enter when price breaks and holds above VWAP.

- Short setups: Short VWAP rejections from below.

Exit targets:

- Profit target: VWAP can be a take-profit area for long and short trades

- Mean reversion trades: When price extends too far from VWAP, it often snaps back. The VWAP can be used as a profit target in these scenarios.

#3 Intraday Trend Confirmation (VWAP Bias Framework)

Since VWAP is meant for intraday trading, trends and market structure can shift rapidly - making it harder to pinpoint strong setups early in the session.

Therefore:

- VWAP becomes more meaningful as the day progresses.

- Using VWAP in the first hour is NOT recommended.

Why?

- Early in the session, volume is low and unstable, which can make VWAP unreliable.

- As the day progresses, more volume accumulates, making VWAP a better reflection of fair value.

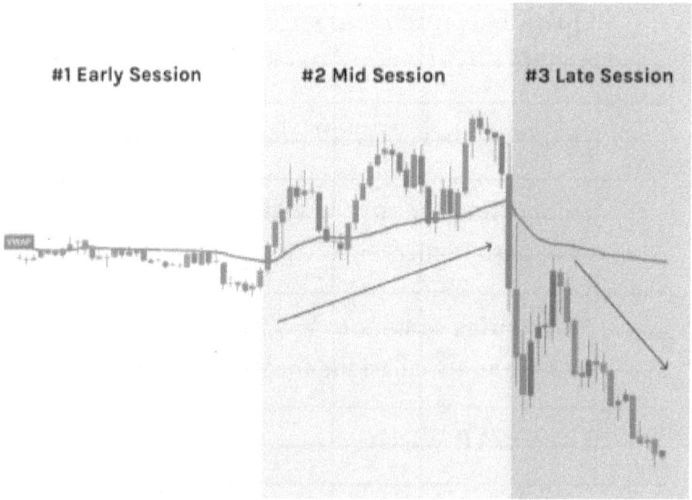

#1 Early Session (Indecision Zone)

• Price consolidates below VWAP with no strong momentum = indecision zone.

#2 Mid-Session (Trend Confirmation)

• Higher lows above VWAP = buyers gaining control. Pullback buy opportunities.

#3 Late Session (Reversals & Trend Exhaustion, Levels For Next Session)

• Price rejects VWAP after a breakdown = Short confirmation

• Failed VWAP reclaim = Trend continuation.

• VWAP Bias set for next session.

Quick Do's And Dont's
Avoid:

- Buying above VWAP without confirmation.

- Shorting the first VWAP touch - momentum can push higher.

- Ignoring volume - VWAP is useless without strong volume backing the move.

Use VWAP Wisely:

- As a bias filter, not a trade signal. With volume, support/resistance, and price action.

- Setting stops near VWAP-below for longs, above for shorts.

Bottom line

VWAP is an useful tool, not a magic bullet. Use it as a supporting element in your intra-day trade analysis.

Lesson 5: Super Trend

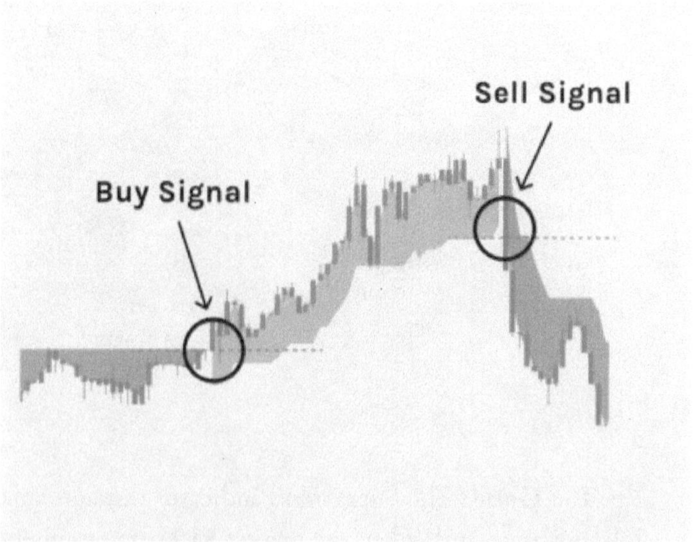

The Super-trend Indicator is excellent at identifying market trends and when they're about to change - hence the name.

It's simple, accurate, and powerful - making it useful both day trading and swing trading.

But what makes it better, is that it doesn't just track momentum. It also factors in ATR (Average True Range), meaning it accounts for market volatility.

And that's a game-changer for traders.

Here's how it works

- **Green Line = Bullish signal**
- **Red Line = Bearish signal**

This makes it incredibly simple to use, but like any indicator, it's not perfect. If you rely on it alone, you could run into issues. Let's talk about that.

The Problem With Super Trend (And Solution)

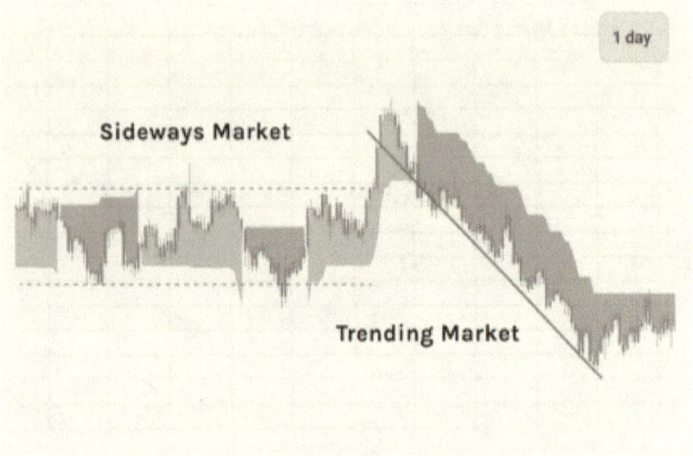

The Good: The Supertrend Indicator does an amazing job spotting trends when the market has strong momentum.

The Bad: But when the market moves sideways, it keeps throwing buy and sell signals, leading to unnecessary losses.

Supertrend in sideways markets = low momentum, unpredictable price action, and poor trade quality.

Solution

Use an additional trend filter - like the MA-200 to confirm trades and avoid weak signals.

The 1-Minute Scalping Strategy with Supertrend

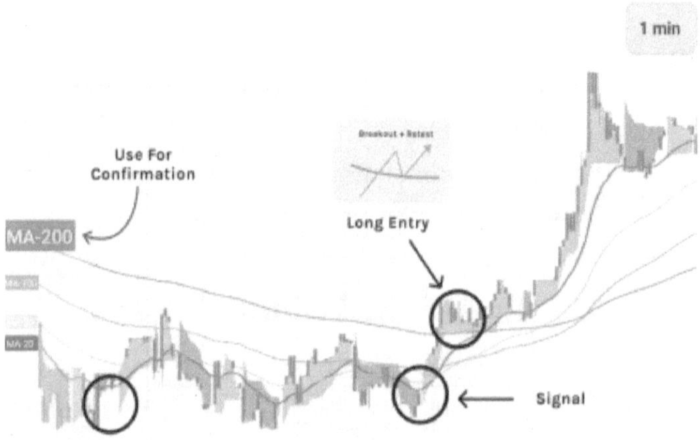

If you're looking for a fast, efficient trading method, the 1-minute scalping strategy using Supertrend is one of the best ways to trade intraday price movements.

Key Rules to Follow:

- Only take short trades if the price is trending below the 200 EMA.

- Only take long trades if the price is trending above the 200 EMA.

How to Trade It Profitably:

- Use the buy/sell signals from the Supertrend Indicator.

- Set a small take-profit target between 0.3% and 0.5%.

- Use the Supertrend lines as your stop-loss level.

- Take profit at supertrend shifts.

This simple strategy keeps you in strong trends while avoiding weak setups.

The 1-minute timeframe allows you to capitalize on fast market moves without overcomplicating things.

Lesson 6: Volume Profile

If you've ever looked at a price chart and felt like something was missing-like you weren't seeing the full picture-you were right.

Most traders focus only on price action and volume. But Volume Profile shows you where traders actually put their money at different price levels.

- Where the most trading activity happens

- Which price levels matter most
- Where price is likely to react, bounce, or break

Let's break down how it works, how to read it the right way, and how to use it to make better trades.

How Volume Profile Works

On a mobile device, Volume Profile may appear simpler than desktop versions but follows the same principles.

It's a fixed-range tool that highlights key volume data for the candles you're viewing.

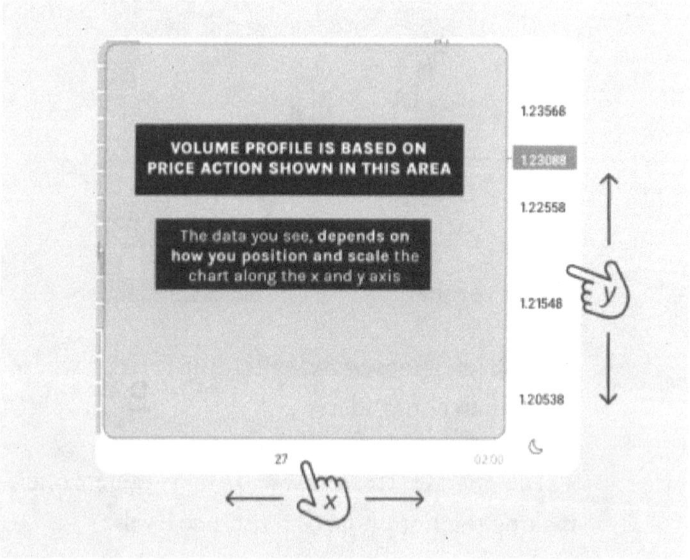

Reading The Data For Trades

To fully understand the key insights of the Volume Profile, we must first separate it's three distinct elements:

- High Volume Areas (HVA)

- Low Volume Areas (LVA)
- Point of Control (POC)

#1 High-Volume Areas

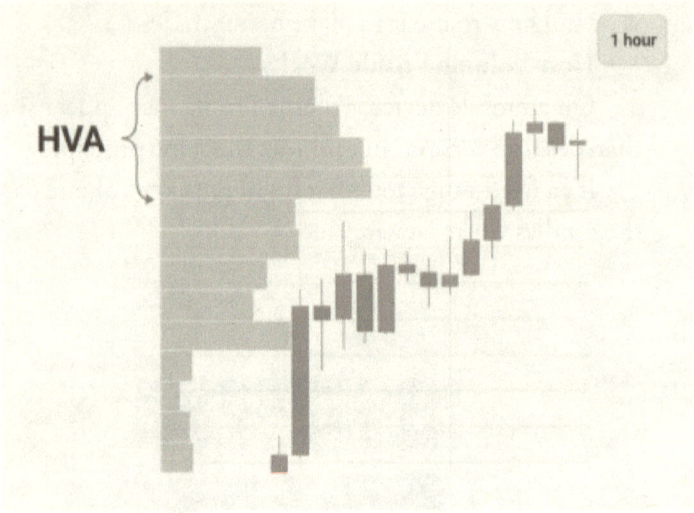

What it means:

- These are zones of heavy trading activity where price often consolidates.
- The market treats these as fair value zones, making them support & resistance levels.

Trading Tips:

- If price retests a high-volume area, expect a bounce or consolidation before moving again.

• If price breaks through, it often retests before continuing the trend.

#2 Low-Volume Areas

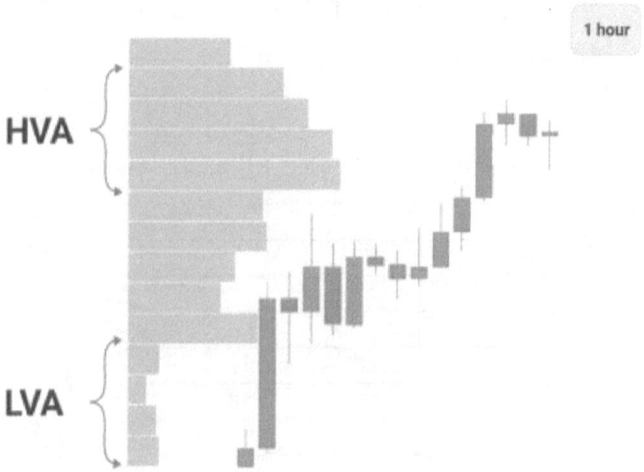

What it means:

• Low trading activity = Price tends to move quickly through these zones.

• These areas indicate a lack of interest, meaning price doesn't linger here.

Trading Tips:

• When price enters a low-volume zone, expect fast movement toward the next high-volume area.

• Use these areas for breakout trades - momentum increases when price moves above/below these levels.

#3 The Point of Control (POC) - The Most Important Level

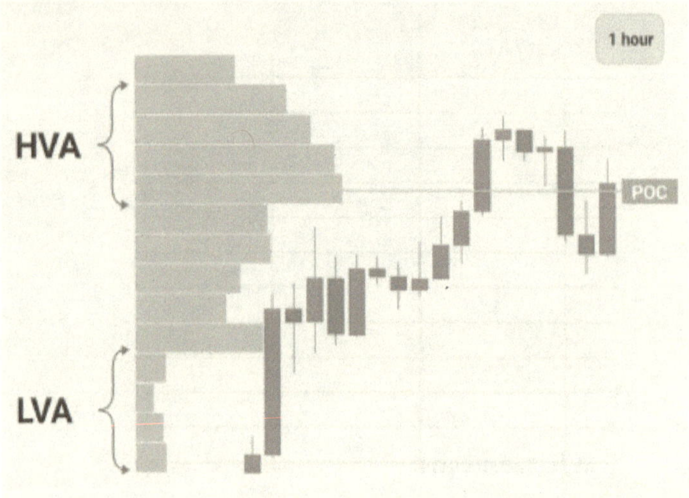

The POC (Point of Control) is the price level where the most volume was traded (longest purple bar).

Why it matters:

- Acts as strong support/resistance.
- Above POC = Bullish Bias.
- Below POC = Bearish Bias.

Pro Tip: The POC is often a key decision zone - watch how price reacts here to predict the next move.

Integrating Volume Profile Into Analysis

Now that you know the key concepts, let's build a simple way to integrate trading strategy using Volume Profile.

Step 1: Identify Key Levels

- High-volume zones = Support & Resistance.
- Low-volume gaps = Breakout zones.
- POC = Major decision area.

Step 2: Plan Your Entry & Exit

Bounce Trades:

- If price rejects a high-volume area, enter a trade in the opposite direction.
- Example: If price bounces off a high-volume zone, enter long with a stop-loss below it.

Breakout Trades:

- If price moves through a low-volume zone, enter in that direction.
- Example: If price breaks a low-volume zone, take a momentum trade to the next high-volume level.

POC Reactions:

- If price rejects the POC, expect a reversal.

• If price breaks the POC with volume, expect continuation.

Step 3: Set Stop Loss & Take Profit

• Place stops behind the nearest high-volume node (strongest support/resistance).

• Take profit at the next key volume level.

Bottom Line:

• Takes the guesswork out of trading - you focus on key price levels.

• Keeps you out of weak trades - you only enter at meaningful zones.

• Lets you see where liquidity is - so you know when price is likely to bounce or break.

• If you're not using Volume Profile, you're missing a key piece of market structure.

Incorporate Volume Profile into your broader analysis for maximum effectiveness.

Exam - Indicators

1. Which time period produces a stronger MA?

- 90 Days

- 200 Days

- 5 Hours

1. What is trading volume?

- Indicator of how many times asset was traded

- A gauge of market interest in a price move

- Both

1. How much of your strategy should be based on indicators alone?

- 90%

- 55%

- There are no such rules

Answer:

1. 200 Days

1. Both

1. There are no such rules

Chapter 6: The Art Of Calculated Risk

Lesson 1: The Psychology Of Risk

In trading, you're not just navigating the market's ups and downs; you're mostly managing your own mindset.

Tackling psychological hurdles

Imagine two monkeys in your mind: one is fearful and the other greedy. The fearful one can't let go of losses, while the greedy one gets overconfident with wins. You have to learn to silence both in order to progress.

The fearful mind monkey

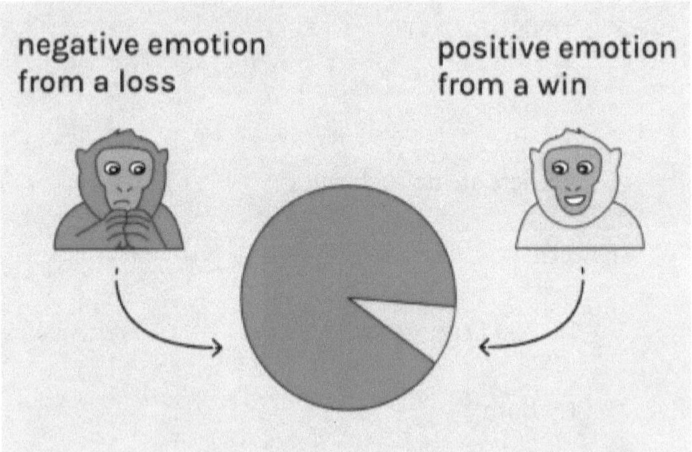

Did you know: losing $100 stings twice as much as the joy you get from gaining $100?

This is due to a psychological bias known as "**loss aversion**". It's a powerful mistake that causes you to hold onto losing trades for too long, hoping for a turnaround.

Hope is a very poor strategy in markets...

Recognizing the brain's loss-aversion monkey is the first step and in a bit we'll teach you how to step over this trap.

The greedy mind monkey

What happens when you hit a winning streak? It is often the case that the monkey in your brain becomes overconfident and greedy, and there's a good reason for it.

Neuroscience labels it the **'winner's effect'** - where success leads to a rush of dopamine, clouding judgment and leading to riskier and riskier trades.

Knowing when to walk away and pocket your gains is just as crucial as cutting your losses, and we have strategy for that too.

Key Takeaways

- **Loss Aversion:** Understanding and countering the tendency to fear losses more than you value gains.

- **Winner's Effect:** Recognizing and managing the overconfidence that comes with success.

Excited to tackle these psychological challenges head-on? Let's move on to the next lesson, where we'll delve into step-by-step strategies for taming these monkeys.

Lesson 2: Trading Safety Harness

Just like rock climbing, trading is exciting and rewarding, but not without risks.

In climbing, a roped harness protects you from falls; in trading, a **'stop-loss order'** does exactly the same.

It's there to protect your money from major losses especially when emotions run high and you're tempted to hang onto a losing trade hoping it reverses.

Setting up the safety gear

Fixed Stops: Think of a fixed stop-loss order as like setting a safety line. If you buy a stock at $100, placing a stop-loss at $95 means you're limiting your risk to $5. It's a predefined escape route if the market turns against you. The stop guarantees that you will never lose more money than you're comfortable with.

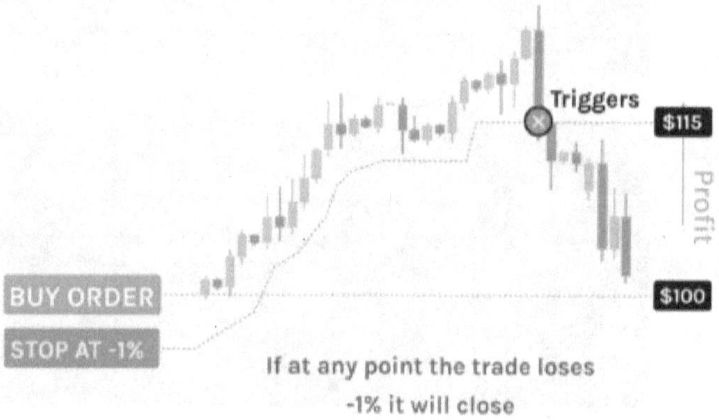

Trailing Stops: Imagine your safety line that moves with you as you climb higher. That's a trailing stop. It adjusts with the market, maintaining a set distance from the highest price reached. For instance, it might close the trade if the price drops by 1%. It's perfect for following trends while keeping your potential losses in check.

There's more to the story

Regardless of your experience level, employing a stop-loss strategy is crucial. You will soon learn that losses in trading are assymetrical and can be disproportionately damaging to your trading account when not controled with a stop-loss. Much like a climber's fall without a rope, can be his last.

Lesson 3: Pocket Your Profits

In trading, where making money is the goal, it's easy to get caught in the grip of greed.

This can lead you to trying to squeeze every last penny from a winning trade, but often risks losing it all. Here's where a **Take Profit (TP) order** comes in - your strategy to lock in those gains.

Better safe than sorry

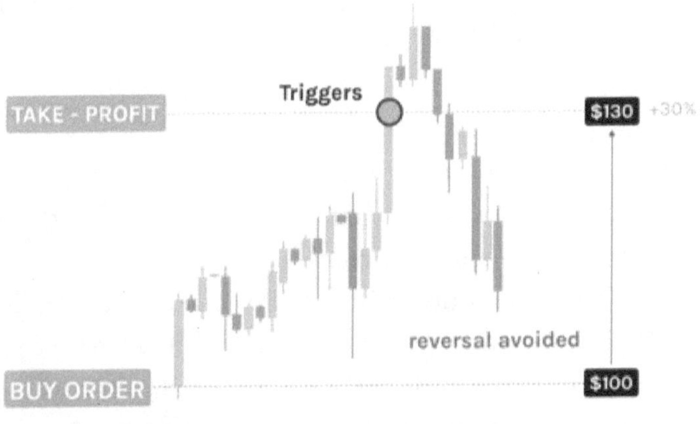

A TP order is your predetermined exit point on a winning trade. It's like setting a goalpost: "If the price hits this point, I'll take my profit and run."

For example, buying at $100 and setting a TP at $130 means you're aiming for a 30% gain.

Taking partial profits

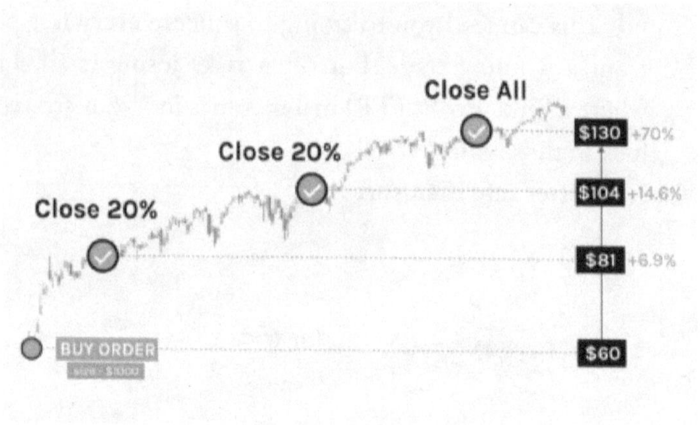

Sometimes, it's smart to cash in profits gradually, especially in long-term trades.

You can set up multiple TP orders at different levels. So for example, if you buy at $60, you might close a part of the trade periodically as the price rises. This way, you secure gains while still giving part of your trade a chance to grow further. A useful strategy when trading strong trends.

Why use both SL and TP orders?

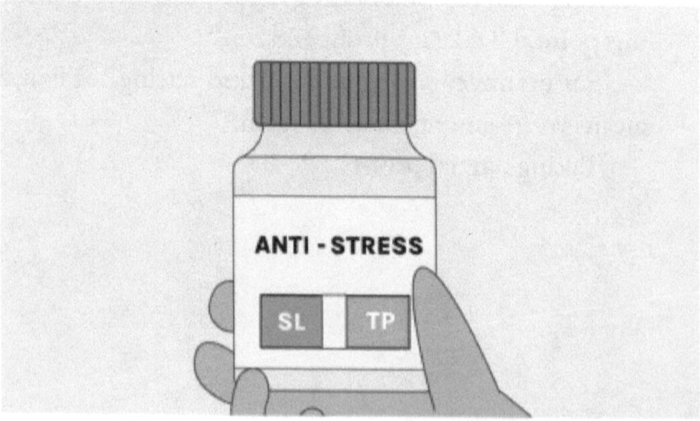

By using both the stop-loss and take profit orders, you effectively program your trading strategy with a fail-safe mechanism. This allows you to step away from the markets, and remain confident that no single trade will go out of control.

This liberates you from the screen, reduces decision fatigue, and mitigates the emotional rollercoaster of watching the charts all day long.

As we move forward, we'll dive into how to strategically place your SL and TP orders for maximum effectiveness. Let's go!

Lesson 4: Placing The Stop Loss

In any military strategy, the most crucial plan isn't the attack; it's the retreat. A successful retreat allows troops regroup and come up with a new attack strategy, if the first one fails.

In trading, this retreat is your stop-loss order. It's what ensures you can "fight another day" if a trade doesn't go as planned. Let's explore how to plan your retreat.

The market structure method

The guiding principle here is simple: **set your stop where your trade idea is no longer valid.**

... and this will largely depend on your strategy. However we can go over a few basic guidelines to consider.

Hypothetical trade thesis:

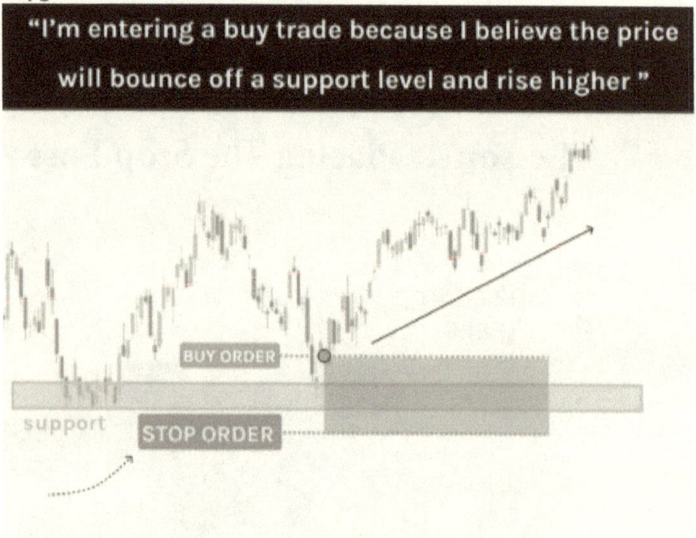

When does the trade idea become invalid?

In our simplified example, if the price breaks down below the support level instead of bouncing higher, your trade has gone off track. That explains the stop placement.

The volatilty method (ATR)

The **ATR (Average True Range)** is a very handy indicator for precise placement of stop-orders.

This indicator measures volatility - how much an asset's price typically moves within a certain period, commonly 14 days. A high ATR indicates high volatility while a low ATR indicates lower volatility and thus smaller price swings.

Where to place the stop?

A rule of thumb is to multiply the ATR by two to determine a stop-loss:

- If you're buying, place the stop-loss at (price - 2x ATR value) below the entry.

- If you're shorting, place the stop at (price + 2x ATR value) above the entry price.

Swing traders require wider stop-losses, while day traders can use stops as tight as 0.1%. That's too much guesswork, so the ATR provides a clear, calculated stop placement for each time frame you might want to trade.

The 1% rule

A fundamental rule in trading is to **never risk more than 1% of your total capital on a single trade**. Why? Because the greater the loss, the harder it is to recover.

Gain required to make up for a loss

Loss	Gain
-1%	+1.0101%
-10%	+11%
-25%	+33%
-50%	+100%
-90%	+1000%

A loss of -1% requires a gain of +1.0101% to break even, and recovery becomes more challenging with larger losses. Placing a stop-loss order at -1% will limit your risk from catastrophic mistakes.

Here's how much that is relative to various account sizes.

1. **$100** - you can lose max $1 per trade.

1. **$500** - you can lose max $5 per trade.

1. **$1000** - you can lose max $10 per trade.

This rule enforces that no single trade sets you back with a massive loss, and hence you should always fall back on this strategy, when unsure about stop placement.

Next Up: Managing the fine line between risk and reward.

Lesson 5: Setting A Profit Target

Once you've set your stop-loss, determining your take-profit (TP) becomes easier. Yet, it's vital to align your TP with market trends and structures.

Striking the right balance is key: be fearful and your profits will be cut short, get too greedy and your target remains out of reach.

Let's explore how to find this balance.

Risk to reward ratio

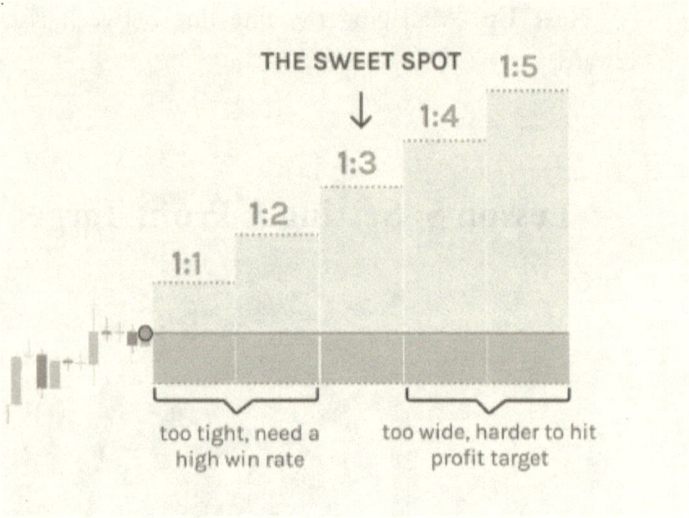

A foundational method for defining profit goals is the **risk/reward ratio (RRR)**.

For example, a 1:3 risk-to-reward ratio (RRR) means aiming to gain three times what you risk. If you risk $1, your goal is to make $3.

This strategy works well with a strong entry strategy and a properly placed stop.

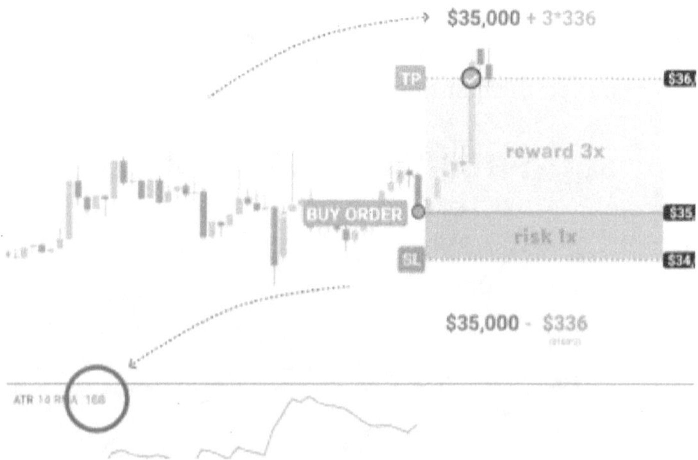

Explanation: Suppose you set a stop-loss using the ATR method, risking a potential loss of $336. With a 1:3 RRR, your take-profit should be $1,008 above your buying price. **The spread was not included in this example!**

Understanding win rate

Profitability doesn't always mean winning more trades than you lose. Renowned trader Steven Cohen points out that even the best traders have win rates around 50-63%.

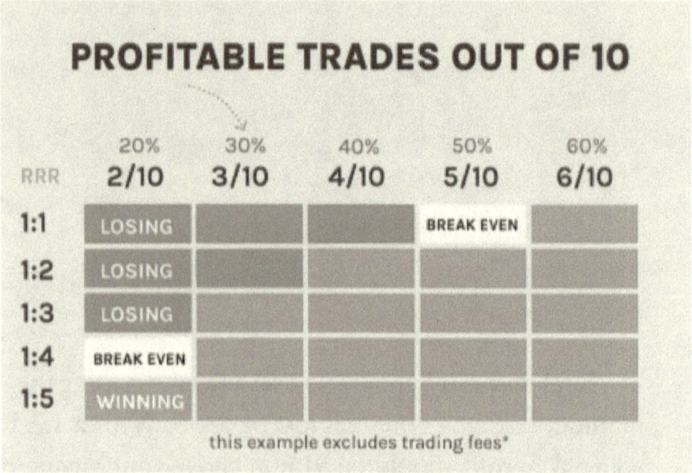

With a 1:3 RRR, hitting your profit target in just 3 out of 10 trades can keep you profitable over time.

Don't limit yourself, be flexible

While risk-reward ratios provide a structured approach to potential profits, they are not unbreakable laws. In fact, follow the rules blindly and you might limit yourself from reaching the target at all.

It's important to consider the market structure and key levels that reflect the current state of price action.

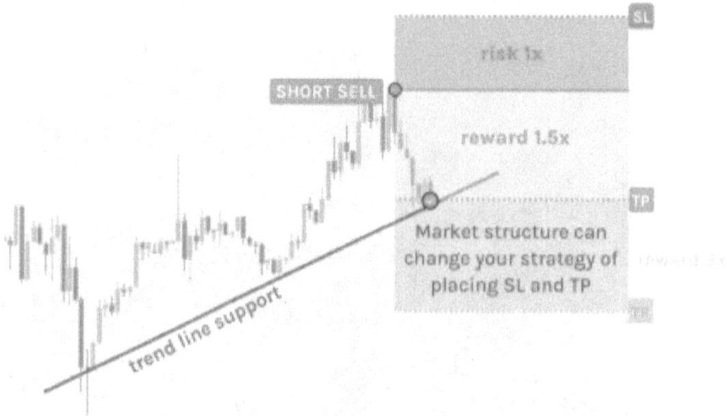

For instance, if a trading setup shows a potential for **1:1.5 RRR** based on historical price movements, using 1:3 would be overly optimistic and may result in missed opportunities or failure to realize gains.

As a trade progresses, be open to adjusting your TP and stop-loss settings. This flexibility can help optimize your trade in response to changing market conditions. With experience, such adjustments will become more intuitive.

Next up: how you can turn $100 into $10,000 in one click. Yes.... really!

Lesson 6: Raising The Stakes

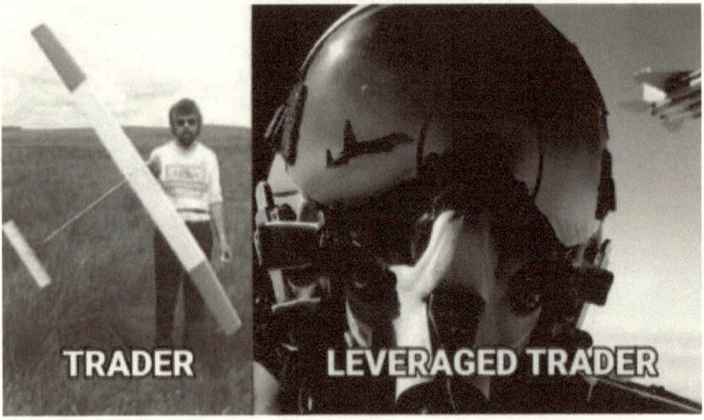

Now that we've covered the boring but very important bits, it's time to inject some excitement into your trading knowledge.

What if I told you that you could open a trade with $10,000 or more, despite only having $100 in your trading account?

That's the power of leverage - but before we begin remember, leveraged trading requires precision and confidence, as the stakes get higher and the room for error much smaller.

What is leverage?

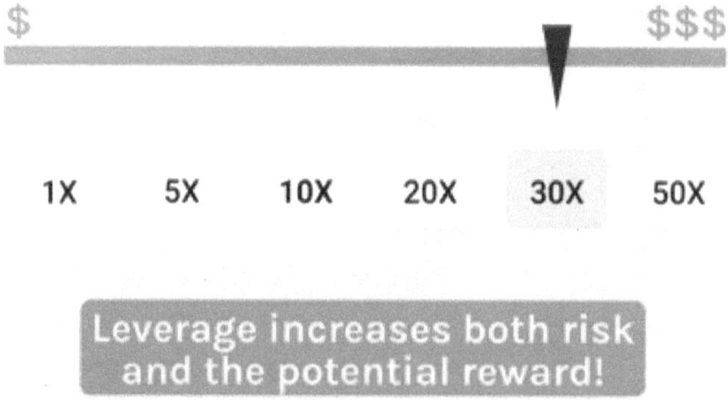

Leverage involves borrowing funds from a broker that let's you trade with more money than you currently have.

The comedic example below precisely illustrates how a well-taken leveraged **(x30)** trade can quickly bring significant profits.

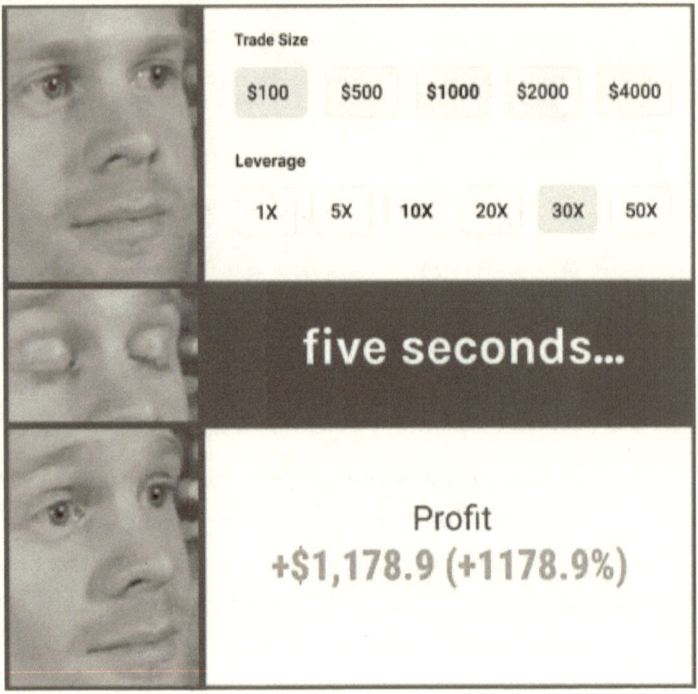

It's important to note that leverage can also lead to fast and substantial losses if the trade goes sour. Here's a detailed explanation of how it all works.

The Math Behind Leverage

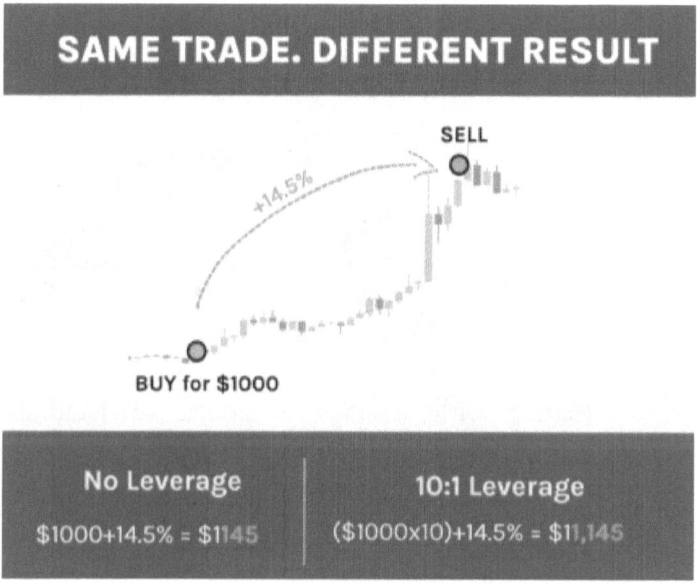

When you buy an asset for $1,000 without leverage, a 1% market movement equates to a $10 profit or loss, but if you leverage your position **10:1 or 10X** your effective market exposure increases to $10,000, making each 1% movement worth $100.

While this amplifies potential returns, it also means that if the market moves against you each 1% move will be a $100 loss from your initial capital. So lose 10% and your $1000 is gone.

Don't even think about touching leverage without enabling the stop-loss.

The real question....

Trading with leverage is similar to handling an expensive, high performance sports car.

The thrill you get is one of a kind, but the stakes are high. Push too hard, lose your focus for a second and you're in for an expensive lesson.

Here are three critical considerations:

#1 The psychological aspect

Cranking on 50X leverage sounds fun, but what if a mere 0.5% move wipes out your whole trading account? With the stakes raised, can you still make the right decision to base a trade on facts not emotion?

Sticking to a disciplined and rational trade strategy is crucial when the pressure mounts. Mix leverage with fear or greed and you're asking for trouble!

#2 Broker risk

Choosing the right broker is critical as you're essentially using the broker's capital to trade with. For instance, with a $1000 investment at 10x leverage, a 20% market downturn would not only wipe out your initial investment but also place you $1000 in debt to the broker.

The key is to choose a secure and regulated broker with "**negative balance protection**". It ensures you can never lose more than your initial deposit More on this soon!

#3 Margin requirements

Margin is the deposit required to enter into a leveraged trade, serving as the backing for your leverage.

This requirement is the broker's way of ensuring that you have a stake in the trade. It dictates the maximum leverage you can utilize.

If the market moves against your position and your account falls below the margin requirement, you'll face a **margin call**, necessitating additional funds or the liquidation of positions.

The bottom line

Leverage is a powerful tool that amplifies your buying power, allowing trades of larger amounts than your actual capital.

However, with the increased potential for profit comes a proportional increase in risk.

Proper use of leverage requires a strong trading strategy, which I will soon build for you.

Lesson 7: The Five Asset Rule

Trying to do ten things at once might look impressive, but it actually slows you down. Research shows that multitasking, especially with complex tasks like trading, makes you less efficient, leads to more mistakes, and wastes time.

The "Five Asset Rule" resolves this by optimizing your trading for less work and better results.

The principle of the greats

The "Five Asset Rule" is built upon principles from ultra-achievers across diverse domains: best results arise from laser-like focus on a few things, instead of everything.

Just as a martial artist hones a single kick to mastery, **excelling in trading only a few financial instruments is more effective.** This approach creates intimate familiarity with these assets over time, increasing your ability to predict daily price movements, short-term patterns and long-term trends.

Supported by data

Average amount of assets traded within a month

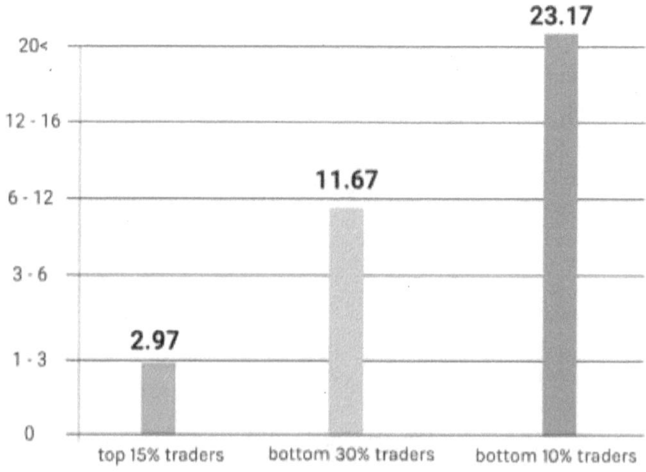

There is a clear discrepancy between the number of assets traded within a specific period and the outcomes achieved in comparison to other traders.

Among the top 15% of traders in the market, an average of 2.97 assets is traded. A market study also revealed the three most popular assets within the group:

#1 EUR/USD - 38% of top 15% traded this.

#2 Bitcoin - 33.1%

#3 Crude Oil - 19.5%

These assets are well-known and have high trading volumes in their respective classes: Forex, Indices, and Commodities. **This supports the notion that successful traders choose assets they know best.**

Contrastingly, the bottom 10% demonstrates inconsistency and a tendency to overtrade. This group tends to switch between assets, attempting to recover past losses. The upcoming segment will explain the problem with this approach.

The proof is universal

In 1906, he unveiled the 80/20 distribution, evident across various life domains.

#1 Personal Finance: ~20% of your expenses can account for about ~80% of your total spending.

#2 Business: ~20% of customers often contribute to around 80% of a company's revenue and ~20% of products typically generate ~80% of a company's sales.

#3 Land ownership: ~20% of landowners possess ~80% of the land.

This idea also applies to trading. In the Nasdaq 100 index, about 20% of the stocks cause around 80% of the price changes. Similarly, the five asset rule shows that roughly 20% of your traded assets, the ones you know best, produce about 80% of your profits.

Start with your strengths

Work in energy? - Commodities like oil, gas are worth considering.

Do you write code? - Tech stocks or crypto might be familiar to you.

Passionate about politics? - Forex is a game of global economics and politics.

Smart trading means **leveraging your strengths**, rather than chasing the latest news hype, you are clueless about.

The Main Takeaway

The Five Asset Rule isn't about restrictions; it's about optimizing your trading for maximum focus and expertise in a select few assets. **This removes distractions and actually reduces your risk.**

The method is fortified by large trading data analysis and universal life observations.

Lesson 8: How Billionaires Trade

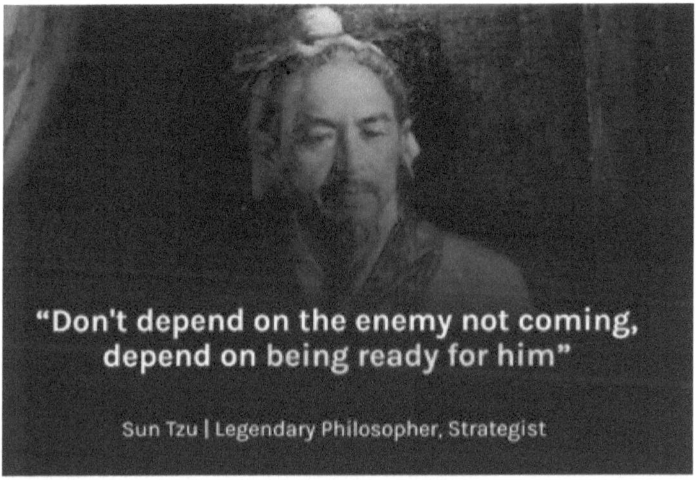

Trading is like preparing for battle, unexpected events can lead to losses just like an unplanned enemy attack.

Sun Tzu, a wise strategist, advised never to rely on the enemy not coming, but to be ready for their arrival at all times. Similarly in trading, **our enemy - losses**, are a part of the game, but we can be ready for them. Either by placing a stop-loss, or through advanced strategies used by top trading firms in the world.

You'll learn one now.

A master of the hedge

Hedge fund manager Bill Ackman is known for making big, bold bets with his firm "Pershing Square".

Recently, Ackman has focused on Alphabet Inc, widely known as Google, betting on the rapidly growing Al sector where Google is expected to lead.

Conversely, he's reducing exposure to more traditional, consumer-facing companies like Lowe's and Chipotle, selling large amounts shares, likely due to risk of inflation impacting their future profits.

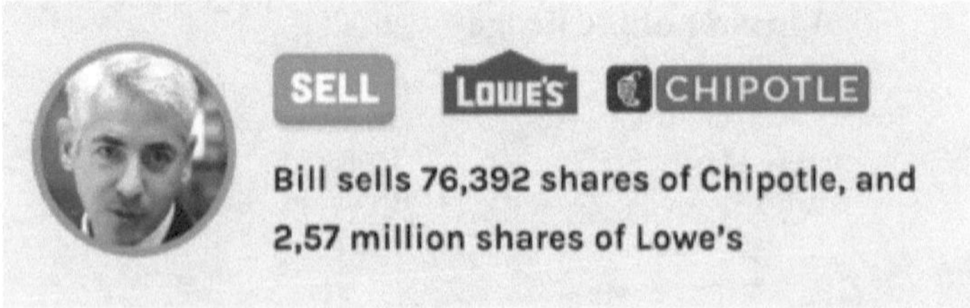

By reducing his stake in one industry where he expects challenges (like Lowe's and Chipotle), he's diversifying into a different industry (Al with Alphabet Inc) that he believes will perform well.

This is how Bill prepares for potential losses on the trading battlefield, with a strategy called: **hedging**, and now let's explore how you can hedge your trades.

The main concept of Wall Street hedge funds

While you don't have access to insider information and billions of dollars, you can still trade with the same principle that big funds use.

Always play both sides

The long/short equity strategy is simple in concept: buy assets you think will rise in value and short those you expect to fall. This way, you aim to make money from one asset while using the other as a safety net, reducing your chances of losing.

Hedging with EUR/USD and USD/CHF

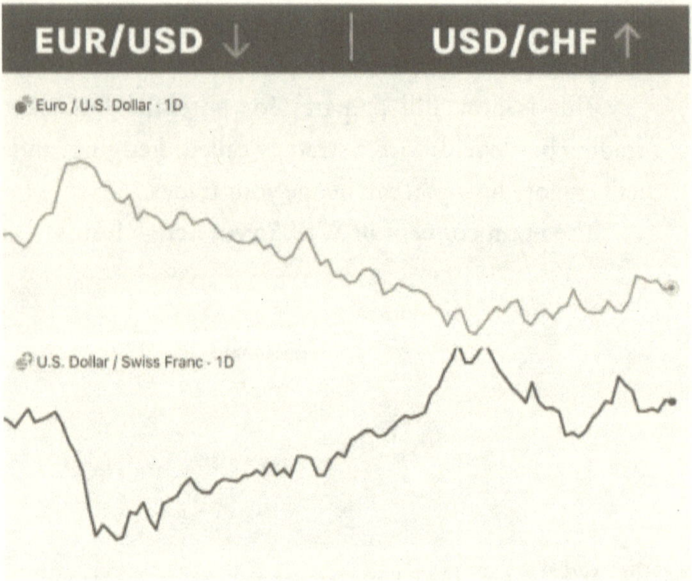

These currency pairs usually move in opposite directions. So, if EUR/USD falls, USD/CHF often rises, and vice versa.

- **Short EUR/USD:** Bet on the Euro losing against the Dollar.

- **Long USD/CHF:** Bet on the Dollar gaining against the Swiss Franc.

Why? The dollar strengthening against the Swiss Franc is often due to the same factors causing its rise against the Euro.

By trading these pairs this way, you're essentially betting on the same market trend from two angles. If the trend changes, you can switch your positions.

Another option, though riskier, is to go long or short on one pair and do the same on the other. This means one trade would be in profit no matter what, but it's a more aggressive approach.

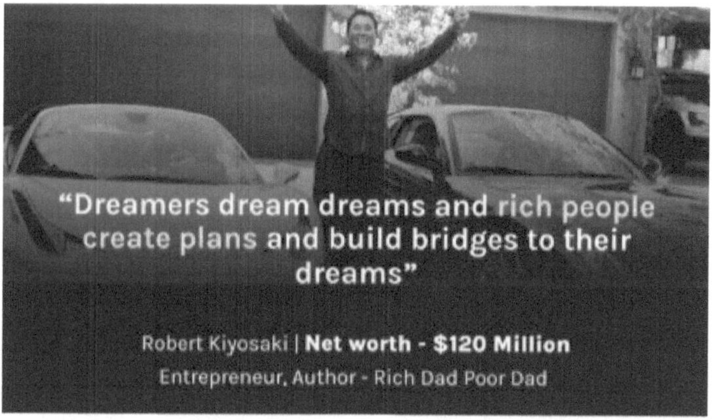

You have successfuly learned the essential concepts of managing the risks of trading.

Now it's about remembering them and sticking to the plan. **No matter what!**

Next up we'll continue with a few crucial chart patterns you should be able to identify.

Chapter 7: Chart Patterns Explained

Lesson 1: Head and Shoulders

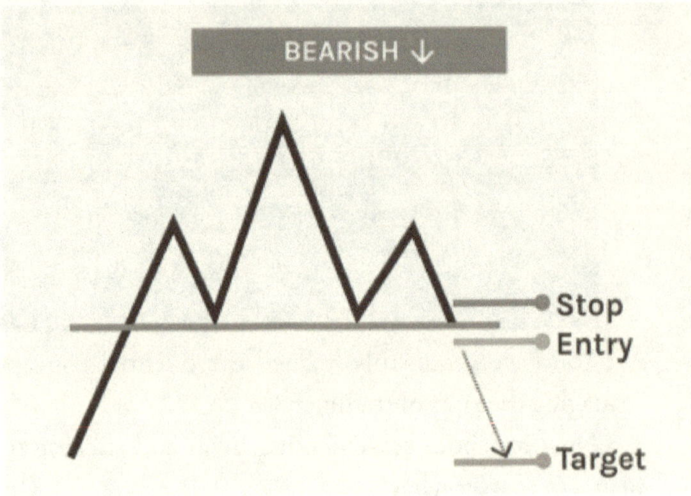

Learn this pivotal reversal pattern in a structured, step-by-step manner, or jump ahead to a specific topic if you feel confident.

Quick Facts

- Among the top three patterns recognized in technical analysis.
- Found in all markets and assets.Serves as a strong indicator for a trend reversal
- Named for its resemblance to the human head and shoulders.

- Average statistical success rate - 68%.

When And Why It Appears

The Head and Shoulders pattern frequently emerges after an uptrend and is sign of a bearish market shift. It signifies a reversal from a bullish to a bearish trend through the following sequence:

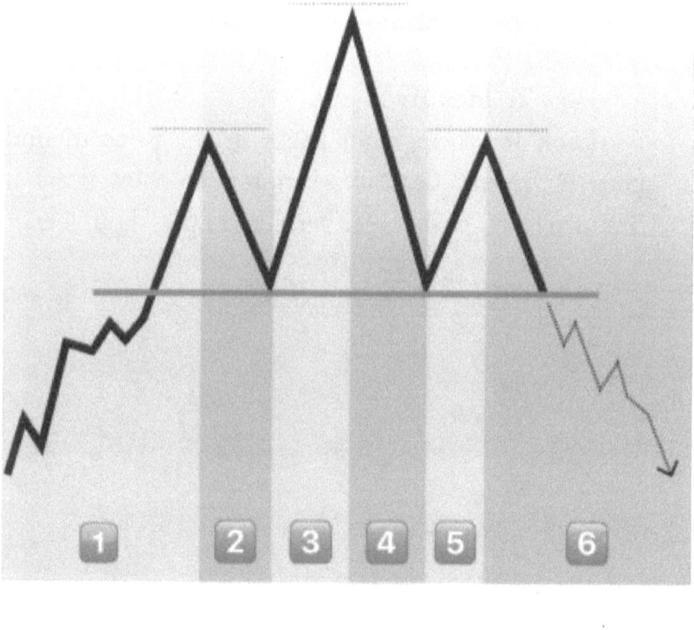

1. **Prior Uptrend:** Buyers push prices higher.

1. **First Reversal:** Early buyers take profits. Reducing demand - the price retreats.

1. **Recovery:** Buyers buy-in at the dip raising the

demand and thus the price.

1. **Second Peak:** Price exceeds prior high, another wave of profit-taking and a second reversal.

1. **Failed Rally:** Bullish momentum falls short of the previous peak.

1. **Final Decline:** Price falls below the lows of both dips, confirming trend reversal.

How To Identify It

Look for three main peaks in the price to find the pattern. The middle peak, which is the highest, is the "head". The two lower peaks on either side are the "shoulders".

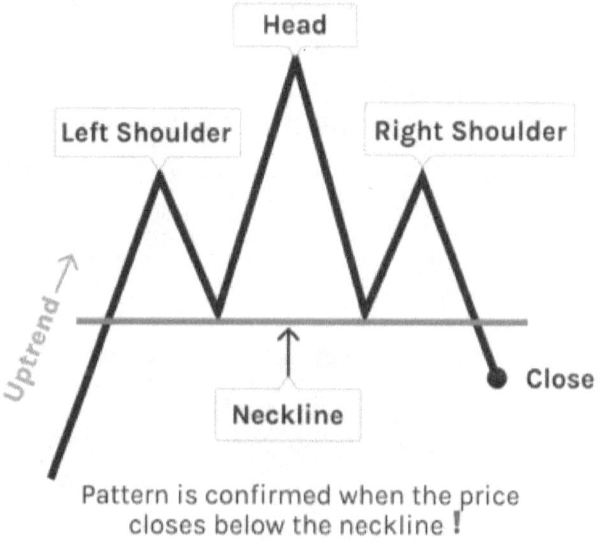
Head
Left Shoulder
Right Shoulder
Uptrend
Close
Neckline
Pattern is confirmed when the price closes below the neckline !

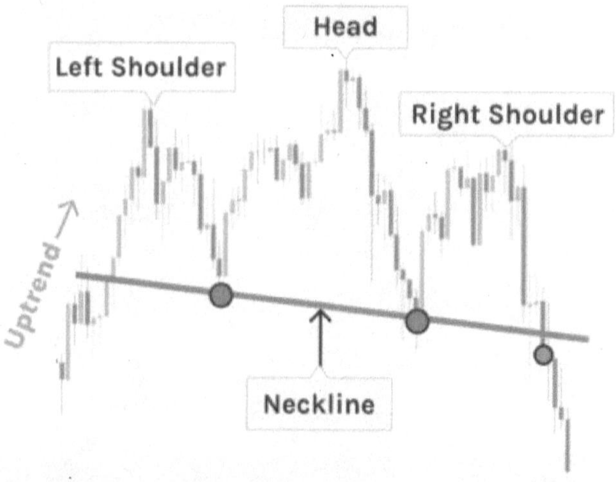
Head
Left Shoulder
Right Shoulder
Uptrend
Neckline

Draw a trend line that joins the lowest points of the dips between the "shoulders." The pattern is confirmed when the price closes below the neckline, confirming a trend reversal.

Volume Analysis

Keep in mind this is an ideal example. Volume can differ depending on market conditions but the pattern can still succeed.

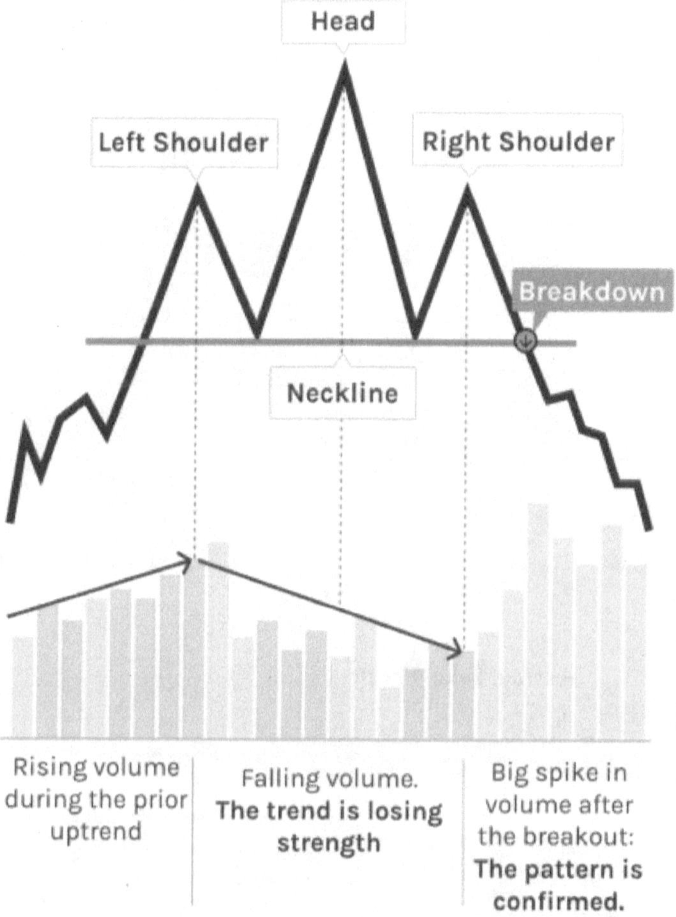

How To Enter The Trade

For a more reliable entry you should confirm a price closure below the pattern's neckline. However, be cautious of false breakdowns-situations where the price moves back above the neckline. To mitigate this risk, consider waiting for the price to retest the neckline before initiating a trade.

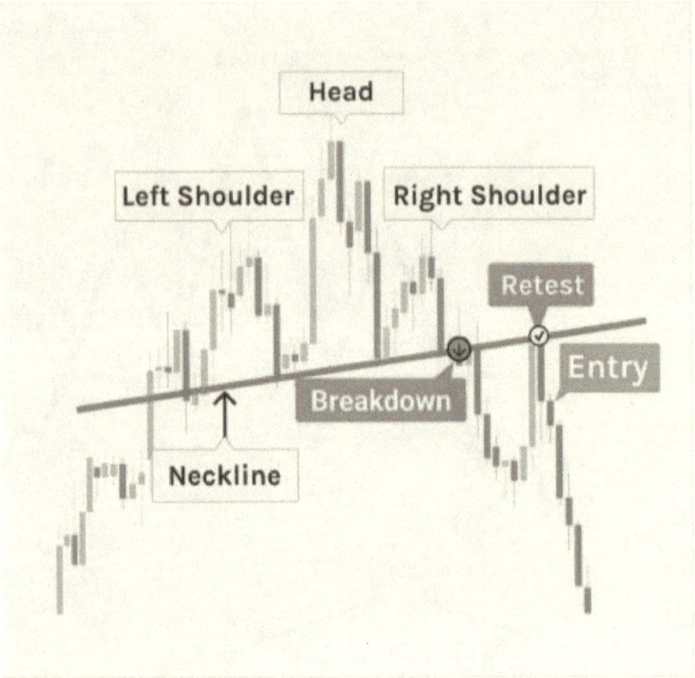

Setting Take-Profit

A reliable method for setting a profit target is to measure the distance between the head and neckline, and use the measurement as a profit target.

Setting Stop-Loss

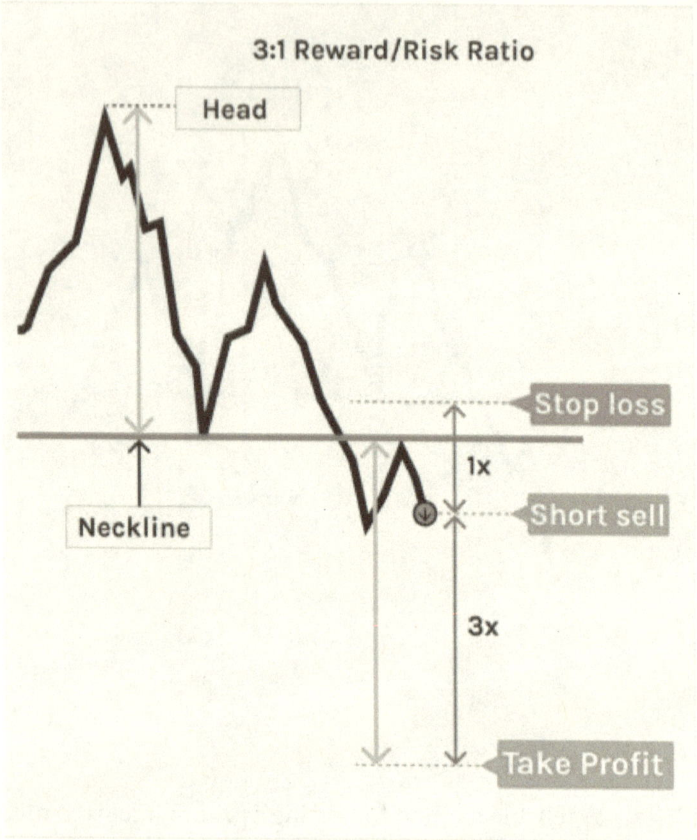

Determine your reward/risk ratio before entering the trade. Knowing your profit target (reward) removes the guesswork from placing the stop - loss. The example above uses the gold standard - 3:1.

Bullish Variation

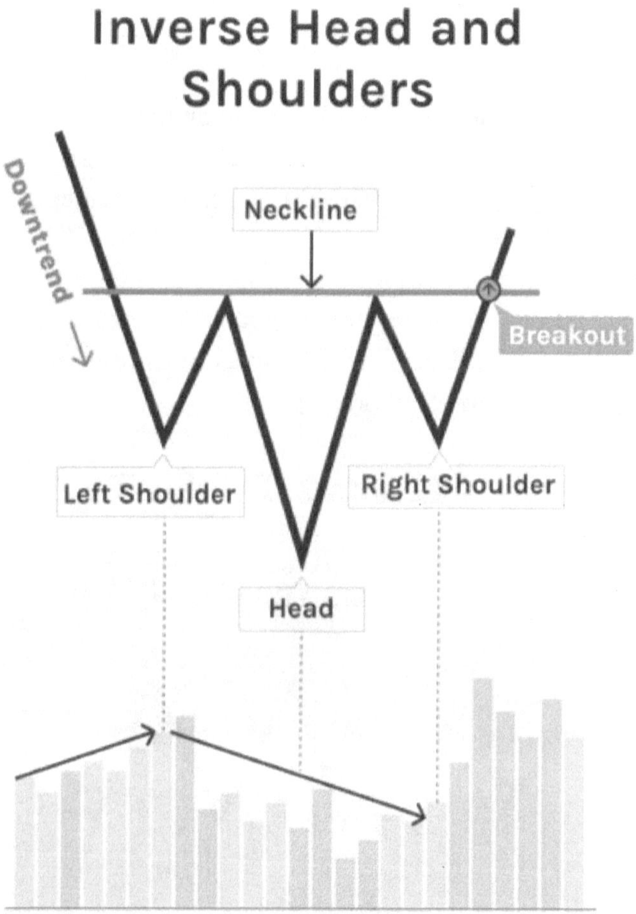

The inverse head and shoulders pattern is essentially the opposite of the standard version. In this variation, it signals the reversal from downtrend to uptrend and the same trading principles apply to both.

Tips For Success

1. The pattern is much more reliable on longer time frames such as daily, weekly or even monthly charts.

1. No pattern looks perfect on the chart. It can be traded as long as it has clear shoulders, head and a breakout below the neckline - the key elements.

1. A downward sloping neckline indicates a stronger bearish reversal pattern, while an upward sloping neckline may result in a weaker reversal or even a false breakout.

Lesson 2: Double Top

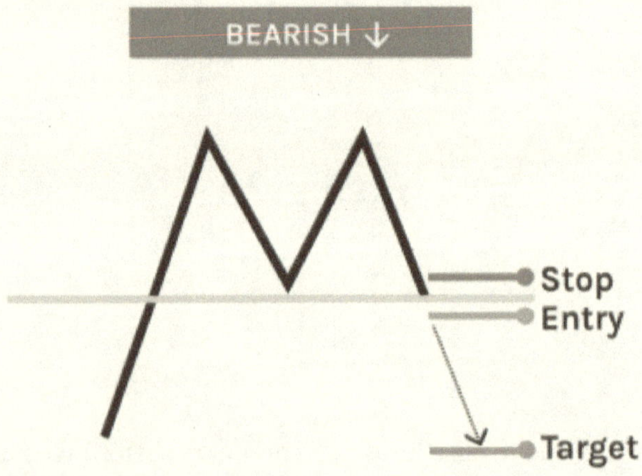

Be cautious when you spot a "double top" on the chart, it can indicate a significant trend reversal and a profitable opportunity to go short.

Quick Facts

- A widely-used chart pattern in technical analysis. Also called M Pattern

- Works best on daily and weekly charts.

- Indicates a trend reversal.

- Average price decline - 15%

- Average success rate - 64%

When And Why It Appears

The double top pattern typically appears after an uptrend signalling a change in market sentiment from bullish to bearish. This leads to a reversal of the uptrend. Take a look at the following explanation:

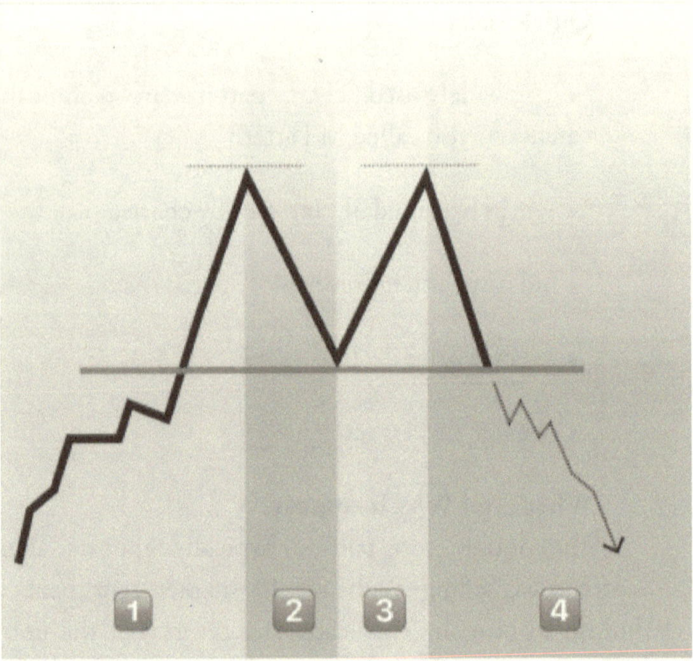

1. **Prior Uptrend:** Buyers push prices higher.

1. **First Reversal:** Early buyers take profits. reducing demand - the price retreats.

1. **Recovery:** Buyers buy-in at the dip raising the demand and thus the price.

1. **Second Peak:** Price meets resistance at the previous top and the trend reverses.

How To Identify It

The double top pattern can be identified by two consecutive peaks that are roughly equal in size, separated by a dip in between.

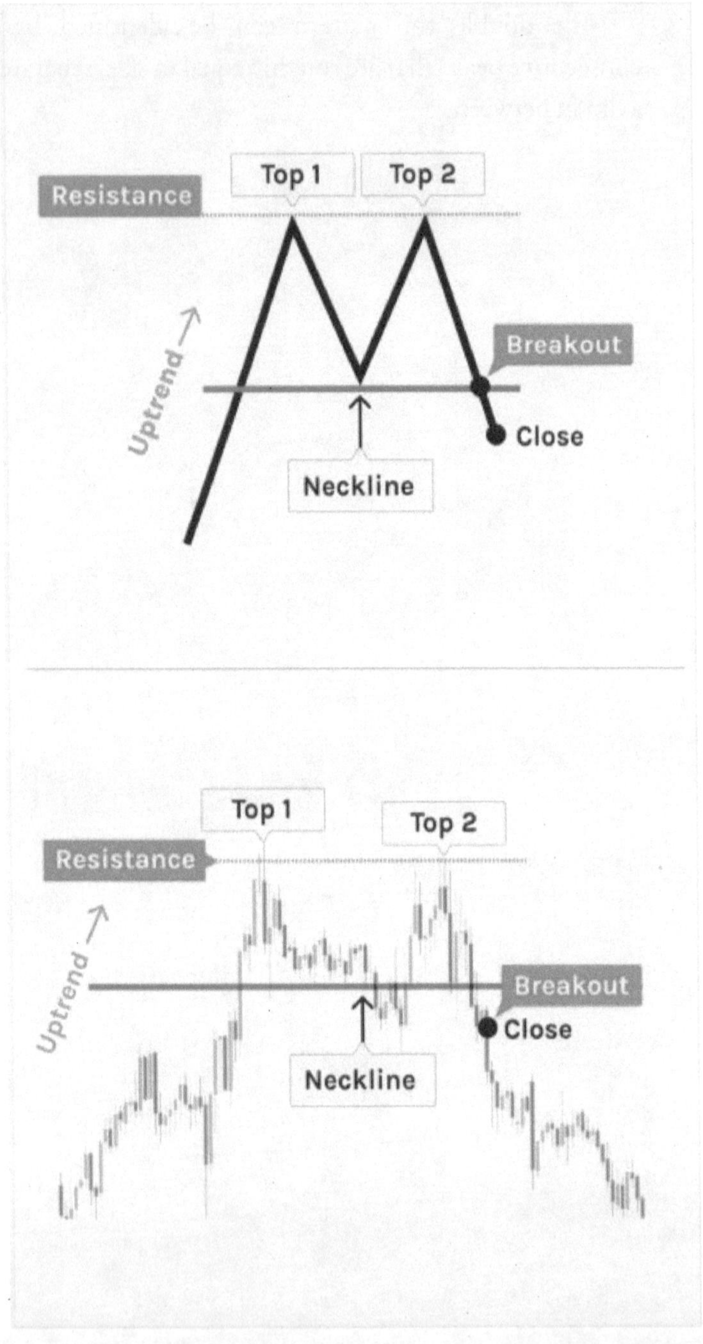
Top 1
Top 2
Resistance
Uptrend
Breakout
Close
Neckline
Top 1
Top 2
Resistance
Uptrend
Breakout
Close
Neckline

The pattern is complete when the price falls and closes below the neck line/support level.

Volume Analysis

Keep in mind this is an ideal example. Volume can differ depending on market conditions but the pattern can still succeed.

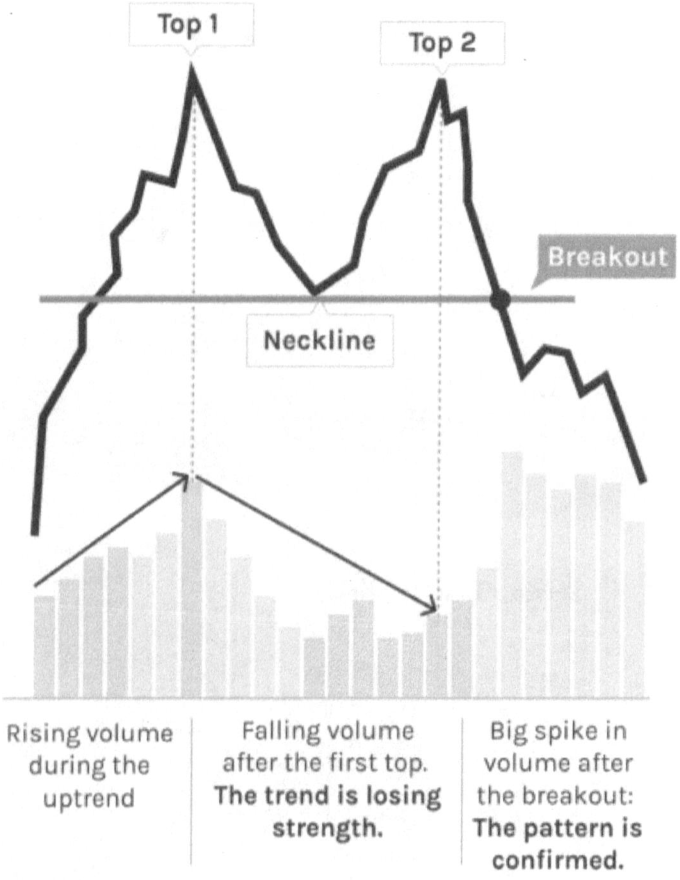

How To Enter The Trade

While a close below the neckline, confirms the pattern, the price can try to reverse back above the neckline. This is known as a false breakout. To increase your odds of success wait for a retest of the neckline before opening a trade.

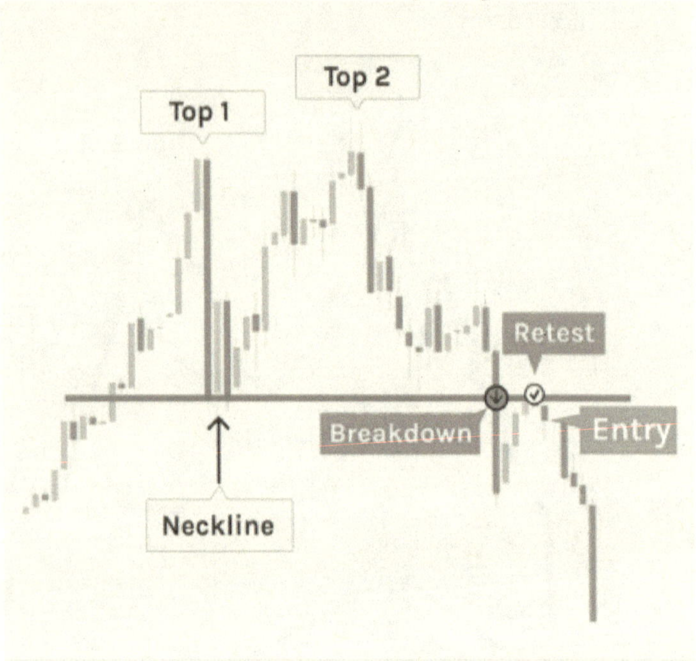

Setting Take-Profit

A reliable method for setting a profit target is to measure the distance between the head and neckline, and use the measurement as a profit target.

Setting Stop-Loss

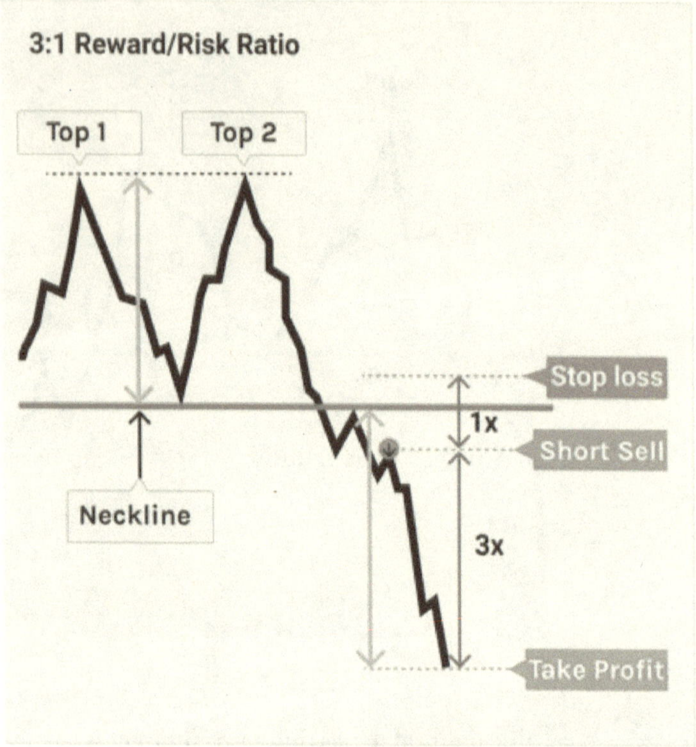

Determine your reward/risk ratio before entering the trade. Knowing your profit target (reward) removes the guesswork from placing the stop - loss. The example above uses the gold standard - 3:1.

Bullish Variation

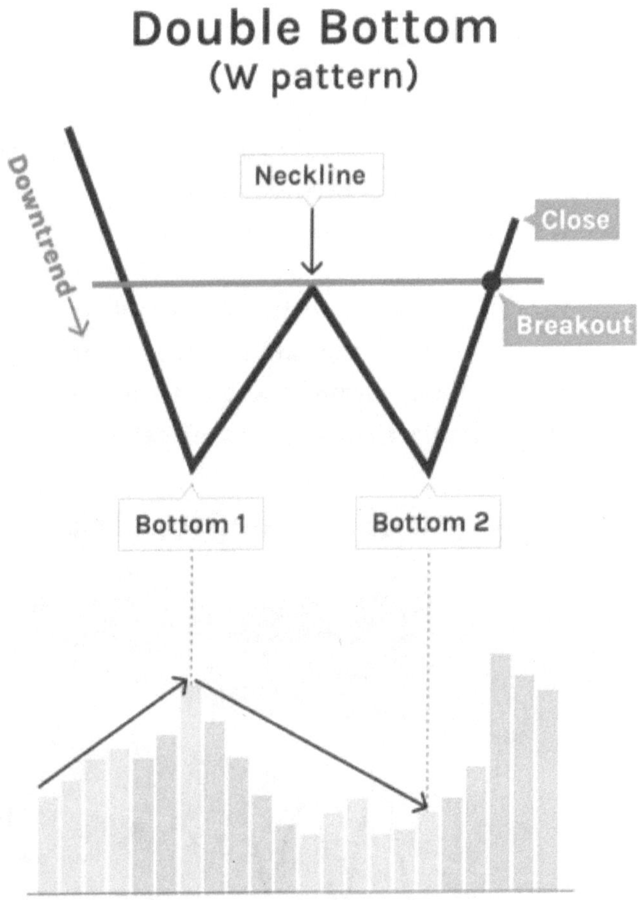

The double bottom pattern is essentially the opposite of the standard version. Instead of signalling a potential trend reversal from bullish to bearish, the double bottom indicates a possible end of downtrend, and the start of an uptrend. The same trading principles apply to both versions.

Extra Tips

1. The pattern is much more reliable on longer time frames such as daily, weekly or even monthly charts.

1. No pattern looks perfect on the chart. The double top pattern can be traded as long as it has clear tops, a valley between them, and a breakout below the neckline - the key elements.

1. The two peaks (double top) or valleys (double bottom) should have a relatively symmetrical shape and size. **Asymmetrical patterns may be less reliable, a more likely a false signal.**

Lesson 3: Symmetrical Triangle

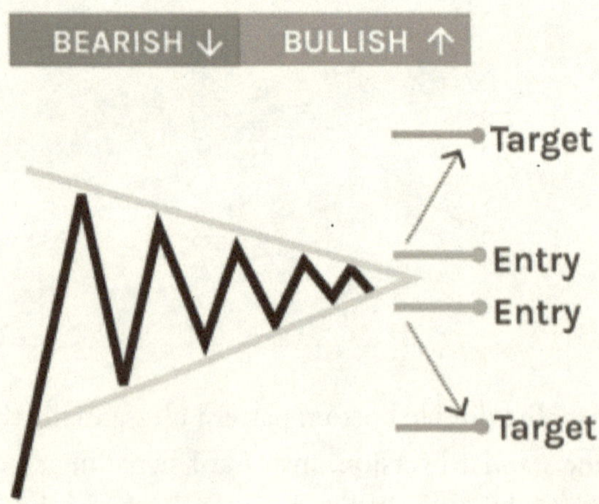

Master the **symmetrical triangle (TS)** to identify profitable long and short trade opportunities in all markets.

Quick Facts

- A symmetrical triangle is formed by two converging trend lines, with **symmetrical slopes**.

- The pattern can signal both a trend reversal, as well as continuation of the existing trend.

- It's harder to find a reliable ST on the charts, as it usually forms over longer time periods. Once identified however, trading it is fairly simple.

When And Why It Appears

The symmetrical triangle is a consolidation pattern. In most cases it signals a loss of momentum for the prior trend. Here's how:

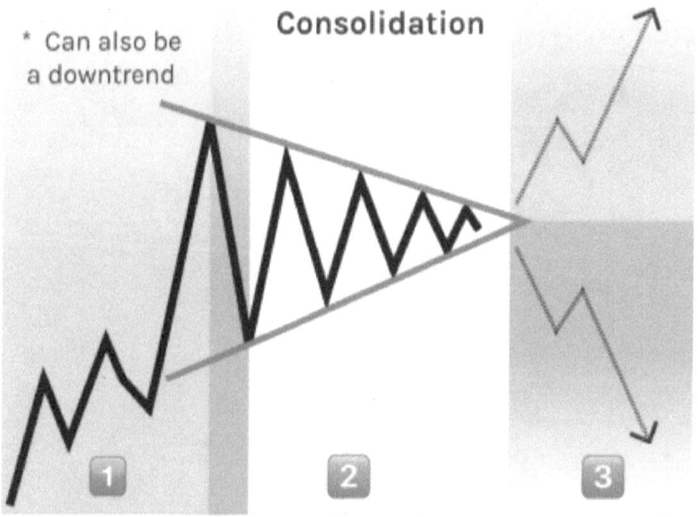

1. **Strong prior trend** and the initial reversal forms the base of the pattern.

1. **Consolidation** - neither buyers nor sellers are in control of the price. The price bounces between the converging trend line support and resistance levels.

1. The consolidation phase is followed by a breakout, where the price breaks above or below either trend line.

How To Identify It

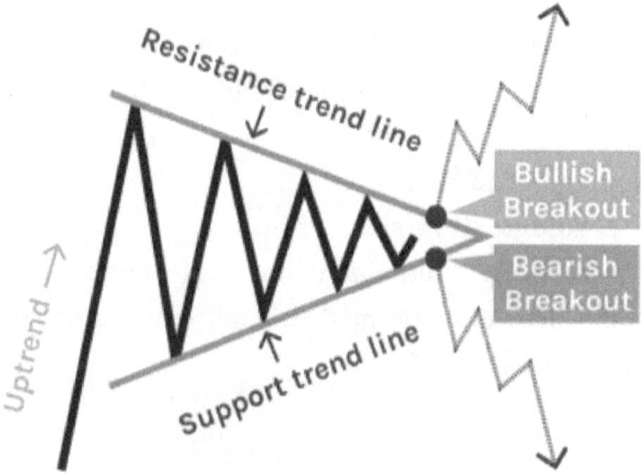
Resistance trend line
Bullish
Breakout
Bearish
Breakout
Uptrend
Support trend line

Resistance trend line
Uptrend
Bullish
Breakout
Support trend line

The symmetrical triangle can be identified by two trend lines that are converging towards each other at roughly the same angle.

The price is making higher lows and lower highs at the same time. The pattern is complete when the price breaks and closes above the resistance trend line or below the support trend line.

Volume Analysis

Keep in mind this is an ideal example. Volume can differ depending on market conditions but the pattern can still succeed.

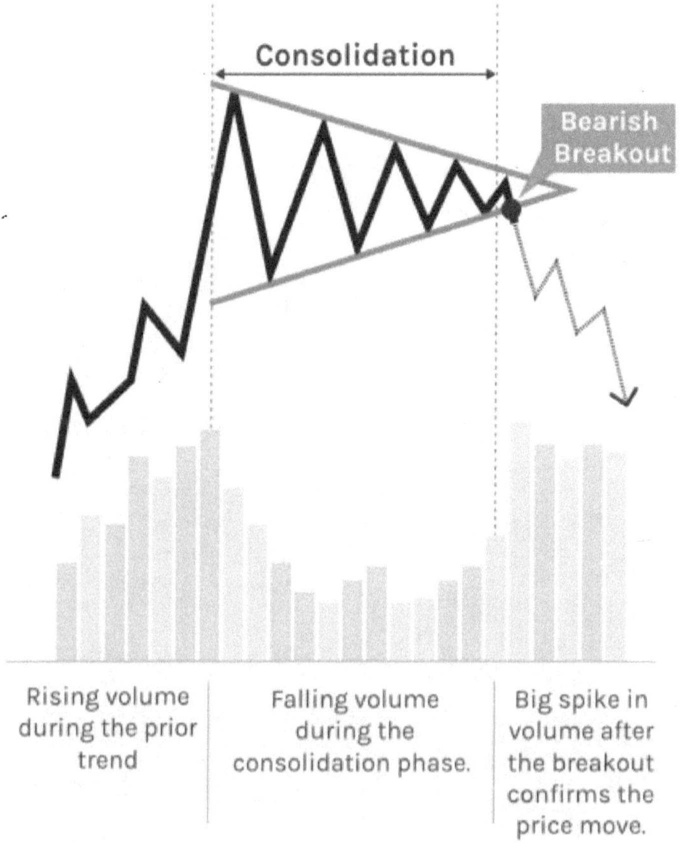

Key To Finding The Direction

Due to the dual nature of this pattern (**it's likely break out in either direction**), it's important to prepare other facts that support the breakout direction. This way you can protect yourself from trading false breakouts.

A reliable method is to check the current trend trend on a bigger timeframe.

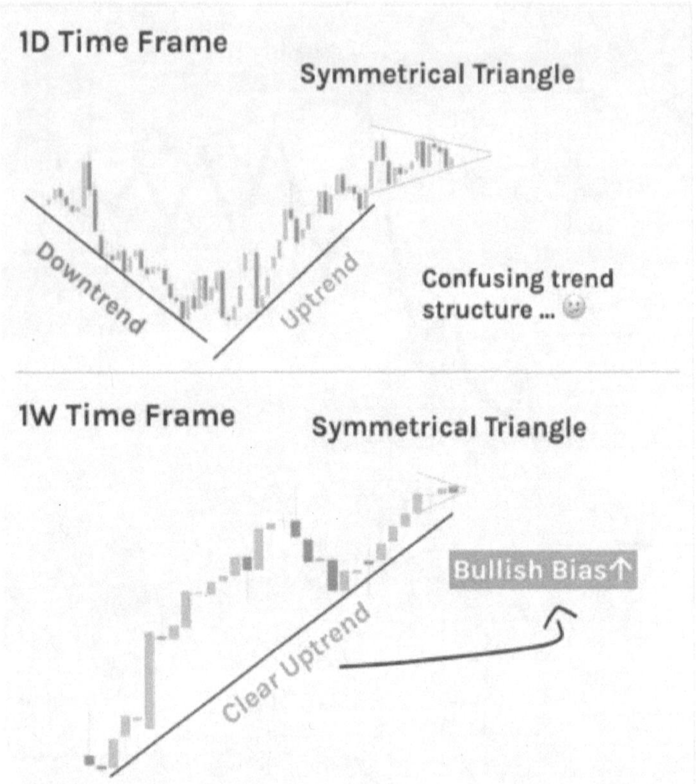

If the higher timeframe shows an uptrend, the symmetrical triangle is more likely to breakout higher.

The opposite is true for a downtrend..

How To Enter The Trade

While a price close above or below either trend line confirms the pattern, the price can often reverse back inside the triangle structure. **This is known as a false breakout.** To increase your odds of success wait for a retest of the either trend line. You can enter the trade on the next exit and price close outside the triangle.

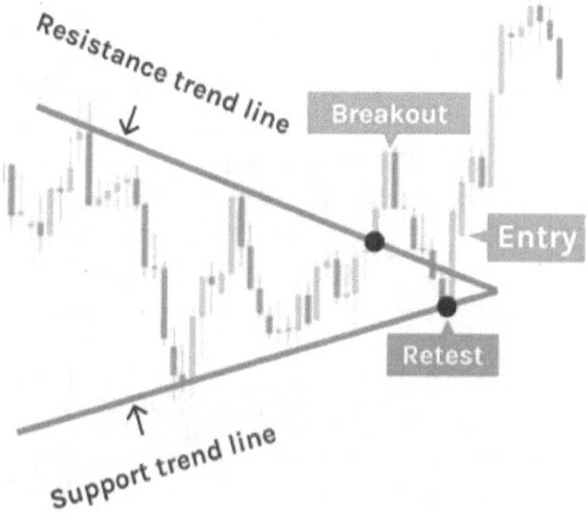

Setting Take-Profit

A reliable method for setting a profit target is to measure the distance at the widest point of the triangle structure, and then copy-paste the distance as your take profit target after the breakout.

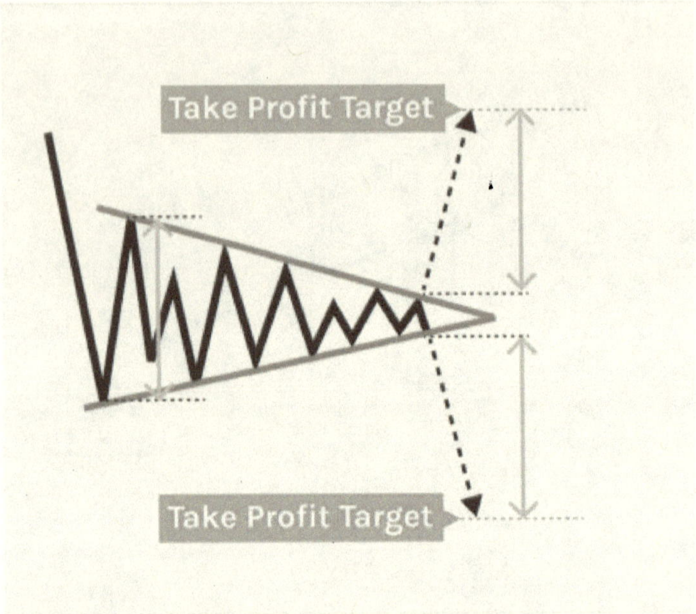

Setting Stop-Loss

First determine your reward/risk ratio before entering the trade. Knowing your profit target (reward) removes the guesswork from placing the stop - loss. The example below uses the gold standard - 3:1.

Extra Tips

1. Use the Moving Average as another metric for predicting the directional bias: If the price is above it's long term MA as it nears the exit of the triangle, a bullish breakout is more likely. On the contrary a bearish breakout is more likely when the price is below it's long term MA.

1. No pattern looks perfect on the chart. It can be traded as long as it has two roughly equal converging trend lines and a breakout and close above or below either.

1. The length of the pattern can range from a few

weeks to many months with the average triangle lasting from 1-3 months. **Shorter triangles can be less reliable for trade entries.**

Lesson 4: Ascending Triangle

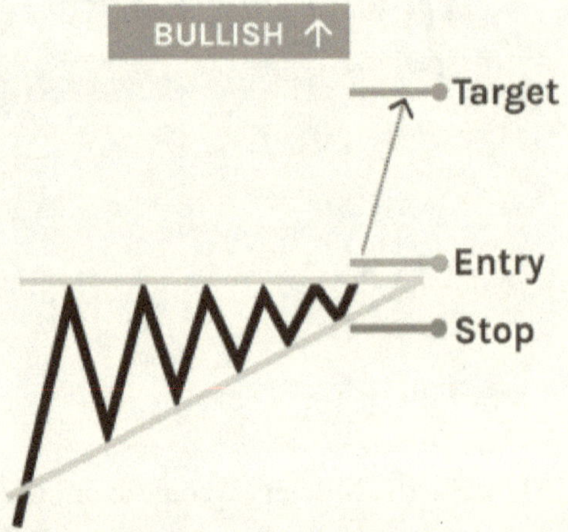

Learn the ascending triangle to find great entry points for long trades during well established trends.

Quick Facts

- The ascending triangle is a bullish continuation pattern that typically forms during an uptrend. It is characterised by a series of higher lows and a horizontal resistance level.

- This pattern suggests that the buyers are getting stronger, and there is a likelihood of a breakout above the resistance level.

When And Why It Appears

The ascending triangle pattern can appear in any timeframe, from intraday to monthly charts and It represents a consolidation period in the uptrend. The buyers are taking a break, and the sellers are testing the market to see if they can reverse the trend.

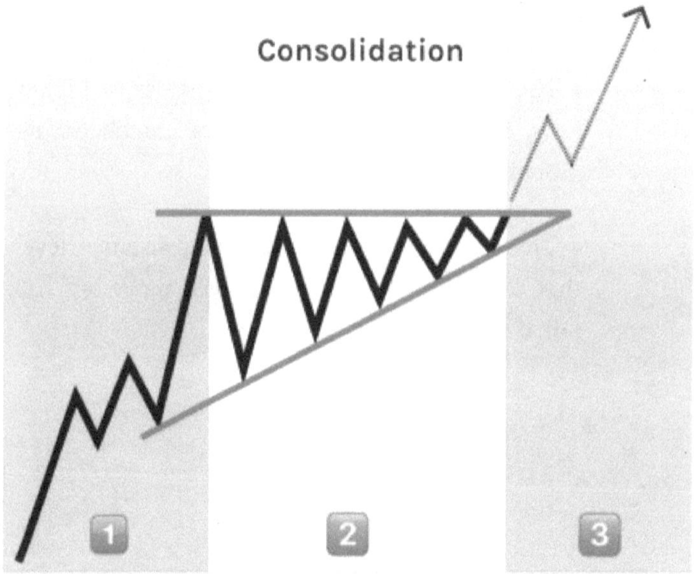

1. **Prior Uptrend** and the initial reversal forms the base of the pattern.

1. **Consolidation:** the uptrend takes a pause and the

price forms a resistance level. The sellers are trying to reverse the price, but lose momentum with each attempt.

1. **Trend continues:** The consolidation phase is followed by a breakout to the upside, where the asset's price breaks the resistance level and resumes the uptrend.

How To Identify It

To spot the pattern you need to look for these characteristics:

- The price should be making a series of higher lows, indicating that the buyers are becoming more aggressive.

- There should be a horizontal resistance level that the price has tested multiple times but has failed to break.

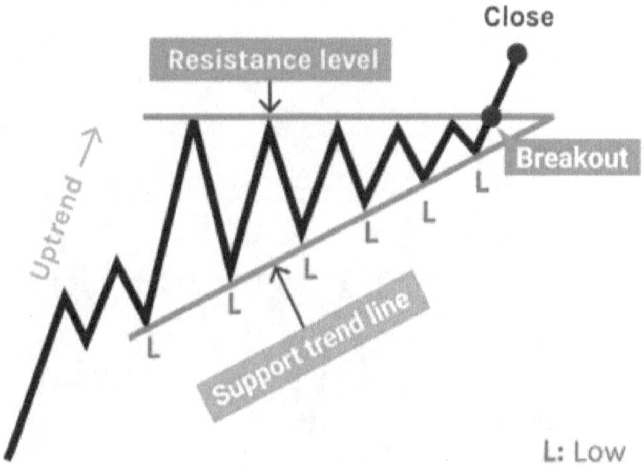
Close
Resistance level
Uptrend
Breakout
L
L
L
L
L
L
Support trend line
L: Low

Continuation
Resistance
Close
Uptrend
Breakout
L
L
L
L
L
L
Support trend line

The pattern is complete when the price breaks and closes above the resistance level.

Volume Analysis

This is an ideal example. Volume might differ depending on market conditions and the pattern can still succeed.

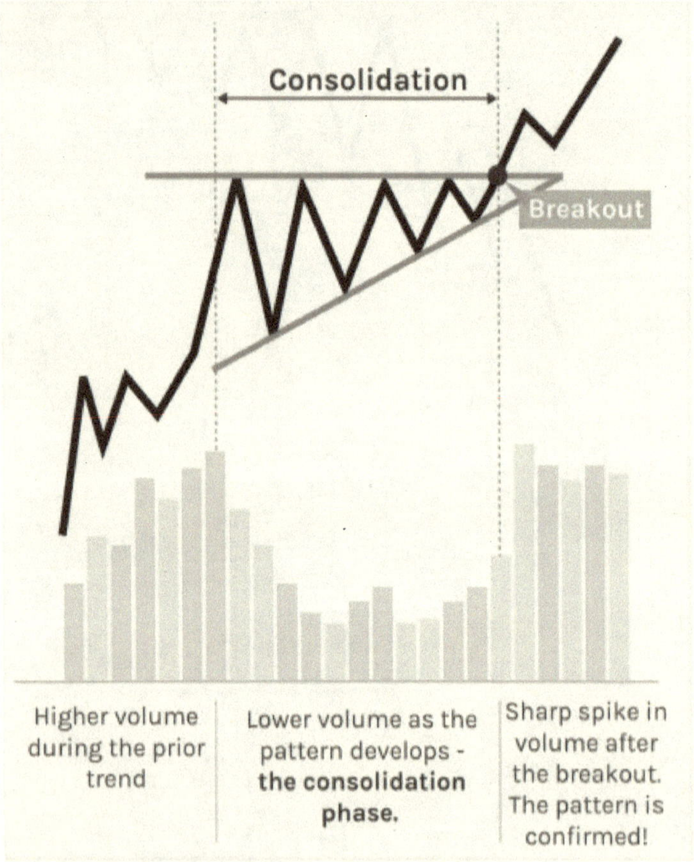

How To Enter The Trade

While a price close outside the pattern structure is the standard confirmation for most patterns, false breakouts can occur. To increase your odds of success, wait for a retest of the triangle structure. This means waiting for the price to reverse back into the pattern and bounce back higher. After the retest, you can enter the trade on a price close after the second "real" breakout, which confirms the pattern's bullish bias and signals a good opportunity to go long.

Setting Take-Profit

A reliable method for setting a profit target is to measure the distance at the widest point of the triangle structure, and then copy-paste the distance as your take profit target after the breakout.

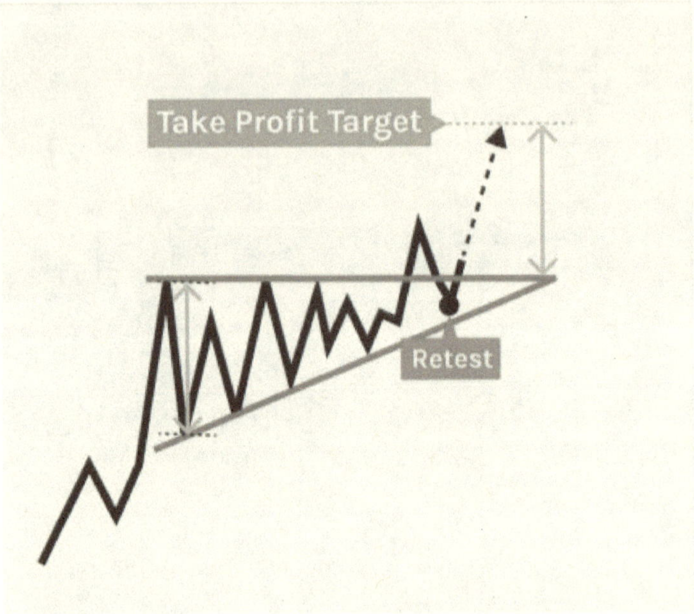

Setting Stop-Loss

Determine your reward/risk ratio before entering the trade. Knowing your profit target (reward) removes the guesswork from placing the stop - loss. The example below uses the gold standard - 3:1.

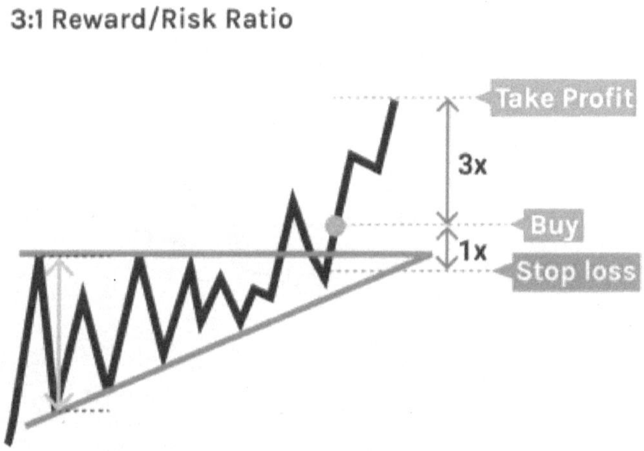

Downtrend Variation

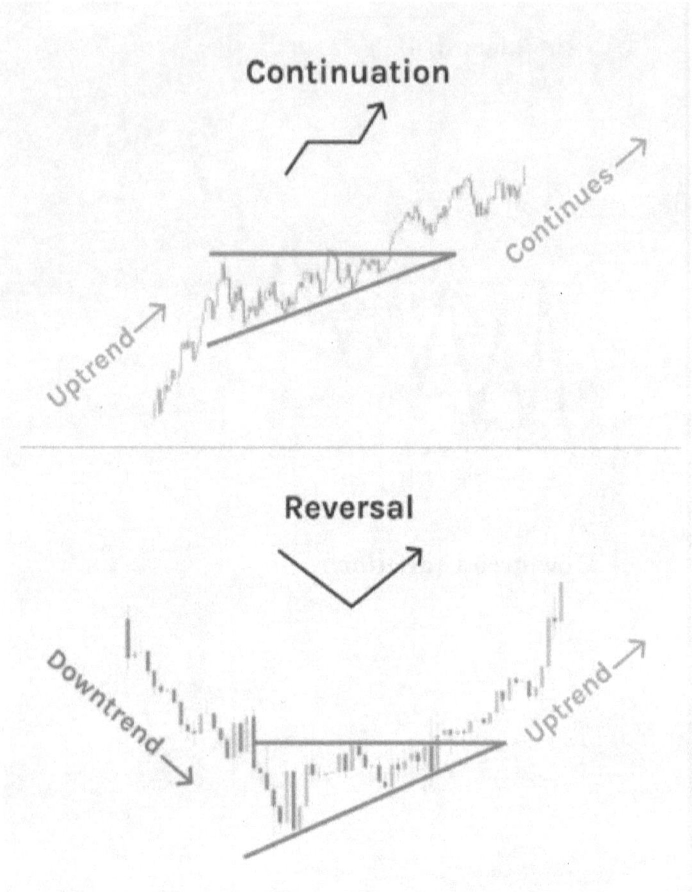

Although the ascending triangle usually forms as a continuation pattern during an uptrend, there are instances when ascending triangles form during downtrends as well. **In both scenarios it indicates a long trade opportunity.** The same trading principles apply.

Extra Tips

1. To predict the direction of a breakout, consider

the price's position relative to its long-term moving average. If the price is above the moving average when approaching the end of the triangle, a bullish breakout is more likely. However, if the price is below the moving average, the pattern may fail.

1. The pattern usually takes a few weeks to months to form.

1. If the duration is only a few days then watch out, the pattern has a higher probability of failing.

Lesson 5: Descending Triangle

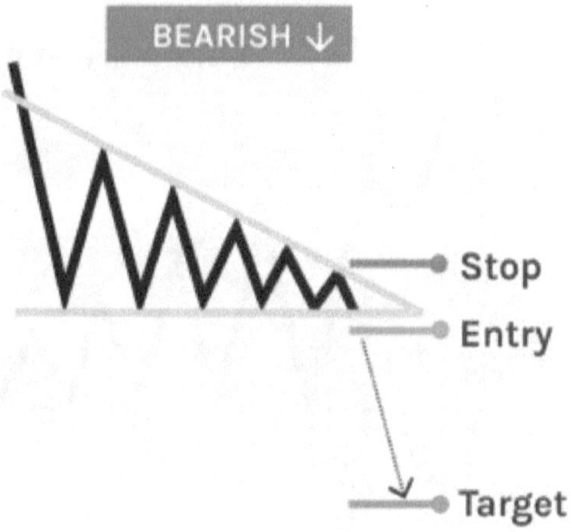

Learn the descending triangle to find profitable opportunities for shorting during downtrends.

Quick Facts

• The descending triangle is a bearish continuation pattern that typically forms during a downtrend. It is characterised by a series of lower highs and a horizontal support level.

• This pattern suggests that the sellers are getting stronger, and there's a high chance of a breakout lower.

When And Why It Appears

The descending triangle pattern can appear in any timeframe, from intraday to monthly charts and it represents a consolidation period in the downtrend. The sellers are taking a break, and the buyers are testing the market to see if they can reverse the trend.

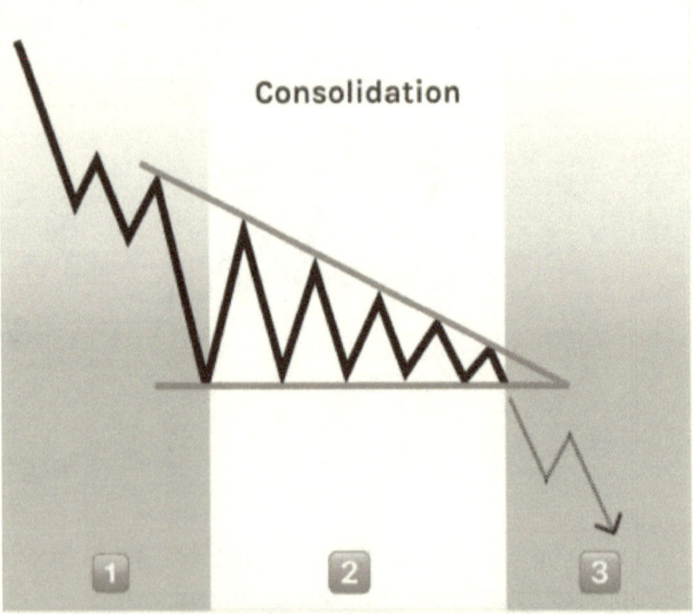

1. **Prior Downtrend and the initial reversal fo**rms the base of the pattern.

1. **Consolidation:** the downtrend takes a pause and the price forms a support level. The buyers are trying to reverse the price, but lose momentum with each attempt.

1. **Trend continues:** The consolidation phase is followed by a breakout, where the asset's price breaks the support level and resumes the downtrend.

How To Identify It

To identify a descending triangle pattern, you need to look for the following characteristics:

- A series of lower highs: This indicates that the buyers are becoming more aggressive.

- Horizontal support: An area on the charts that the price has tested multiple times but has failed to break.

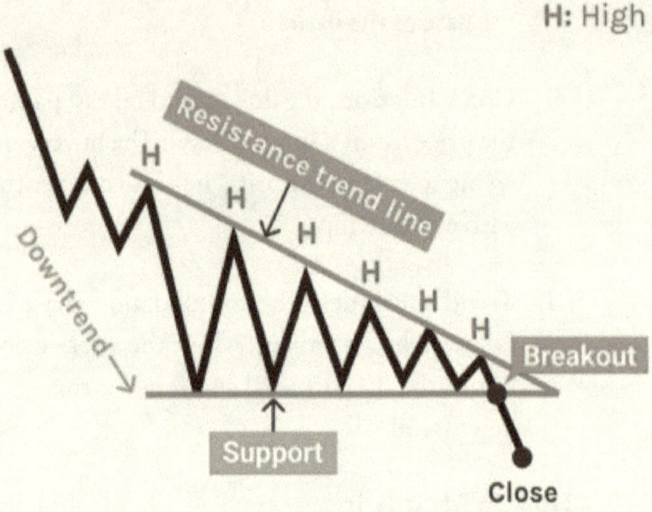
H: High
Resistance trend line
H
H
H
H
H
H
Downtrend
Breakout
Support
Close

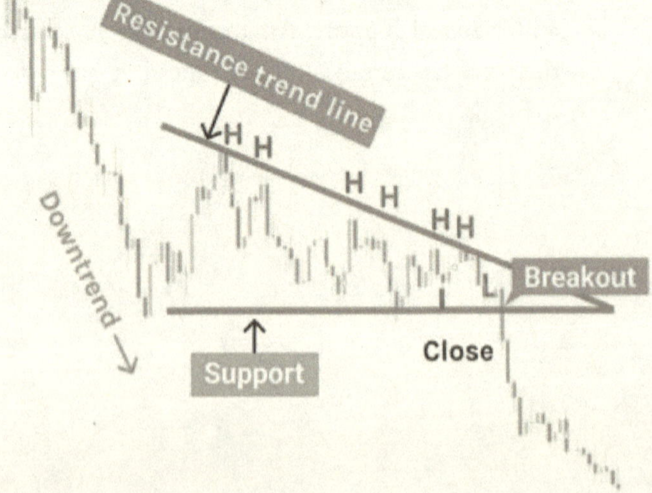
Resistance trend line
H H
H H
H H
Downtrend
Breakout
L
Close
Support

The pattern is complete when the price breaks and closes below the support level.

Volume Analysis

This is an ideal example. Volume might differ depending on market conditions and the pattern can still succeed.

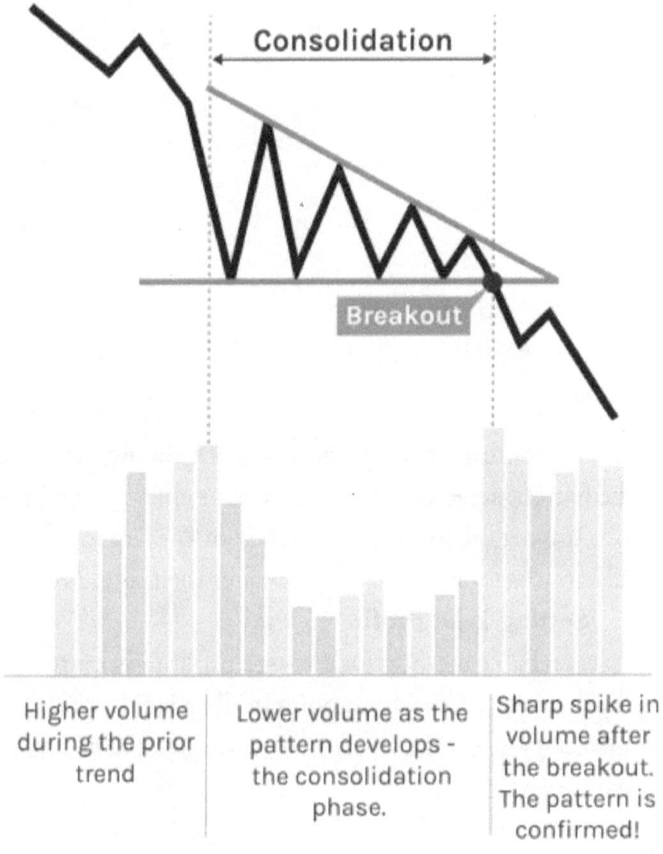

How To Enter The Trade

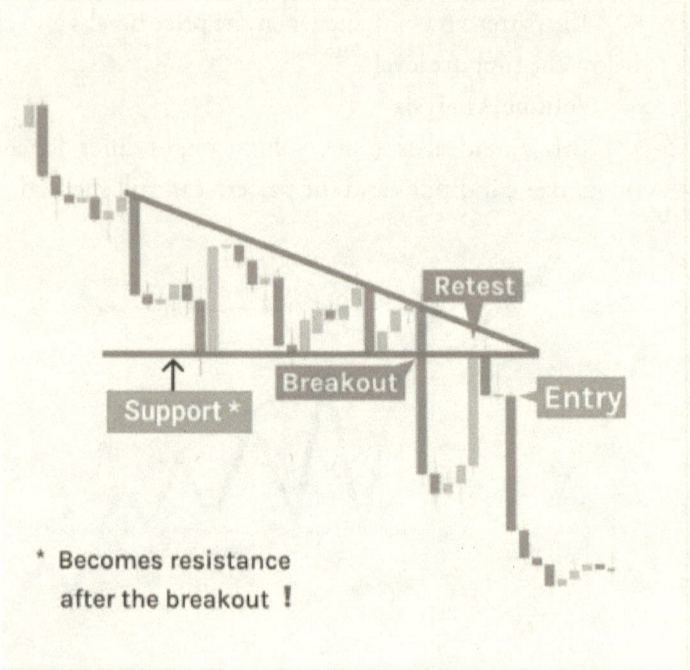

To confirm the pattern, the price should close outside the pattern structure. To increase your chances of success, it's also important to look for a retest of the support level that has now become resistance and enter the trade after.

Setting Take-Profit

A reliable method for setting a profit target is to measure the distance at the widest point of the triangle structure, and then copy-paste the distance as your take profit target after the breakout.

Setting Stop-Loss

Determine your reward/risk ratio before entering the trade. Knowing your profit target (reward) removes the guesswork from placing the stop - loss. The example below uses the gold standard - 3:1.

Uptrend Variation

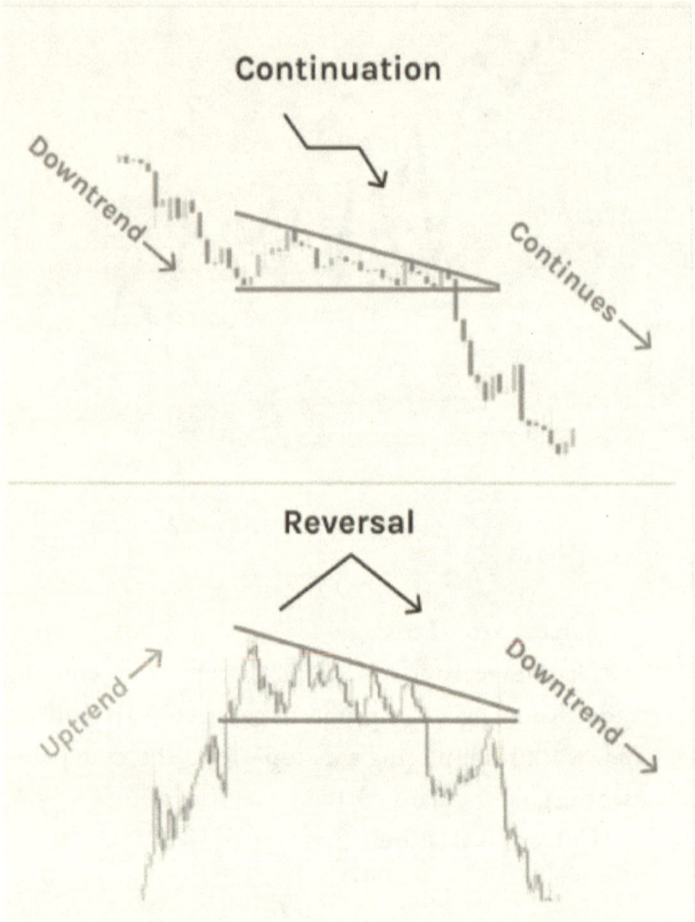

Typically, a descending triangle forms as a continuation pattern during an downtrend. However, there are instances when it forms during an uptrend indicating a potential trend reversal. **In both scenarios the main opportunity is a short trade.** The same trading principles apply to both cases.

Extra Tips

1. Use the Moving Average as another metric for

predicting the directional bias: If the price is below it's long term MA as it nears the exit of the triangle, a bearish breakout is more likely. On the contrary the pattern may fail if the price is above it's long term MA.

1. No pattern looks perfect on the chart. It can be traded as long as it has a sequence of lower highs and breakout below the horizontal support level.

1. The pattern usually takes a few weeks to months to form, so be aware of lower time frame triangles. They may have a higher likelihood of breaking out in either direction.

Lesson 6: Rising Wedge

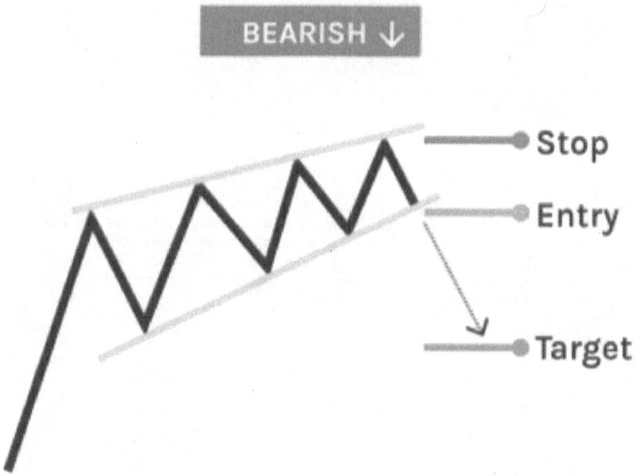

The rising wedge is a commonly observed chart pattern that indicates a potential short trade from a trend reversal.

Quick Facts

- It is called a "rising" wedge because the price is rising, but the trading range is getting narrower, indicating a loss of buying momentum.
- The pattern is very common and can be seen in all time frames, from intraday to monthly charts.
- The rising wedge pattern is often seen in markets with strong bullish sentiment, where traders become overly optimistic and ignore warning signs of a potential reversal.

When And Why It Appears

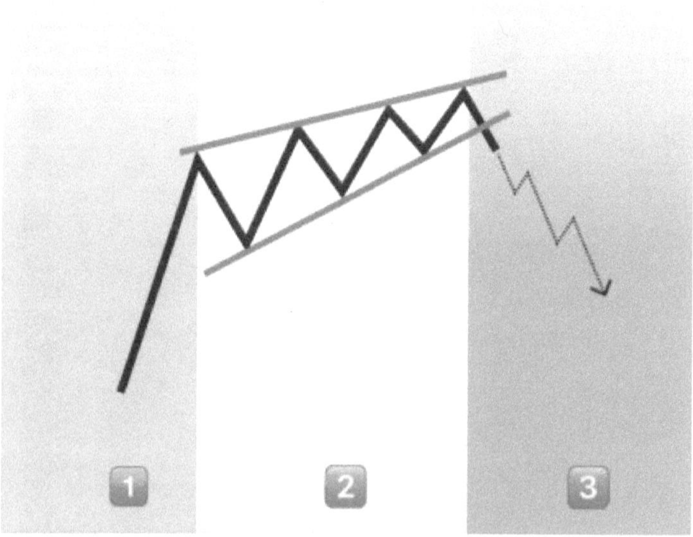

1. **The patterns starts with a strong uptrend.** During this phase, the buyers are in control and the demand is high.

1. **The buyers start losing their strength,** and the price movement becomes less decisive. At this point, the price consolidates between two converging trend lines that slope upward, forming a rising wedge pattern.

1. **As the pattern narrows, traders look for a break of the lower trend line** as it indicates that the sellers have exhausted the buyers, and the uptrend

is likely to reverse.

How To Identify It

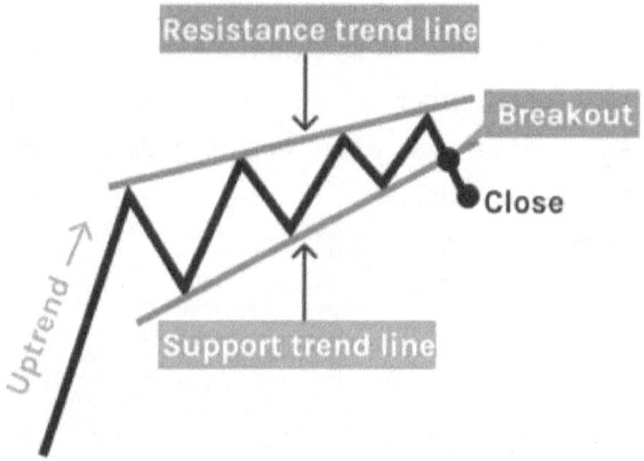
Resistance trend line
Breakout
Close
Uptrend
Support trend line

Resistance trend line
Breakout
Close
Uptrend
Support trend line

The pattern is identified by two converging trend lines that slope upward. The upper trend line connects the highs of the price action, while the lower trend line connects the lows of the price action.

These trend lines should be parallel and narrowing towards each other as the price nears the breakout area. The pattern is complete when the price falls and closes below the support trend line.

Volume Analysis

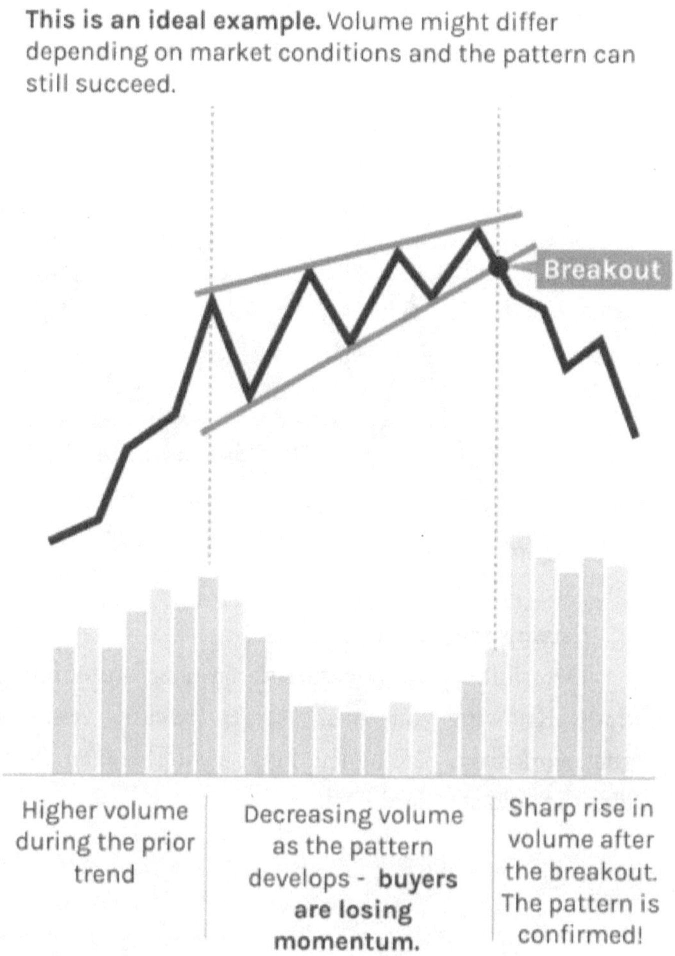

How To Enter The Trade

The rising wedge pattern typically results in a quite sharp breakout lower. Compared to other patterns, retests of the wedge structure are less common. The confirmation to enter a short-trade is a candlestick close below the support line.

Setting Take-Profit

A reliable method for setting a profit target is to measure the height of the rising wedge at its widest point and use the measurement as a profit target.

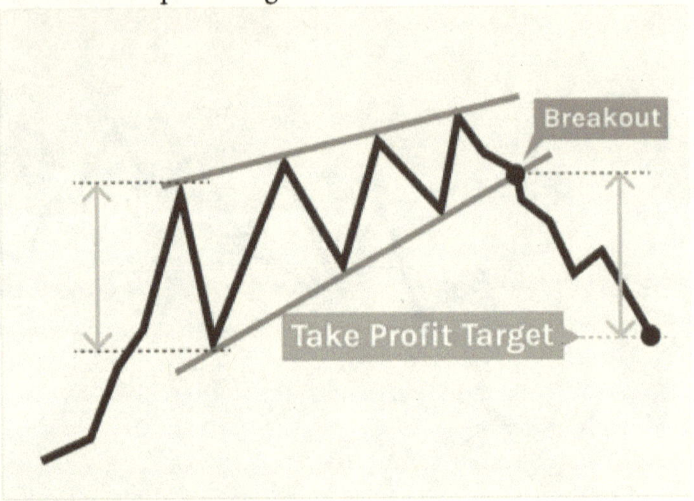

Setting Stop-Loss

Determine your reward/risk ratio before entering the trade. Knowing your profit target (reward) removes the guesswork from placing the stop - loss. The example below uses the gold standard - 3:1.

3:1 Reward/Risk Ratio

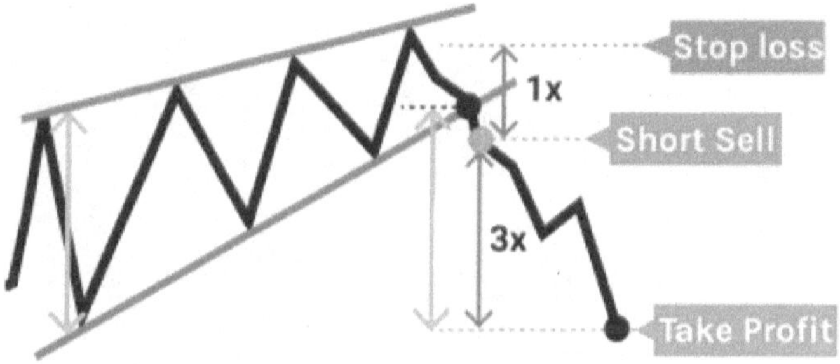

Downtrend Variation

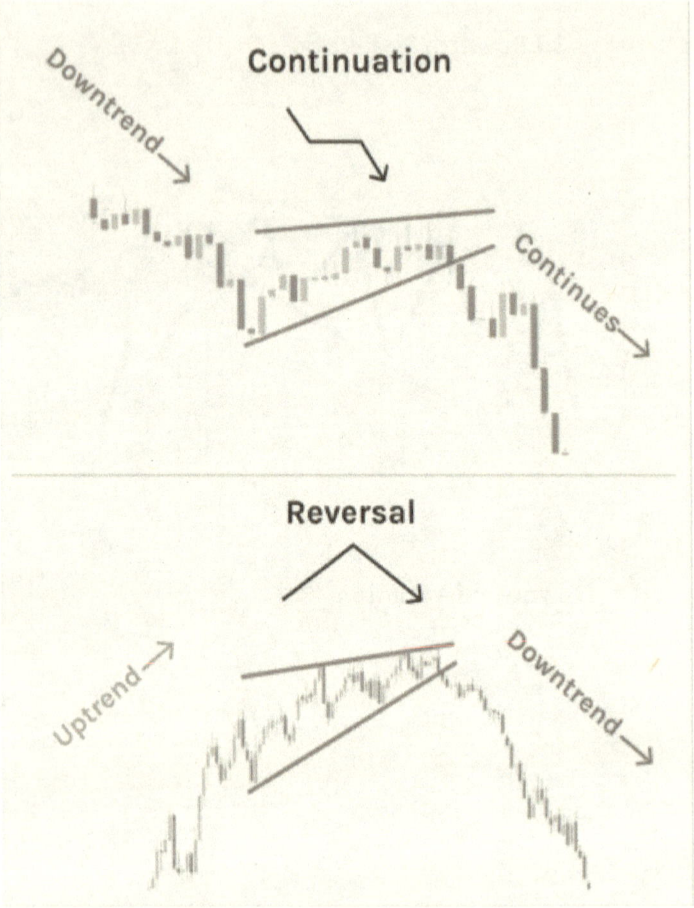

In instances when the rising wedge appears in a downtrend, it usually forms as a continuation pattern. **In both scenarios it indicates a short trade opportunity,** and the same trading principles apply.

Extra Tips

1. When using a longer time frame to identify the rising wedge pattern, it tends to be more reliable

compared to shorter time frames.

1. As this pattern can be identified easily and often, you may be tempted to overtrade. Stick to the guidelines of this lesson and trade only when you are 100% sure it's a rising wedge, and the volume on the breakout confirms it.

Lesson 7: Falling Wedge

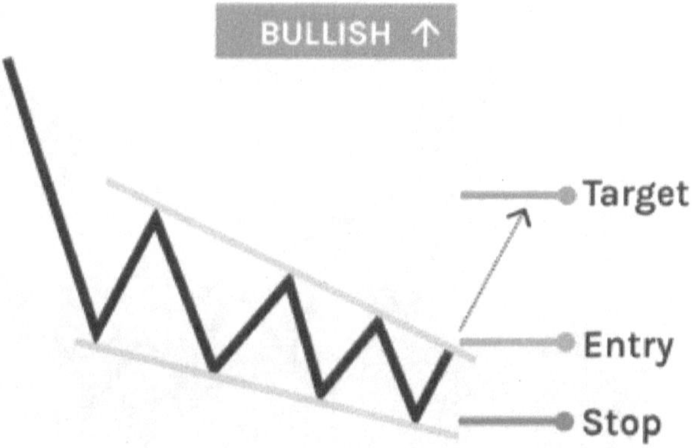

The falling wedge is common bullish reversal pattern found during strong downtrends.

Quick Facts

- It is called a "falling" wedge because the price is falling, but the trading range is getting narrower, indicating a loss of selling momentum.

• The falling wedge pattern is less common than its counterpart - the rising wedge, as well as other chart patterns. Nevertheless it offers great buying opportunities when spotted.

When And Why It Appears

The falling wedge typically appears during a downtrend and indicates a potential bullish reversal. Here's how:

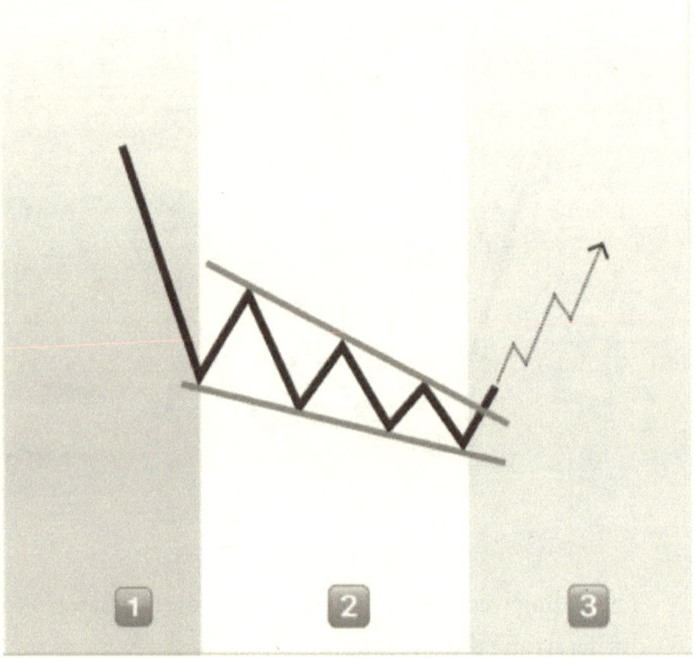

1. **The patterns starts with a strong downtrend.** During this phase, the sellers are in control and the demand is weak.

1. **The sellers start losing their strength,** and the

price movement becomes less decisive. At this point, the price consolidates between two converging trend lines that slope downward, forming a falling wedge pattern.

1. **As the pattern narrows, buyers look for a break of the upper trend line** as it indicates that the downtrend is likely to reverse.

How To Identify It

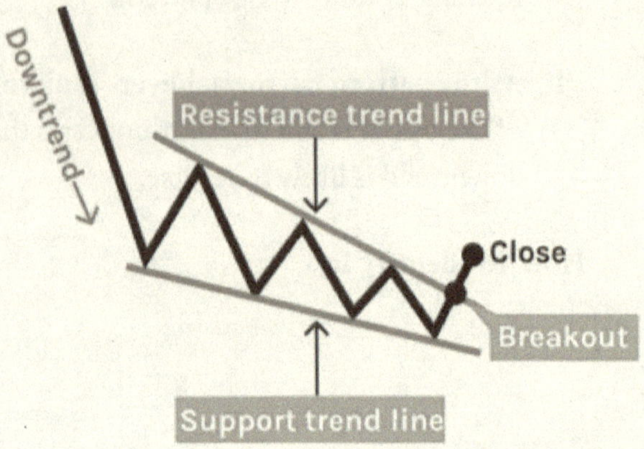
Downtrend
Resistance trend line
Close
Breakout
Support trend line

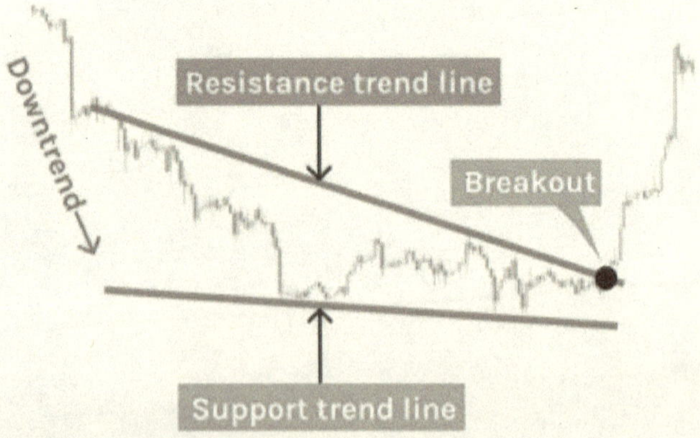
Downtrend
Resistance trend line
Breakout
Support trend line

The pattern is identified by two converging trend lines that slope upward. The upper trend line connects the highs of the price action, while the lower trend line connects the lows of the price action.

These trend lines should be parallel and narrowing towards each other as the price nears the breakout area. The pattern is complete when the price falls and closes below the support trend line.

Volume Analysis

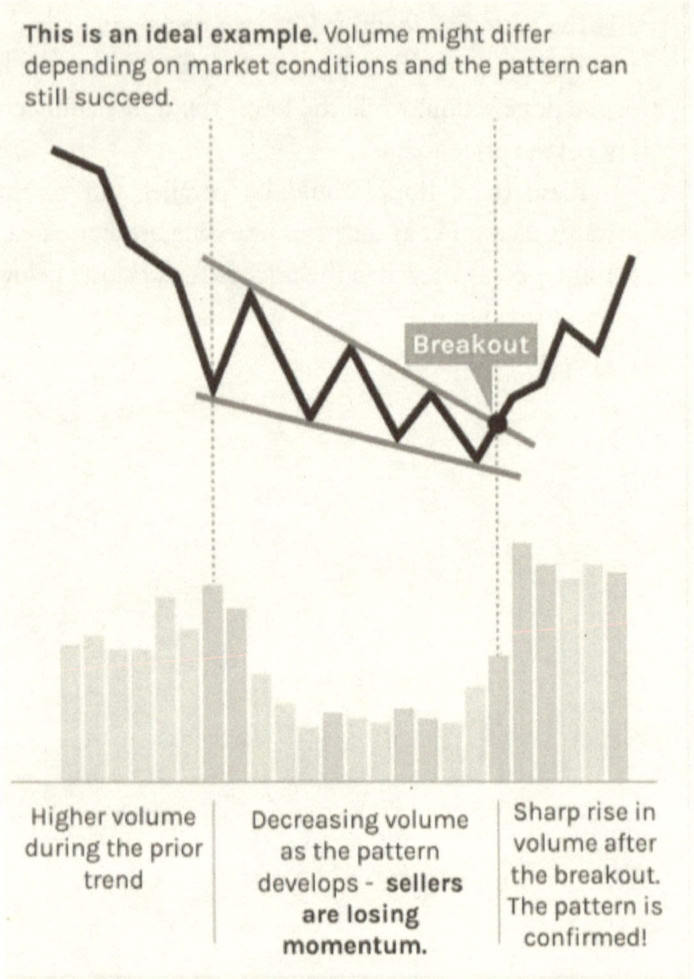

How To Enter The Trade

The falling wedge pattern typically results in a volatile breakout higher. Compared to other patterns, retests of the wedges are less common. To confirm a long trade entry, wait for the price to close above the resistance trend line.

Setting Take-Profit

A reliable method for setting a profit target is to measure the height of the falling wedge at its widest point and use the measurement as a profit target.

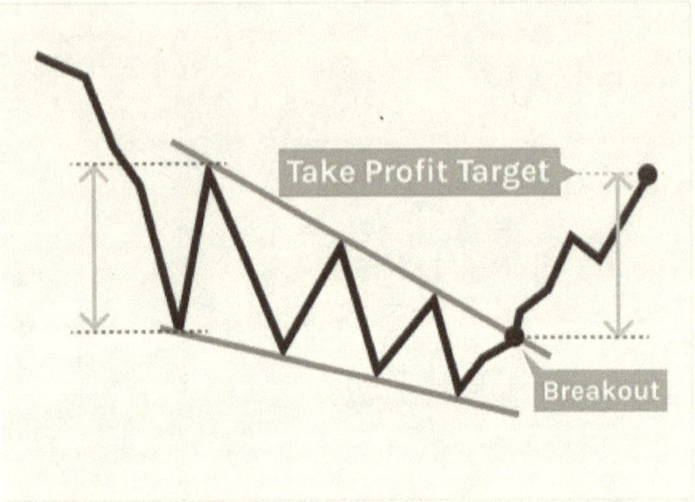

Setting Stop-Loss

Determine your reward/risk ratio before entering the trade. Knowing your profit target(reward) removes the guesswork from placing the stop - loss. The example below uses the gold standard - 3:1.

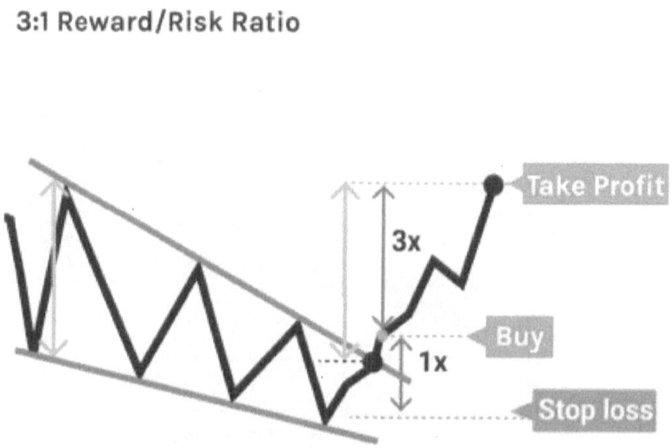

Uptrend Variation

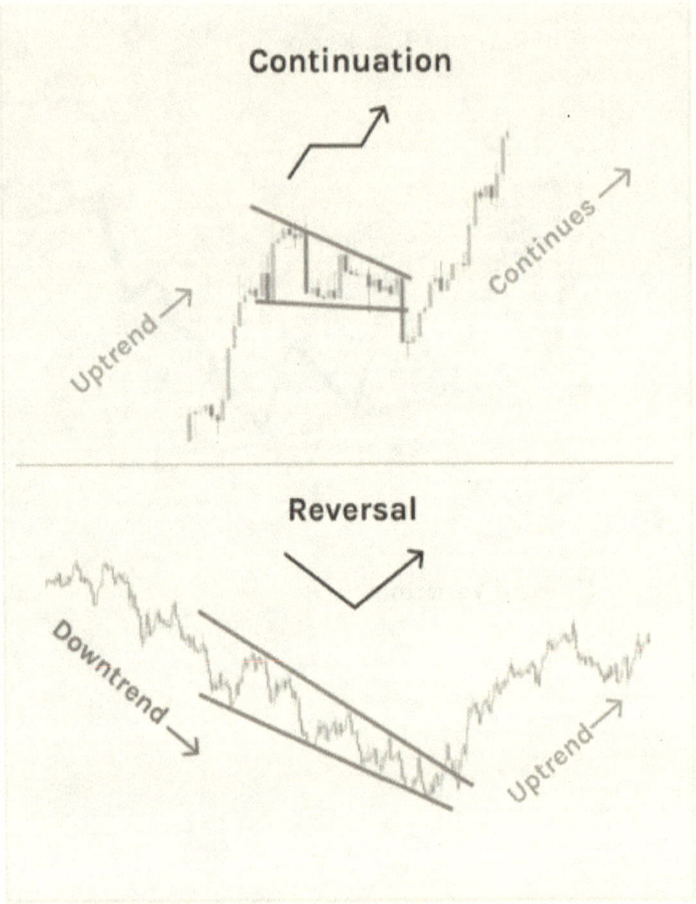

In instances when the falling wedge appears in an uptrend, it usually forms as a continuation pattern. **In both scenarios it indicates a long trade opportunity,** and the same trading principles apply.

Extra Tips

1. When using a longer time frame to identify the falling wedge pattern, it tends to be more reliable

compared to shorter time frames.

1. As this pattern can be identified easily and often, you may be tempted to overtrade. Stick to the guidelines of this lesson and trade only when you are 100% sure it's a falling wedge, and the volume on the breakout confirms it.

Lesson 8: Top 10 Candle Patterns

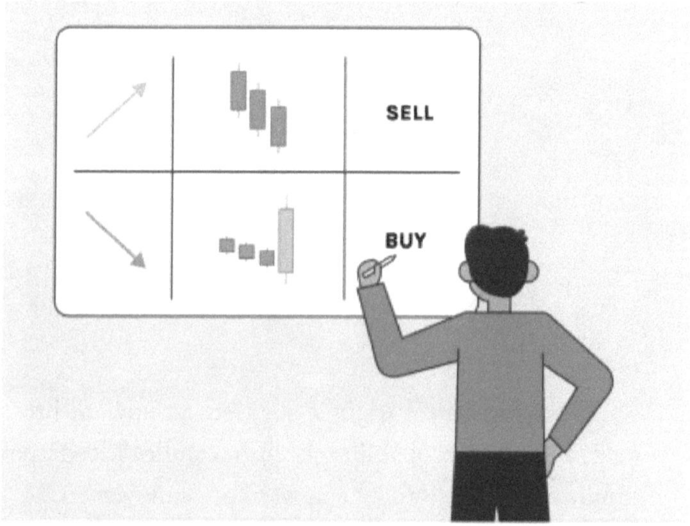

The truth is, all chart patterns can go either way. While a reversal pattern is more likely to change the direction of a trend, it is not a 100% guarantee.

Fortunately, there is another signal available that can assist you in making the correct trading decision.

Entry confirmation signal

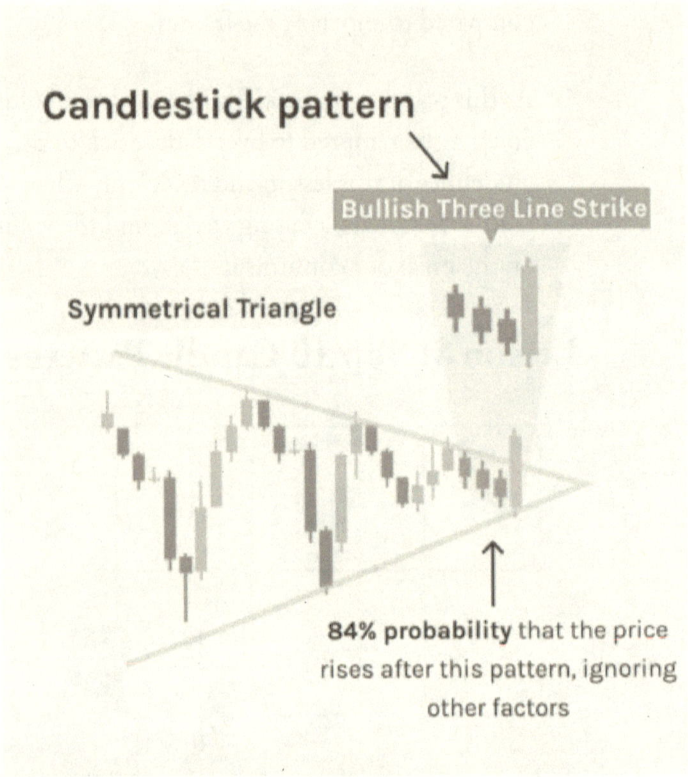

If a symmetrical triangle suggests an upward breakout, seek a high - probability bullish candlestick pattern to support your thesis for the upward price movement.

There are hundreds of patterns. However, very few patterns have a historical success rate of more than 50%.

Trading is all about probabilities. If you were to stop learning and randomly enter a trade without any analysis, your odds of making a profit would be like flipping a coin. Around 48% accounting for fees. The price can only go up or down, after all.

To overcome this, I have carefully selected 10 patterns that have historically exceeded the baseline probability of trading.

Top 10 candle patterns

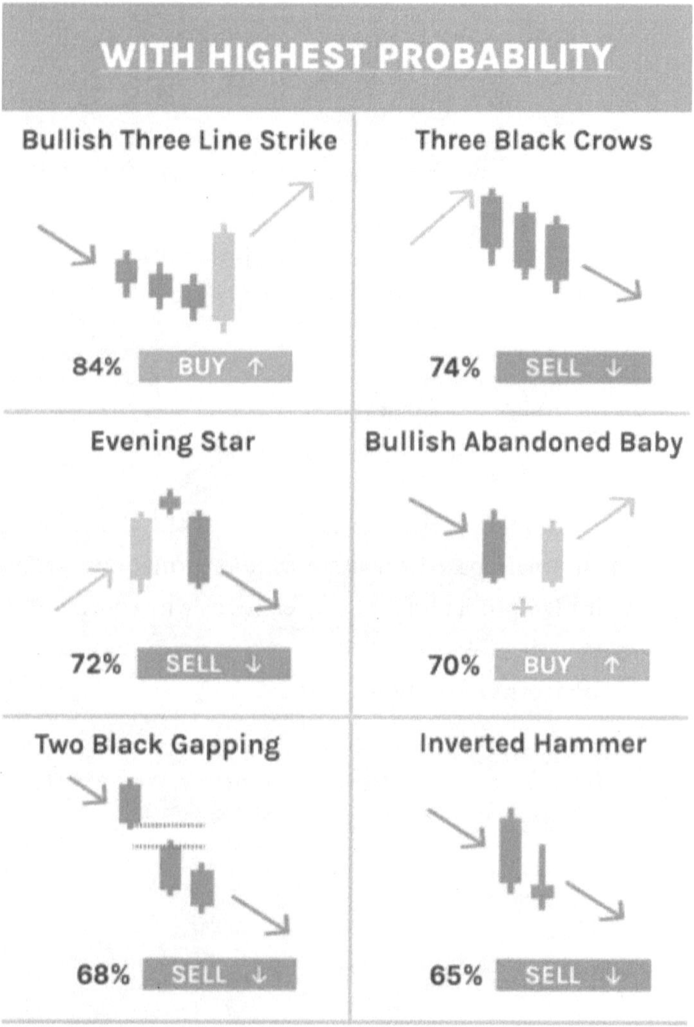

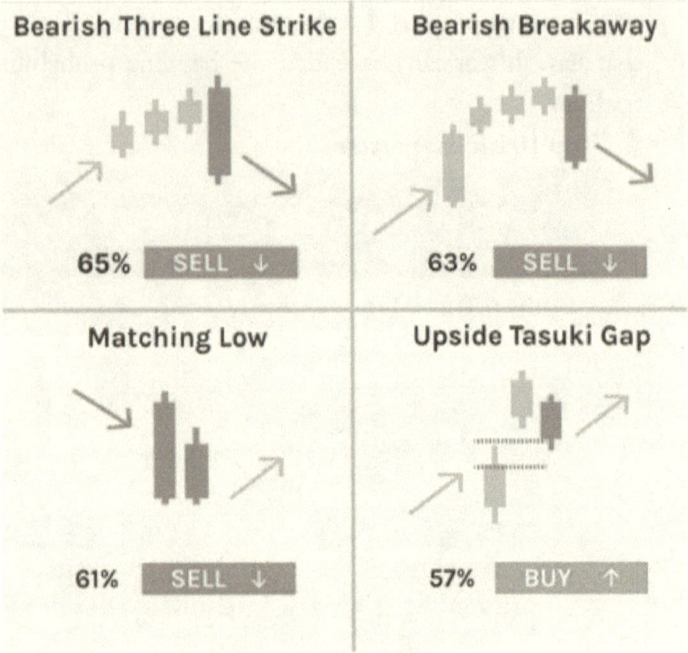

You might feel tempted to look at the charts and make trades solely based on these candle formations because of their high probability. However, here's why you shouldn't do that:

Patterns never work alone

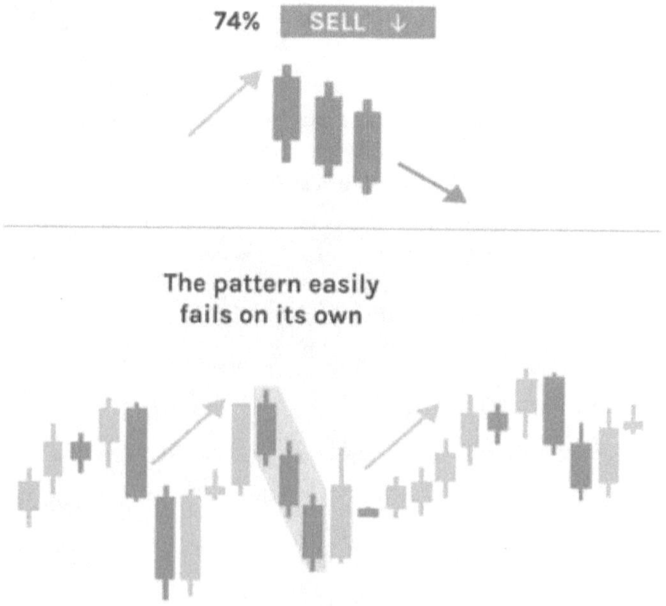

To yield highest possible chance of success, use candlestick patterns within proper context - as extra confirmation for the direction of a chart pattern, or a reversal from support or resistance level.

In other words, aligning with market structure!

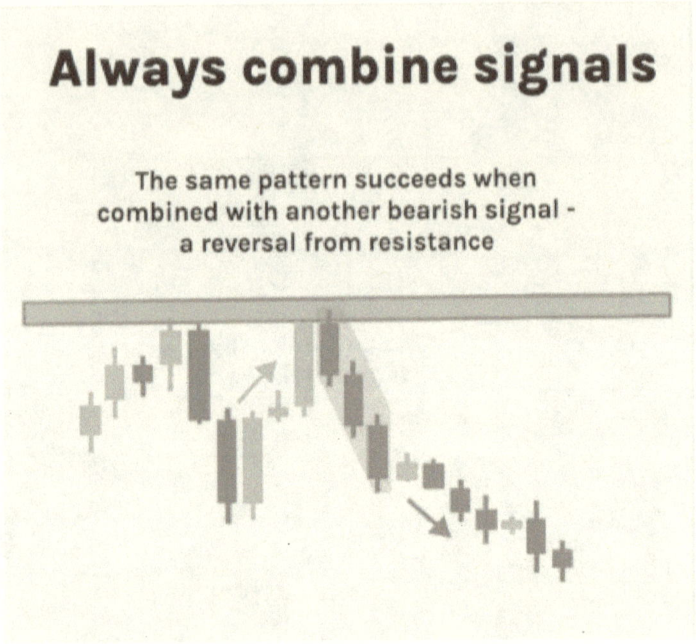

As with any technical analysis concept, candle patterns work best when used together as one element of your overall strategy.

Exam: Chart Patterns Explained

1. Does the size of a pattern have any meaning in your trades?

- No, it has no meaning at all

- Yes, it tells how many buyers and sellers trade

- Yes, it can guide the placement of SL and TP

1. You can base trade decisions on candle patterns alone?

- False

- True

1. Candle patterns never fail, they always move as in the examples

- False

- True

Answer:

1. Yes, it can guide the placement of SL and TP

1. False

1. False

Chapter 8: Best Losers Win

Lesson 1: Samurai Wisdom

Miyamoto Musashi was a 15th century Japanese samurai who wrote "The Book of 5 Rings" on sword-fighting strategy and **the philosophy of excellence.** The book is a favorite among entrepreneurs like Tim Ferriss and Joe Rogan, as well as top executives and athletes.

Musashis's philosophy

Musashi's philosophy is centered on **'the way,'** a relentless pursuit of excellence in one's art rather than the outcome.

This approach suggests that mastering one discipline, such as a sport or an art, can unveil a universal path to excellence in all fields, including trading.

Musashi himself, besides being a lethal samurai, excelled in painting, gardening, dance, philosophy, strategy, and writing.

Parallel to trading

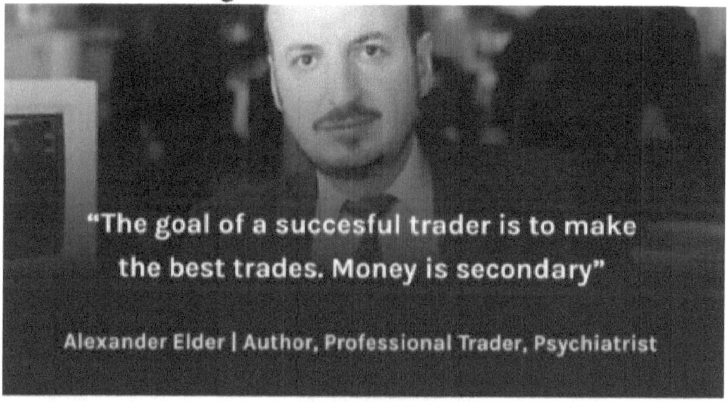

Echoing Musashi's philosophy, Alexander Elder remarks - **making money and profits, are simply a side-effect of mastery.**

- Consider a great dentist: is their main focus to earn money, or in **doing the best possible dental work to fix a painful tooth?**

- Does an experienced pilot prioritize their salary, or **the safety and precision of landing the plane?**

- Does a boxing world champion in a fight think about the paycheck, or keeping his hands up and **avoiding a fight-ending blow?**

Focus on "The Way"

To be profitable, you must master the way of trading: focusing on the process of trading - the strategies, decisions, and discipline - over the pursuit of profits.

There are no shortcuts to excellence.

You cannot simply read a book, including this one, and expect automatic greatness.

While I provide effective tools and techniques in this book, your inner drive and commitment are what will ultimately determine your success.

This chapter delves into the psychology of a successful trader, offering practical insights and a strong focus on helping you adopt the 'way' - a mindset of disciplined strategy and decision-making.

Lesson 2: Success Through Failure

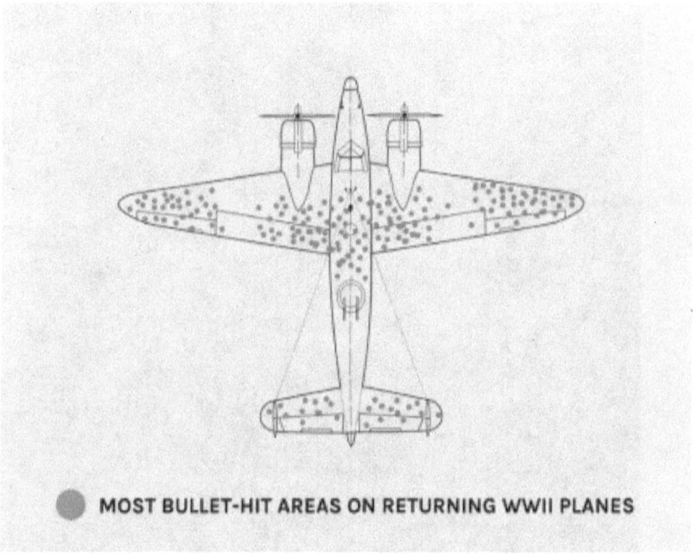

During World War II, allied military experts analyzed fighter planes returning from battles. Noticing more damage in certain areas, they first thought, "These parts are getting hit the most, let's reinforce them."

However, statistician Abraham Wald challenged this notion, pointing out the crucial areas were actually those without bullet holes.

Planes hit there likely never returned. This shift in perspective, **focusing on failures rather than visible successes,** allowed the Allies to save more planes and pilots, ultimately leads to their victory.

Jordan's philosophy on failure

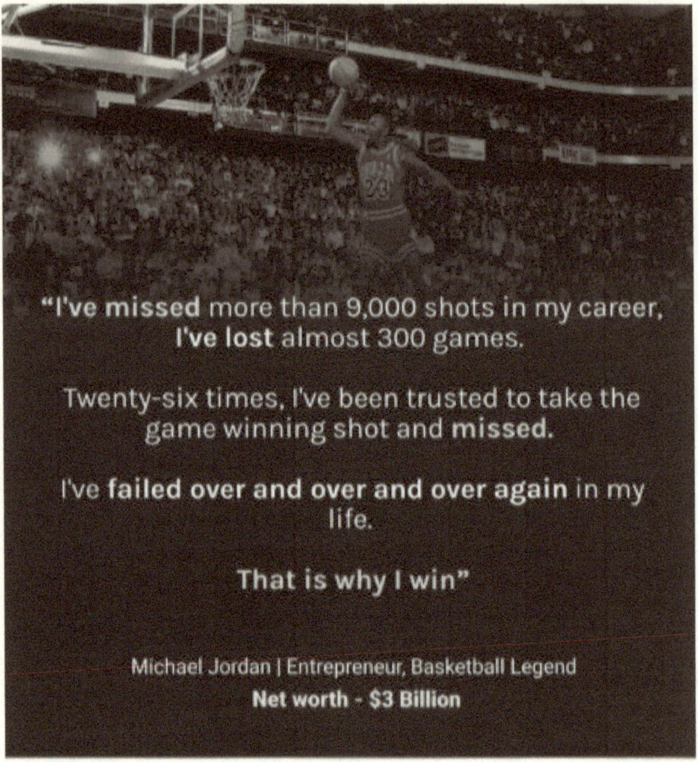

Michael Jordan views each missed shot as a crucial learning step shaping him into a legendary athlete, traders should view each loss in the market similarly.

Every lost trade, like each missed shot, is not just a setback but an opportunity to recognize a mistake and correct it.

This mindset mirrors Wald's approach to analyzing fighter planes in WWll - focusing on what's missing ultimately lead to victory.

Trading: a mental game

Jordan dedicated years to developing his physical skills in the gym, but a significant part of his work was mental training with George Mumford, a psychologist and mindfulness coach.

Jordan credits Mumford's guidance as pivotal in **building his mental resilience despite losses and composure under pressure** - key factors helping him secure 6x NBA championships with the Bulls.

In trading, we don't have the physical stuff - it's all in your head. Your success rests on how you handle the ups and downs, stay disciplined, and keep your cool. Just like Jordan, it's about training your mind to be as strong as your game.

Win or learn

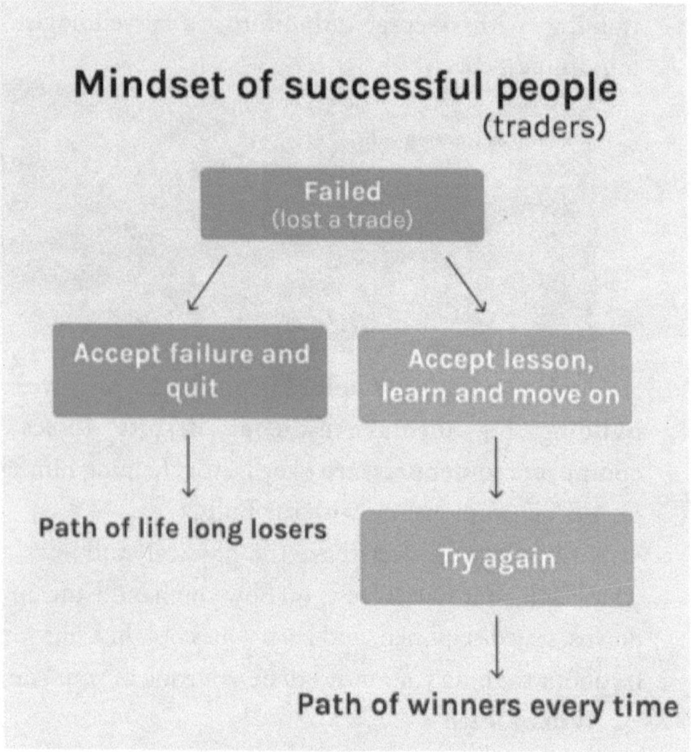

When it comes to trading, think 'win or learn', not 'win or lose.

Every trade that doesn't work out? That's your chance to learn and improve. The 'Best Loser Wins' philosophy is all about using each setback as a stepping stone.

The best traders like the best athletes don't give up, they learn and get better.

Lesson 3: Everyday Habits

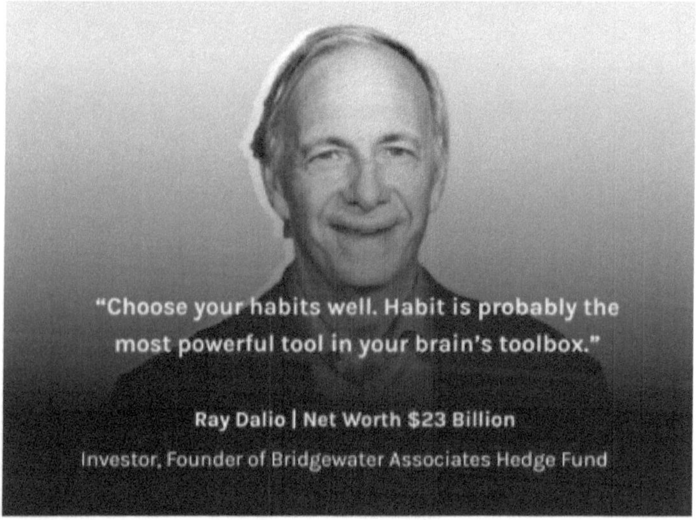

Discipline is the cornerstone of mental strength whether in trading, business or professional sports. For example, pro athletes' dedication to sleep, nutrition, and recovery outside of training training hours is what distinguishes them from people who just work out.

Similarly, in trading, it's not just the time spent on trades but also what you do with the rest of your day that matters.

Key habits to build discipline and help you trade better

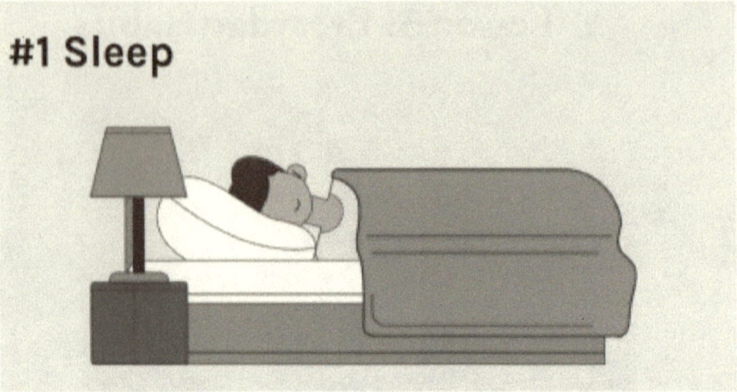

Mental Benefit: Improved Decision-Making and Risk Assesment

It's much easier to swipe your phone, than shutting it off and going to bed. Quality sleep is essential, and it takes discipline. Missing just 2 hours, leads to riskier behaviour, impaired judgment, mood issues, and overall health problems - all detrimental to winning in the markets.

Aim for 7-8 hours nightly - this ensures your brain operates at peak performance.

Mental benefit: Stress Management and Improved Focus

Just 30 minutes of exercise is proven to lower cortisol levels - a damaging stress hormone. Less cortisol means a calmer and more focused mind for concentration on the charts.

Be it a walk, yoga, a gym session, or just stretching at your desk, exercise will reduce stress and anxiety, two common issues among traders.

Quality sleep and exercise are two key habits that cost nothing, but help you feel better, trade better and thus win more.

Build a disciplined winning routine

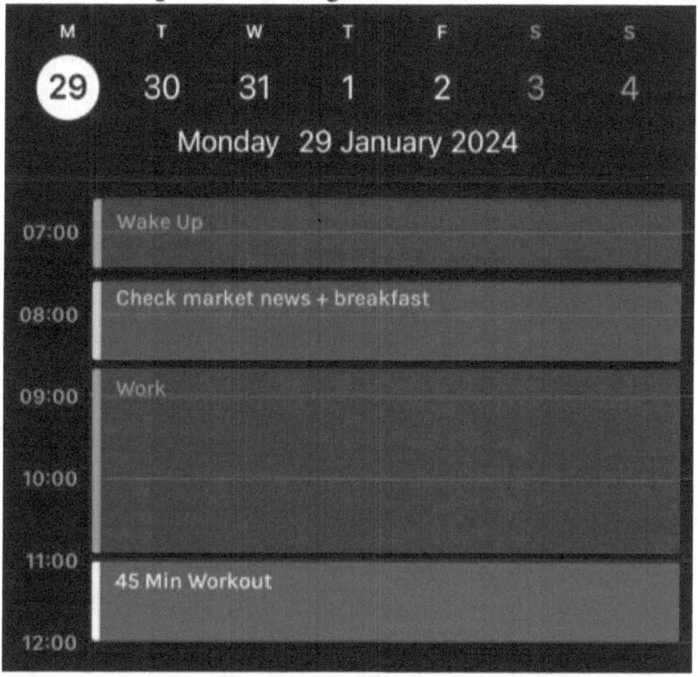

Developing a routine like in the example above, which includes both mental and physical preparation, lays the groundwork for a clear, and organized trading day.

For instance, Ray Dalio attributes much of his success to a daily meditation routine.

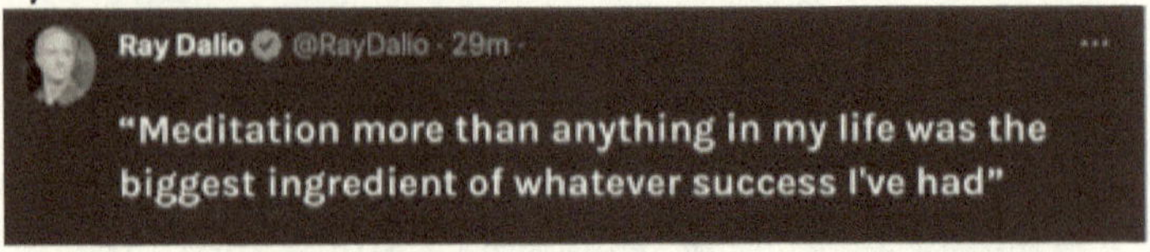

Build a healthy routine that suits your needs and schedule. **And stick to it!** The discipline you build will not only aid in your market performance but also contribute to your overall success and well-being.

Lesson 4: Strong Trading System - Your Edge

In trading, having an 'edge' means having a strategic advantage. This edge could be a well-defined strategy, mental strength, risk management, or even simple lifestyle habits like a disciplined sleep routine we discussed earlier.

By optimizing your sleep, you could theoretically gain some edge over a large portion of the population, including traders. And simple tricks like these can be one part of strong but easy to follow trading system.

System = Routine + Rules

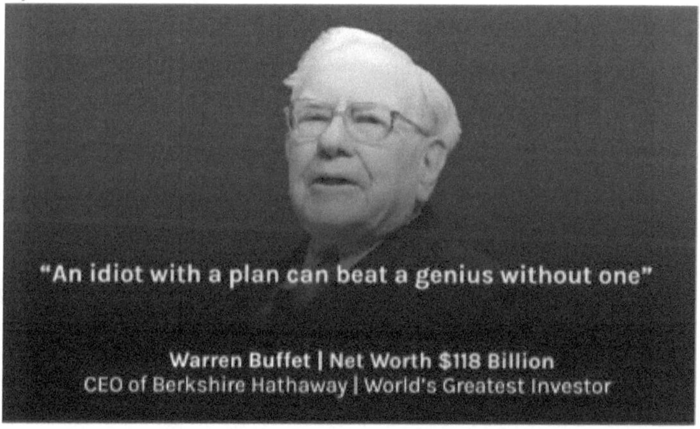

Your trading system should be a blend of a disciplined routine and rules - a structured approach that fits your style and goals.

For instance, you might decide to trade only certain assets or set specific times for trading. The system is unique to every trader, thus we cannot give you one-size-fits-all answer. But we can give you pointers:

Where to test your system?

Did you know that commercial jet pilots spend about **~ 100h in flight simulators** before taking control of a real plane?

First to build a pilot's skills and confidence without risking life and property and second - because it is much cheaper to train in a simulator than it is to fly a plane during training. Flying a Boeing 747 costs about $30k per hour.

Similarly in trading, confidence grows from hands-on practice. **Research shows that simulated trading is more effective for understanding and capitalizing on market movements than just pure theory.** Thus you can use any real-time market simulator, for testing, building and implementing your own personal trading system.

Don't do it in the real markets, where mistakes can be very costly.

A crucial component of any trading system is the preparation before each trade. To assist you in this, I've developed a simple yet effective pre-trade checklist.

Follow a pre-trade checklist

Research data suggests that following a pre-trade checklist can help reduce total losses by up to 70% and decrease the average loss from 8.3% to -0.9%. I've made this checklist, so you can keep it handy, print it, or share it with friends!

PRE - TRADE CHECKLIST

- **MINDSET** — ARE YOU MENTALLY STABLE AND NOT INFLUENCED BY FEAR OR GREED?
- **LOGIC** — DO YOU HAVE A LOGICAL BASIS FOR TAKING THE TRADE?
- **TREND** — ARE YOU AWARE OF THE CURRENT TREND IN YOUR TARGET TIME FRAMES?
- **S/R** — HAVE YOU IDENTIFIED KEY SUPPORT AND RESISTANCE LEVELS?
- **STRUCTURE** — ARE YOU VISUALLY AWARE OF THE MARKET STRUCTURE?
- **CAPITAL** — ARE YOU NOT TRADING WITH MONEY ABOVE YOUR COMFORTABLE LIMIT?
- **ENTRY** — DO YOU KNOW WHERE TO ENTER THE TRADE AND WHY?
- **S/L EXIT** — DO YOU HAVE A PLAN FOR PLACING THE STOP - LOSS?
- **T/P TARGET** — IS YOUR TAKE-PROFIT TARGET SET, IS IT WITHIN YOUR RISK/REWARD RATIO?

IF ALL BOXES ARE CHECKED:

TAKE THE TRADE

Adhering to a pre-trade checklist is like a pilot running through pre-flight checks. It ensures you're fully prepared for the trade.

Next up we'll close this chapter with 5 key psychological traps traders fall into.

Lesson 5: Five Traps To Avoid

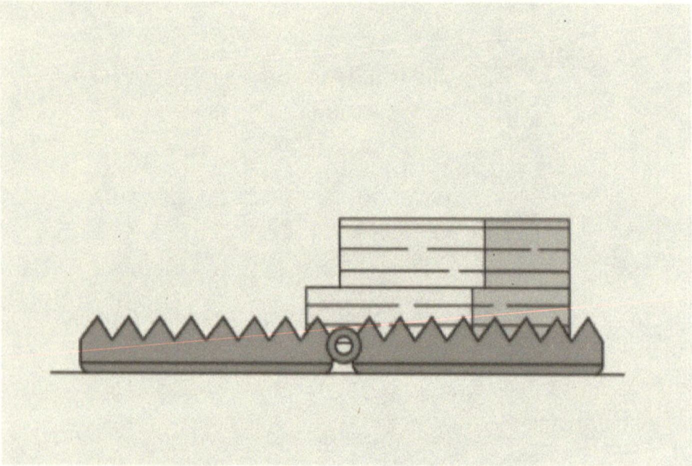

As we wrap up this chapter, I hope it's clear to you that your mental strength is as crucial as mastering the technical aspects.

Here, I'll highlight five common traps that, if avoided, will significantly improve your edge in the markets:

#1 Trading on a bad day

Life's ups and downs impact us all. When work, health or relationships weigh you down it's best to use the time to learn and observe the markets but don't open trades.

Otherwise if you lose, you've got another problem, bad mood and lost money on top of it. Don't let a bad day lead to a bad trade.

Tip: Feeling down - take a break from the markets.

#2 Revenge trading

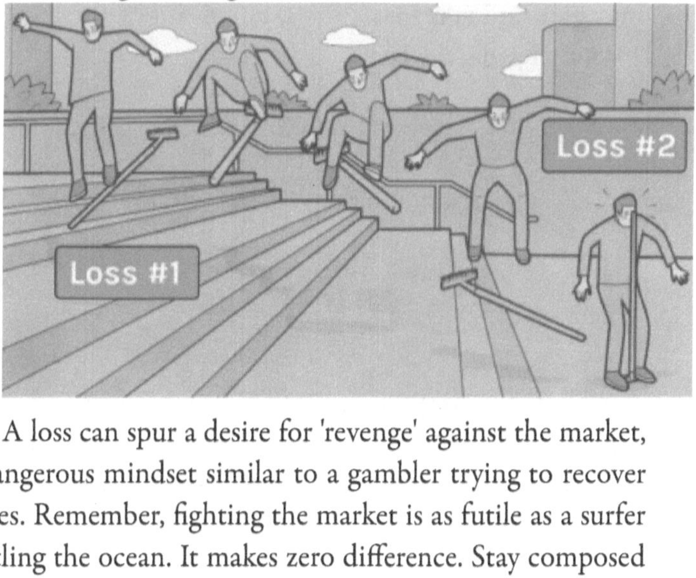

A loss can spur a desire for 'revenge' against the market, a dangerous mindset similar to a gambler trying to recover losses. Remember, fighting the market is as futile as a surfer battling the ocean. It makes zero difference. Stay composed and return with a clear mind.

Tip - Lost two trades in a row, take a break!

#3 Overtrading

Overtrading often stems from a dopamine-driven desire for excitement, leading to impulsive, high-frequency trading. This leads you to trade without thinking, often so much so, that managing trades or setting calculated stops becomes impossible.

Tip - Quality, not quantity, is the key. Set your daily max gain and max loss.

#4 Chasing the bag

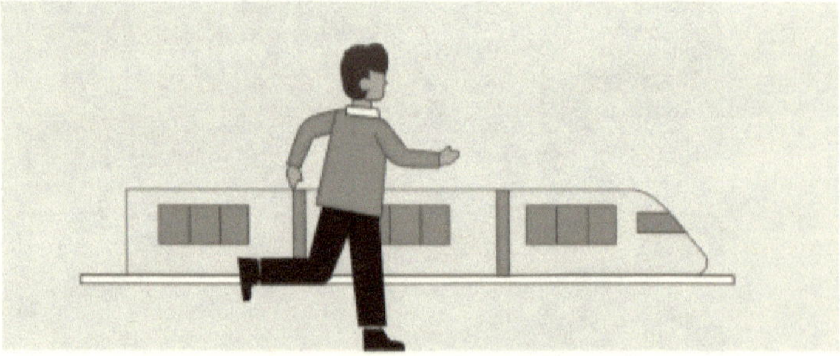

Timing is everything, a trade is meaningless unless you can buy/sell the at the correct time. Fear of missing out, (FOMO) during strong rallies or peaks, can lead you to trade when it's too late.

When you realize that there are usually 1-3 high-quality opportunities every day, you don't have to have a mindset of scarcity.

Tip - If an asset is overly hyped, it's often too late to enter profitably.

#5 Taking it too seriously

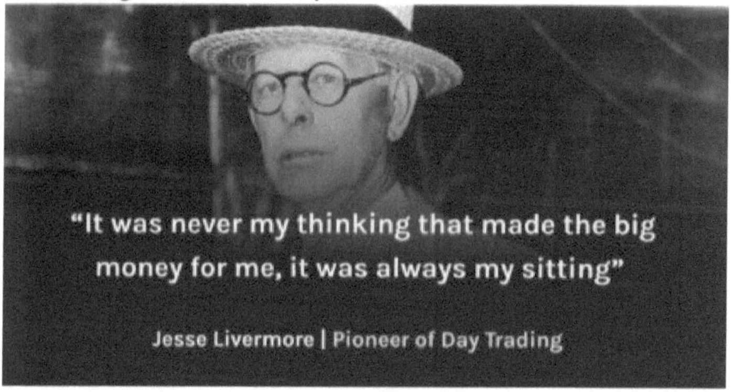

Jesse Livermore's wisdom reminds us that patience, beats constant action. You're not a stressed hedge fund manager in charge of billions, so don't overthink it.

Start small, manage your risks, apply the lessons learned in this chapter and you will already have a substantial edge.

Main learnings

Focus on 'The Way': Aim to become a skilled trader by focusing on the process, not just the profits.

- **Win or Learn Approach:** Embrace every outcome as a learning opportunity.

- **Winning Routine:** Develop a consistent routine that enhances your trading efficacy.

- **Find Your Edge:** Sleep, checklist, risk management, build a strong trading system.

Exam: Best Loser Wins

1. What should a trader do on a bad day?

- Increase trade size to recover good mood

- Trade as much as possible to mask bad feelings

- Avoid trading, at most check up on market news

2. What it means to have a "win or learn" mindset?

- Win or lose each trade is a chance to learn

- Only winning trades matter

- Losses should be avoided at all costs

3. Which habit is NOT recommended for traders?

- Overtrading to gain experience

- Working on quality sleep and fitness

- Approaching losses as lessons

Answer:

1. Avoid trading, at most check up on market news

1. Win or lose each trade is a chance to learn

1. Overtrading to gain experience

Chapter 9: Dopamine Battles

Lesson 1: Hacking Your Brain

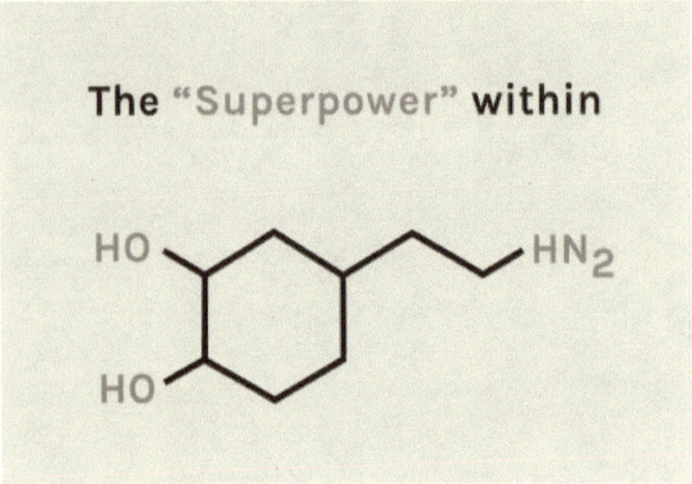

This lesson will take you on a journey through the inner workings of your mind. You'll learn how a tiny chemical in your brain - dopamine, motivates you to get good at trading. I'll explain how to harness its power and make it work for you.

Quick science on dopamine

Dopamine is closely related with feelings of reward and pleasure. It's essentially a cycle of motivation, reward, and reinforcement. Here's a brief overview of how it works:

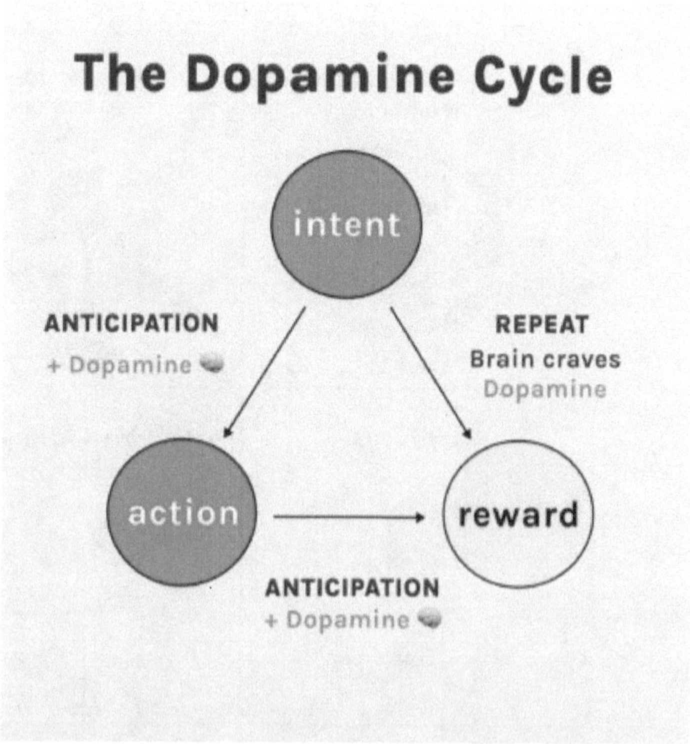

Scientists discovered that when we set goals and anticipate a reward for achieving them, our brain releases a hit of dopamine. We feel this as motivation and a sense of accomplishment when doing hard tasks - like learning how to trade.

Your brain then associates these pleasurable feelings with the reward, and motivates you to repeat that behavior - to get that next dopamine hit.

It's not about the reward

Earlier on we discussed how succesful trading is less about the reward part, and more about the process. The answer to why that's the case can be found in the dopamine system.

Theres a common misconception that dopamine is released when we obtain a reward, but it's NOT true.

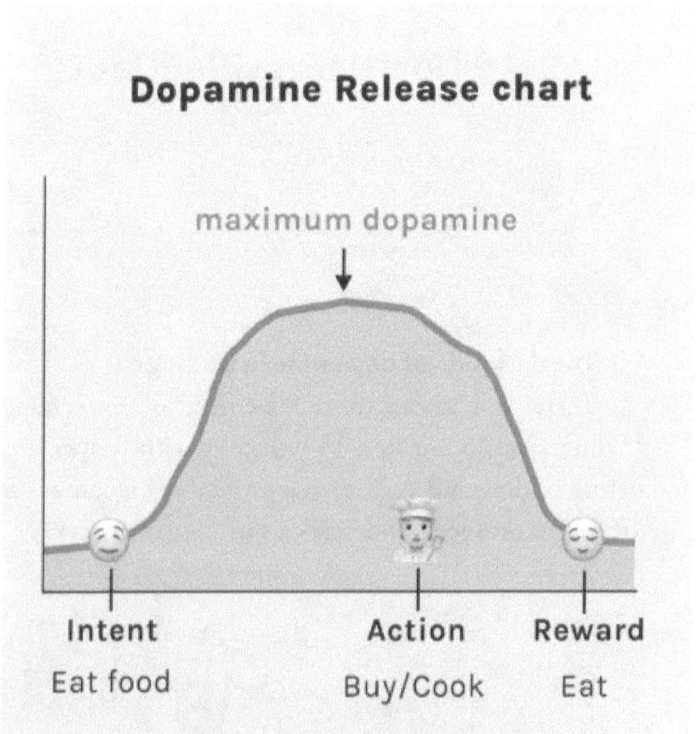

Research in neuroscience has proved that dopamine is actually released in the **anticipation phase.** You feel this in every day life too, when you're hungry, the expectation of food excites you and motivates you to get it. When you eat, the dopamine release lessens and as you return to baseline, you seek another hit.

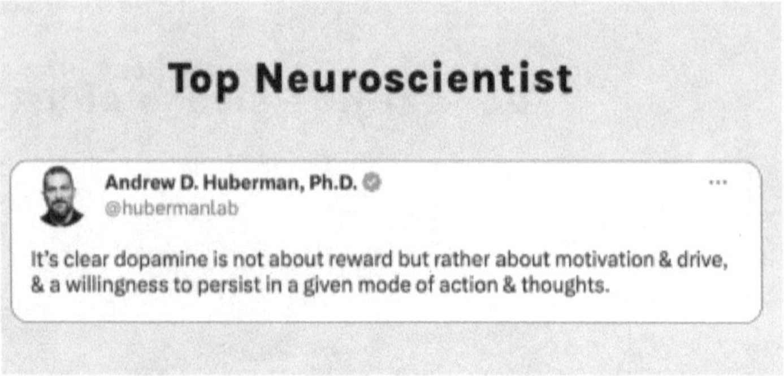

The dark side of dopamine in trading

There will always be an element of uncertainty in trading. We do our best to reduce it with proper analysis before trading and even then a profitable outcome is **never 100% guaranteed.** And here's a shocking discovery:

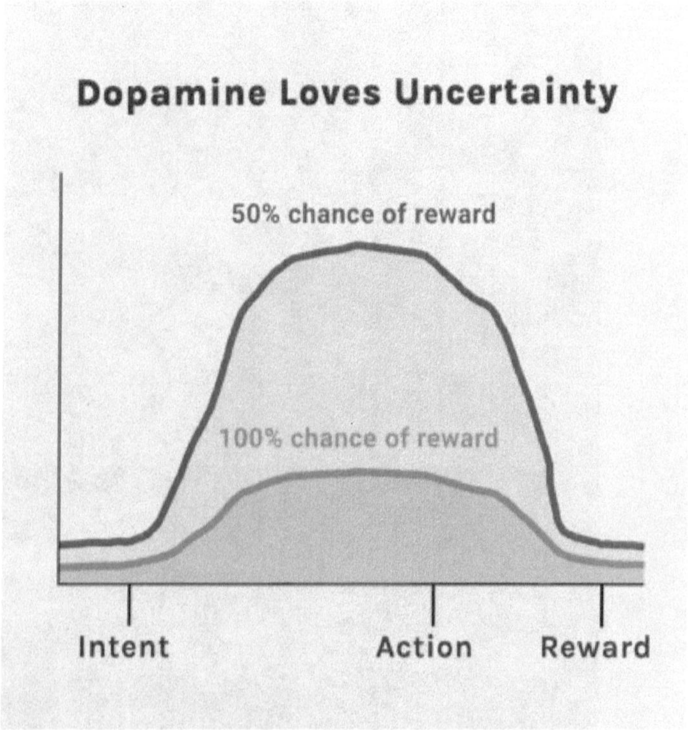

Researchers found that if the reward part of the dopamine cycle, is uncertain, like in trading, the spike in dopamine release is greatly increased. This explains how undisciplined traders get hooked on chasing "the rush" with risky trades. **It's no different than gambling.**

The bottom line

To help maximise dopamine in a healthy way, remember these three principles:

- Make a goal of becoming a good trader and making the best possible trades. Money will come naturally.

- Embrace and look forward to the challenge of learning how to trade.

- Your dopamine system will help you focus and learn better as you move closer to that goal.

But if that's not convincing enough, I've researched the science and found another amazing discovery that can boost your dopamine system even further. Read on.

Lesson 2: The Power Of Competition

In this lesson, we will explore the science behind competition and how it can vastly increase the odds of you becoming a highly-skilled trader. First, a little back story.

Life is about competition

Competition is an integral part of being humans and life itself. In the natural world, plants compete with each other for resources such as sunlight, water, and nutrients.

The competition can be fierce, with some plants even secreting toxins to prevent other plants from growing nearby.

In pro trading, it's no different.

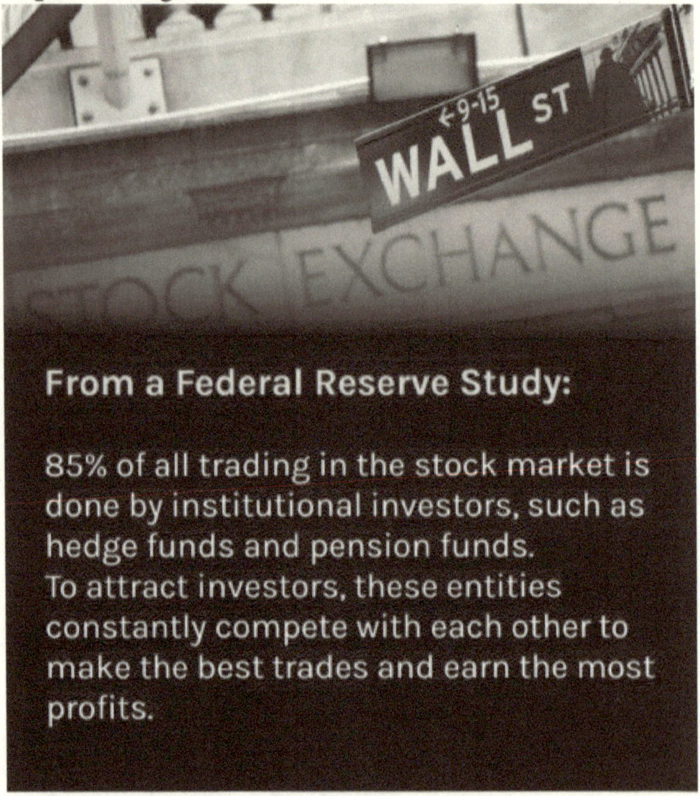

Hedge funds go to extreme lengths to compete and beat each other. They also do everything in their power to outsmart retail traders like you. Think about this - have you ever picked stocks from space?

One shady method used by hedge funds is buying real-time satellite imagery of parking lots to predict retailers' sales. Based on the data, they make decisions to invest in the most profitable retailer, like Walmart, Costco and others. It's a clear example of the fierce and often unfair competition.

But is there a way you can gain an edge by competing? There is one.

The effects of competition on the dopamine system

Surprise surprise... studies have shown that competition activates the brain's dopamine system, which as you learned is responsible for motivation, focus, and learning.

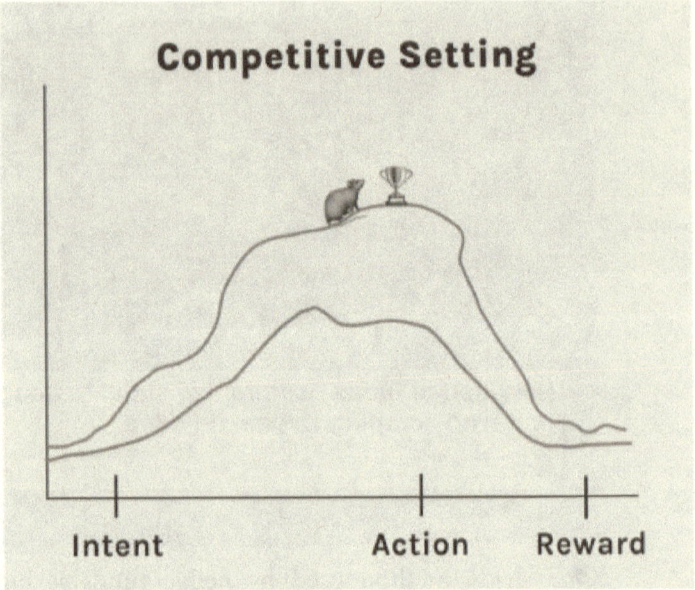

A study by Dr. John Salamone of the University of Connecticut found that rats who were in a competitive environment had higher levels of dopamine in their brains than those who were not, thus leading to more focus and motivation for certain behaviours.

Similar findings can be observed in cognitive studies on humans:

Cognitive improvement from competition

Competing improves cognitive performance by **5-10%**, by rising **dopamine levels** in the brain.

(Study published in: Social Cognitive and Affective Neuroscience)

Competition improves effort and focus. Subjects competing in a memory task saw **15-20%** improvement in results.

(Study published in: Psychological Science)

Competition improves mental performance in children: **15%** increase in a competitive group vs 7% in non-competitive group.

(Study published in: Intelligence)

Older adults competing in a brain training program saw **25%** mental improvement vs 12% in a non-competitive group.

(Study published in: PLOS ONE)

The data is undeniable, competition boosts mental performance from 5 - 25%. In trading that can be the difference between success and failure.

This is why trading battles in trading simulators, are the most unique and novel approach to become a smarter trader, in a fun and exciting way. I recommend the following trading simulation platforms:

www.ninjatrader.com[1]

www.investopedia.com[2]

Now go out there, and climb the leaderboard. I believe in you!

---

1. http://www.ninjatrader.com
2. http://www.investopedia.com

Chapter 10: Beginner Strategies

Lesson 1: The 4 Hour Per Year Strategy

Can you believe you can set up future wealth in just half a workday per year? Sounds crazy, right? But it's possible!

Understanding the misconception

- **Active Investing:** This is where you're deep-diving into company analysis, economic trends, and data overload. This takes time and skills.

But, here's the kicker: You don't need to do this! Even the big hedge fund gurus, with their insider info and fancy analytics, find this challenging.

FINANCIAL TIMES

86% of active equity funds underperform

Large study raises more questions about the value stockpicking managers add

What's the alternative?

Smart, stress free investing

Indexes = Economic Thermometers

- They reflect the overall health of the economy. Index price is rising? Good times! Falling? Uh-oh...

Instead of picking stocks, why not go big and invest in the entire market? It's like betting on the entire sports league instead of one team.

Imagine a basket of the top companies (like the S&P 500 or DAX) that you can invest in. This removes the need for painstaking analysis and research. But there's a catch, you can't buy an index directly.

Enter ETFs - the easy investment

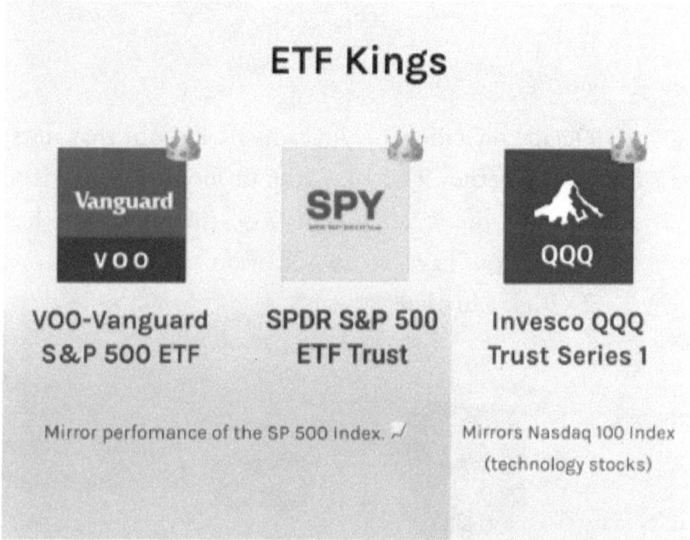

Think of an **exchange-traded fund (ETF)** like a shopping basket full of different stocks.

Basically its an easy way to invest in the whole stock market and let it grow without any babysitting, and there's a good reason why ETF prices are highly likely to grow over time. Read more about it at "**stock market indices**".

Step by step ETF strategy

1 - Set your budget

Decide on a monthly investment amount that suits your finances, whether it's $10, $100, or more. The key is to not sacrifice on life quality otherwise investing will become something you "have" to do not "want" to do.

2 - Pick a broker

Select a broker offering zero-commission investing, like **Etoro**. The choice of broker is crucial for your investment journey. More on brokers in the chapter "the wrong broker".

3 - DCA in an ETF

Dollar cost averaging (DCA) is fancy name for a basic but effective investing strategy.

It involves investing a fixed amount at regular intervals, regardless of market fluctuations. It's an effective way to mitigate market volatility. For example $50 at the same date each month. Also, if there are months you want to invest less it's ok, you're not tied to a contract, and the strategy is not suddenly "broken".

4 - Compound your gains

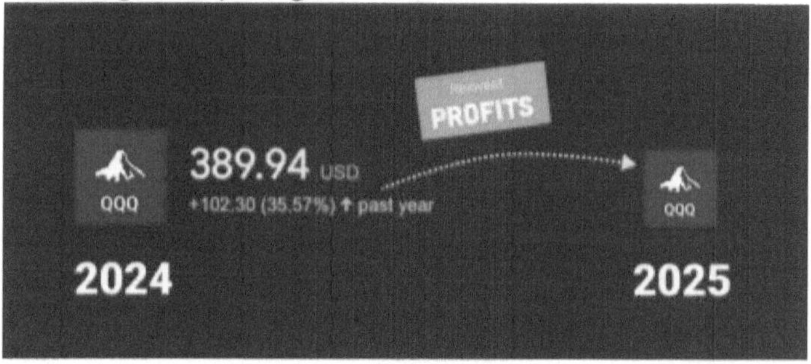

Reinvest your profits back into the ETF, typically annually. This approach amplifies your returns as you earn profits on your reinvested earnings.

Some brokers automate this process, but to be sure about your broker, you should message the broker to confirm if that is an option.

5 - The number 1 ingredient for success

Welcome to the Club: You're now part of the smart investor community, but remember **successful investing is a long-term game.**

Set a timeline for your investment and resist the urge to exit prematurely. The longer you stay invested, the more you can benefit from market growth. Remember, **time is your ally** on the road to financial security.

Lesson 2: Top Down Strategy

In this lesson, let's examine a real case study that demonstrates how the concepts you have learned so far can be applied to conduct proper trade analysis and execute successful trades.

Through a step-by-step example, I will illustrate how to combine various elements to confirm a move before entering a buy or sell position. Let's dive right into it with step one.

Step 1: Early research

To stay updated on the assets in our watchlist, we explored financial news to find important new stories or developments. Since the stock market was closed, our focus shifted to Forex and Crypto. It didn't take long for us to stumble upon a significant headline with potential implications for the crypto industry.

> **Coinbase Announces Very Bad News**
>
> The cryptocurrency exchange says it received a warning from the Securities and Exchange Commission (SEC), suggesting a possible enforcement action.

Explained: As the crypto industry is new and lacks regulation, news of Coinbase receiving a warning from the SEC (USA's top regulator) can create uncertainty for the industry.

In summary, if there is negative news and regulatory scrutiny surrounding a major American crypto exchange, it could result in selling pressure and cause Bitcoin's price to decrease. Thus, we decided to focus on finding opportunities within BTC.

Step 2 - Pick a time frame and identify the current trend

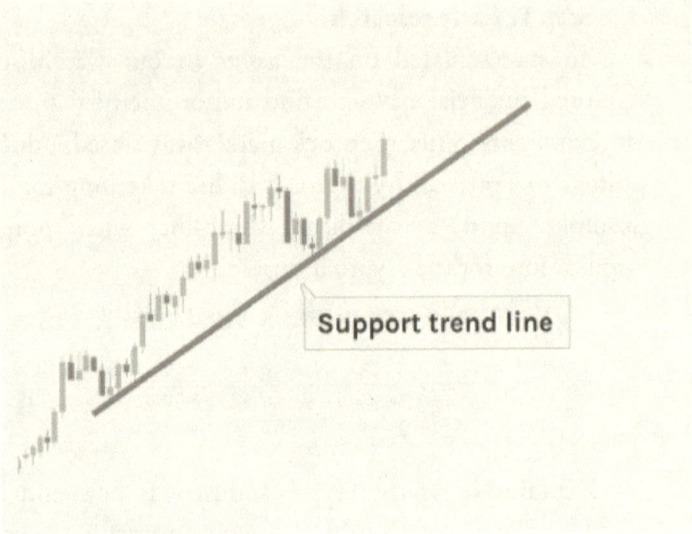

We started with a simple trend line and noticed that the price is trending higher at a very steep angle.

It could be a sign of excessive optimism among traders who are disregarding negative news. Let's keep monitoring the chart.

Step 3 - Identify S/R

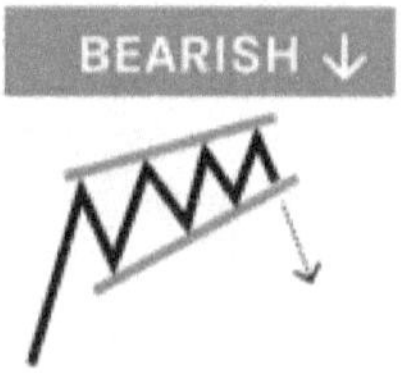

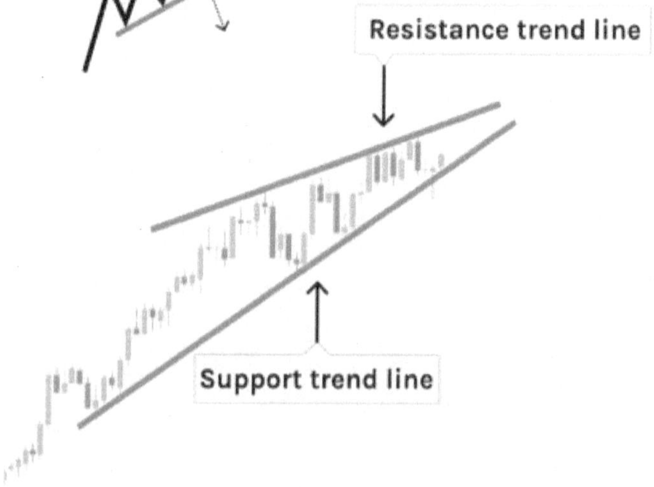

We let the price run for a few more hours, and noticed that the volatility of price swings is narrowing.

These trend lines clearly acted as support and resistance levels, as part of a broader rising wedge pattern.

Step 4 - Double check with indicators

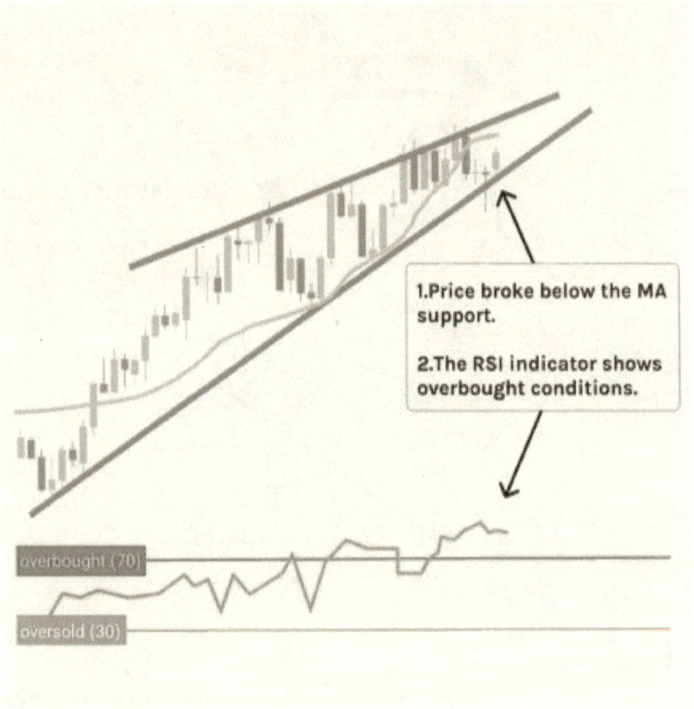

We noticed further bearish signals. At this point we've observed:

- **bearish news,**
- **bullish uptrend,**
- **bearish reversal pattern.**

A perfect combination to enter the trade, but we were not done yet... We looked upon indicators to help our analysis further.

Step 5: Look for a breakout, and confirm with volume

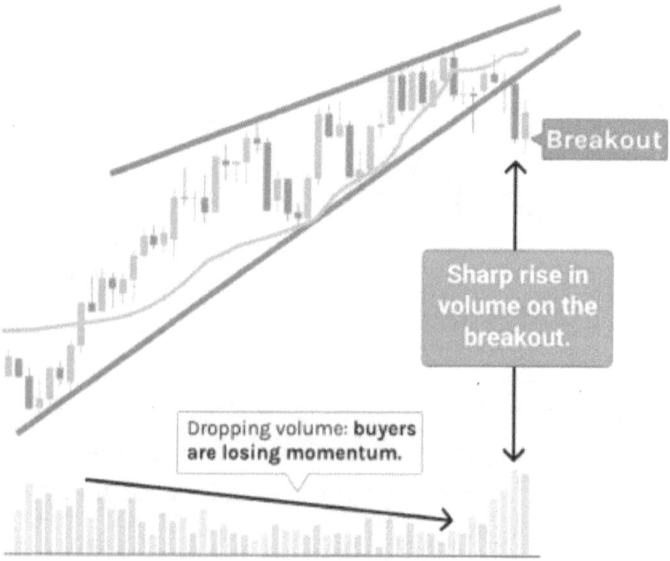

We've built a strong case so far. The volume indicator acts as the final check point to see if the market is ready to trade this move as well.

And it is! We're ready to enter the trade.

Step 6: Entry with 3:1 risk/reward ratio

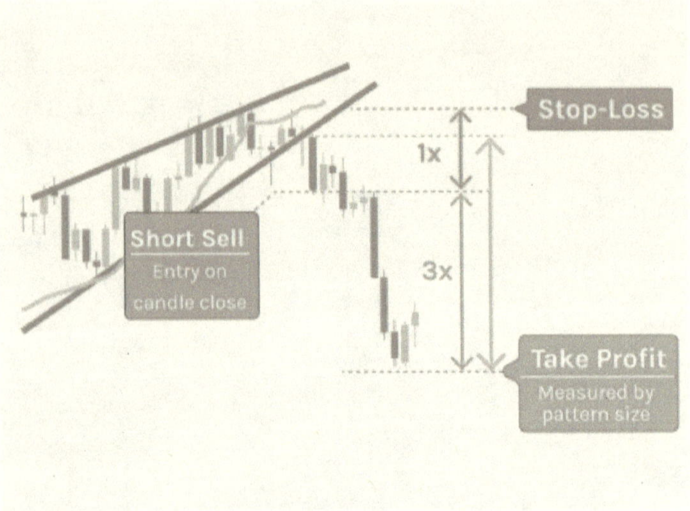

What you just saw, is called the **top down approach.** We began by identifying the trend and looked for a weakness due to bearish news.

Then we systematically added other signals to assess market interest in a downward movement. Our case for a bearish breakout was constructed step-by-step, with a calm and rational approach.

Entering the trade became the simplest part.

If you want to succeed in trading, this methodology can be a good start for you.

Lesson 3: Copy Trading Strategy

Copy trading is super straightforward, especially when following a few key guidelines. But you should never copy a professional trader blindly!

This concise guide will equip you with a safe strategy for identifying proficient traders to copy.

1 - Social Trust

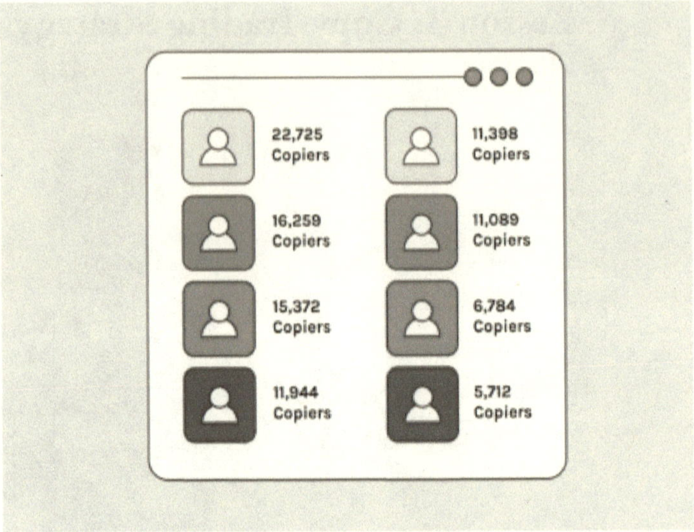

A critical factor in assessing a trader's proficiency is the level of trust they have garnered from other investors. It's not just about the number of copiers; the total amount of money invested in a trader can be a more telling indicator.

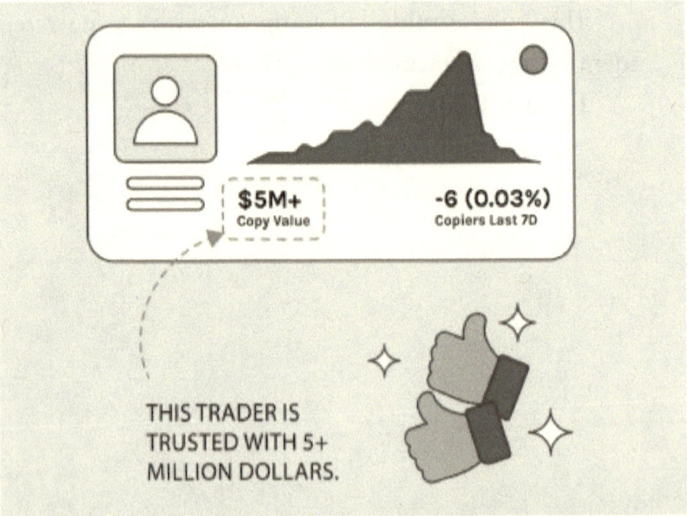

- **Positive Indicator:** A trader trusted with a significant sum (e.g., over $5 million).

- **Red Flag:** A trader with a minimal number of followers or copiers.

2 - Realistic, consistent returns

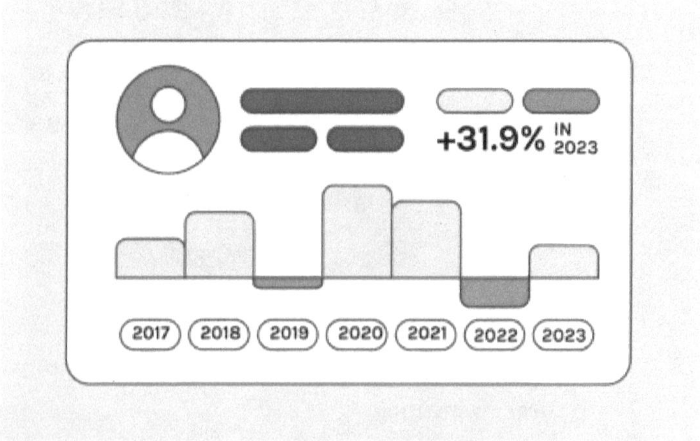

The nature of a trader's returns is revealing. While negative returns are obviously a bad sign, extremely high returns can also be deceptive, often indicating high risk or mere luck, which doesn't equate to stable long term perfomance.

• **Goal:** Target traders with smaller, consistent returns over time.

3 - Low risk score

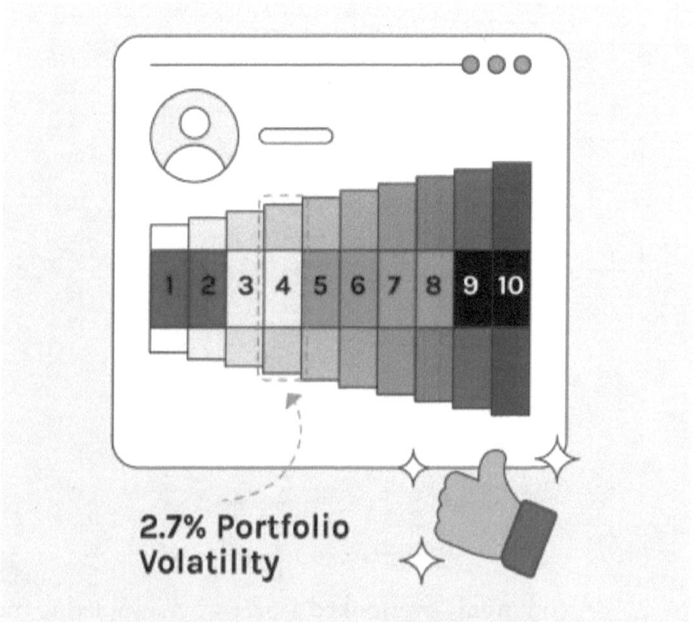

Understanding the risk-return trade-off is key. A lower risk score usually indicates a more consistent and potentially sustainable trading approach.

- **Target Range:** A risk score between 0-5, especially one that remains stable over time, is preferable.

4 - Examine open trades

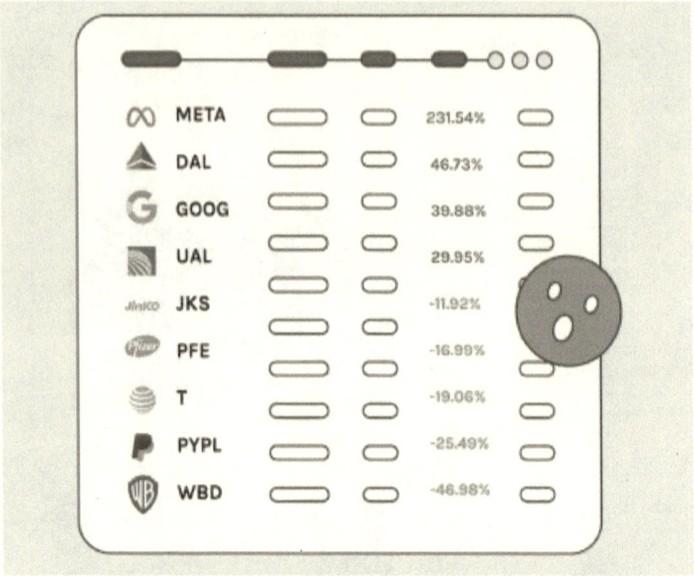

A commonly overlooked aspect when evaluating traders is the state of their open trades.

Skilled professionals understand the importance of cutting losses and using stop levels to minimize them before they escalate.

However, some traders may **leave losing trades open for extended periods to avoid negatively impacting their performance statistics.**

It's essential to scrutinize their open positions. A pattern of numerous running losses, indicated by several "red" trades from weeks or months past, can be a concerning sign of poor trading strategy or risk management.

5 - Copying with safeguards

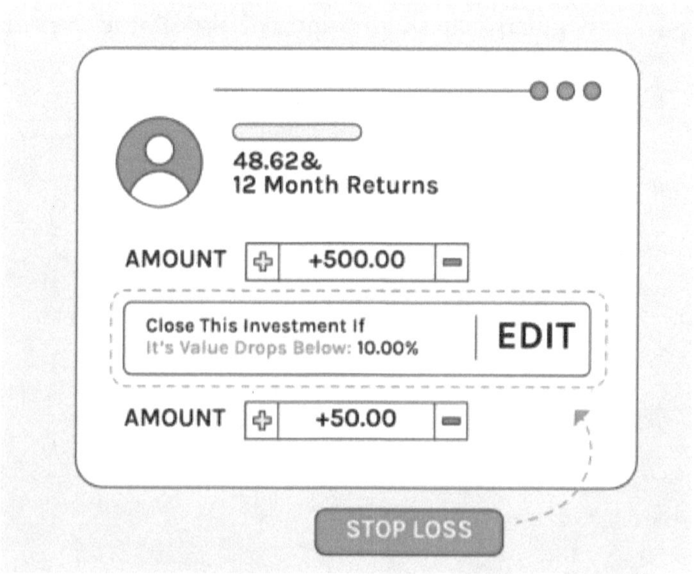

Not everyone feels safe to trust their money to a stranger. Before fully committing, you can consider a cautious approach to copy trading.

Trial Period: Use a demo account at Etoro to copy a trader's performance for a few weeks. This allows you to assess their strategy with zero financial risk.

Copy Stop-Loss: Implementing a stop-loss on your copy trades can significantly reduce potential losses. This tool automatically ceases copying if your investment falls below a set threshold.

Bottom Line

Copy trading can save you enormous amounts of time spent learning the markets.

While losses are always possible in the markets, copying a pro trader with a few simple guidelines in mind, can be a relatively safe way to be participate in trading.

Regularly check the updated list of top performers, available in the main menu under "Top Brokers"" to see the safest picks.

Chapter 11: Pro Strategies

Lesson 1: Order Block Strategy

In trading, orders are how we buy, sell, and make a profit.

But what if you could spot where the big players are placing their orders? And then trade along with them?

That's where **order blocks(OB)** come in.

OB's are specific chart levels where banks and institutions - the guys who move the market - place large buy or sell orders.

And these areas where they build positions - that's where we want to be.

Why this matters?

To understand the opportunity here, you must know why order blocks form.

Institutions have deep research and data, so they know the best prices to buy and sell at.

But even with the best data, and unlimited money, **a strategy is required.**

Quick example below:

Unlike us, the traders at Citibank, can't just fire up a trading platform and hit sell. There's two simple reasons why:

- There's not enough liquidity to fill such a large order at Citibank's desired price.

- An order of this size will tip off other institutions and retail traders.

So instead they do this:

As Citibank's large order sells at $1.0850, buyers at that level get 'used up.' To keep selling, Citibank lowers the price, creating a **zone of intense selling pressure.** That's an order block in essence.

How You Make Money:

These OB's act as support or resistance, creating bounce or reversal opportunities.

- A buy order block can act as support. When price revisits, you can buy, expecting a bounce.
- A sell order block can act as resistance. When price returns, you can sell or short, anticipating a reversal.

As these institutions drive most of the price movements, this strategy aligns you with "big money", so you can trade "with them", not against them, with higher accuracy.

We'll do this in three steps:

1. Finding the order block
1. Narrowing down for accuracy
1. Taking the trade and managing risk.

Lesson 2: Step 1 - Finding Order Blocks

Before you trade an order block, always identify the market's overall direction, beforehand. Without this clarity, you'll have no basis for gauging the next potential momentum:

Upward (bullish) or downward (bearish), or the setup to look for: long or short.

Observe Momentum And Direction

Step A: Zoom out to the 4H chart

This higher time frame eliminates noise from smaller moves, revealing the broader trend.

Step B: Identify the Trend

Use recent price history to assess the market's trajectory:

- **Bullish Trend:** The market forms higher highs and higher lows consistently.

- **Bearish Trend:** The market forms lower lows and lower highs steadily.

If you're unsure - refresh the details in lesson "surfing market trends".

Finding the Order Block

With the trend identified, you can, in theory, better predict whether the momentum will likely continue upward or downward.

Step C: Spotting consolidation (a pause in momentum)

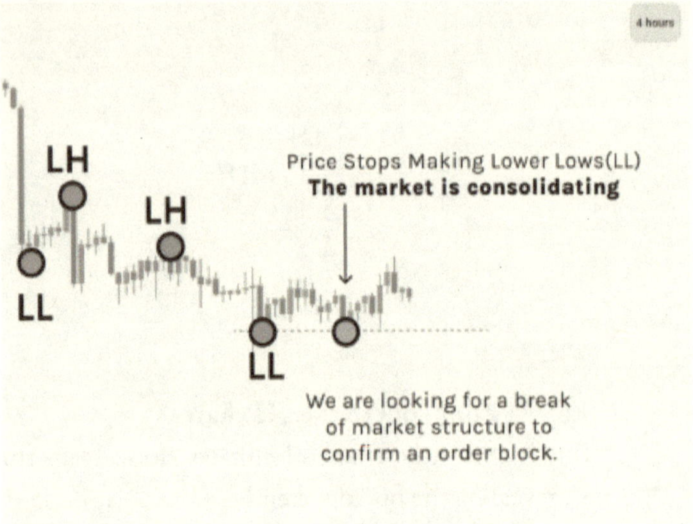

Example:

In a bearish trend (as shown in the chart):

- Price stops making lower lows (LL).

- The market consolidates sideways.

- We await a break of structure to confirm the order block.

Remember, market structure can be:

- **Trendlines:** Connecting highs and lows.

• **Support & Resistance:** Horizontal levels where price reacts.

• **Patterns:** Triangles, wedges, channels.

• **Swing Highs/Lows:** Key turning points in price action.

Step D: Break of structure

In order block trading, a strong breakout is signaled by a break of structure, often by a sharp, sudden, move in price.

Typical Pattern:

• A single large candle breaks through the structure (as shown above).

• Alternatively, multiple smaller candles moving in the same direction can confirm the breakout.

This break is a clear sign of momentum continuing, aligning with the established trend.

Step E - Marking the order block

The next step is to identify the last opposite candle before the break of structure.

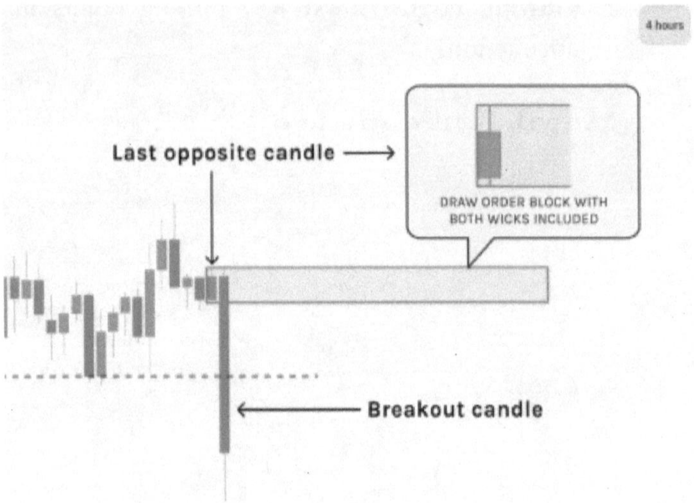

- In a bearish example, this would be the last bullish candle before the breakout.

- In a bullish example, you would look for the last bearish candle.

This opposing candle becomes the foundation for marking your order block, as it represents the final pause or counter-move before momentum shifts decisively.

Next up, we'll improve the accuracy to get ready for trading this setup.

Lesson 3: Step 2 - Improving Precision

Identifying the 4H order block is a great start, but it's still too broad for precision entries.

This lesson focuses on refining your OB by zooming into the 1-hour chart, allowing you to:

- Tighten your stop losses.
- Improve your risk-to-reward ratio.

We begin by marking a second order block.

Marking the 1H Order Block

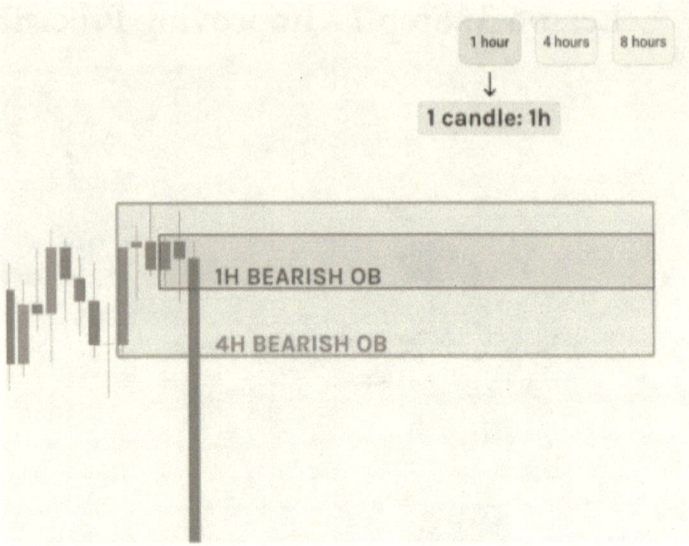

Step A: Switch to the 1H chart

Focus on the 4-hour OB zone identified earlier. This step lets you spot smaller, high-precision zones.

Step B: Mark the second order block

Look for the last counter candle (e.g., a bullish candle in a bearish trend) before the breakout. This marks where momentum shifted, helping you define a smaller OB within the larger zone.

Remember, this is the same exact price movement, just from a more detailed perspective.

Bullish example

As this strategy creates setups in both directions, here's a bullish example to help you understand the entire process:

A: Trend + Structure

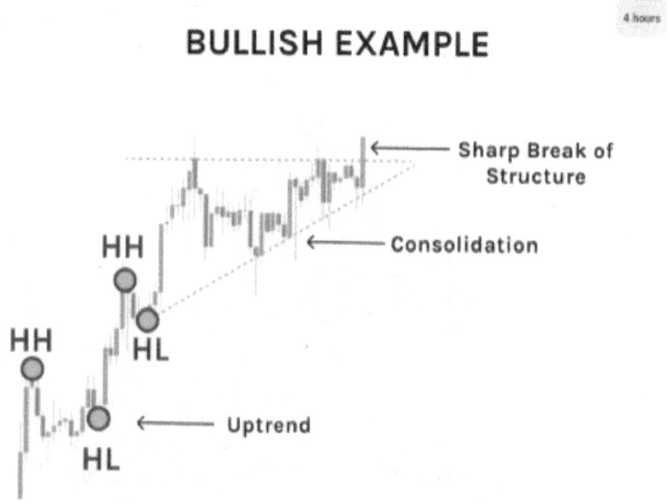

In an uptrend scenario:

- Price stops making lower lows (HH).
- The market consolidates in an ascending triangle pattern.
- There is a sharp break of structure.

B: Mark both order blocks

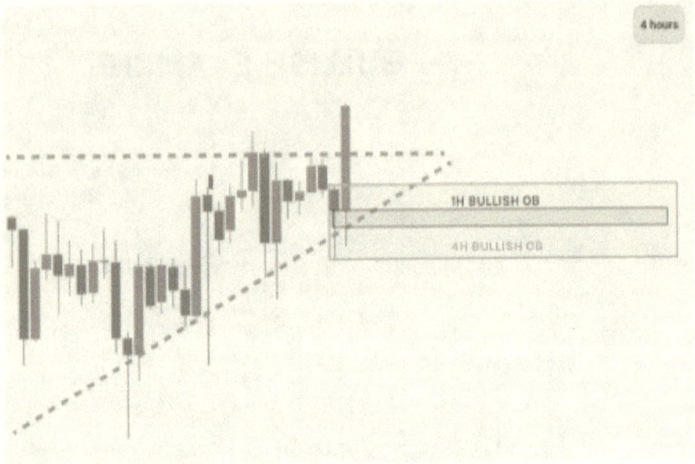

The same principles you learned before apply:

Mark the last bearish candle on both the 4h and the 1h time frame.

Once your two order blocks are drawn, we can proceed with trading this setup.

Lesson 4: Step 3 - Entry And Exit

Once all the previous steps have been completed, it's time to execute the trade. But there's one last thing to clarify:

Two ways to trade OB's

For optimal precision, this strategy works best with limit orders:

- **Limit Order:** Automatically execute at your set price.

- **Manual Entry:** Require monitoring charts for the best entry point.

For safety and education purposes, some simulators may not support limit orders. Trades must be placed manually as this improves your timing skills as a trader.

If you'd like to practice with limit orders, I advise you choose a trusted broker to explore this feature in a demo account. Once confident, you can transition to live trading with real money.

When to execute the trade:

Many retail traders assume price will fully pull back into the order block - this is known as the "retail trap".

Instead, institutions often cause a bounce off this level, catching retail traders on the wrong side of the trade. By anticipating this and entering strategically, you align with the "smart money" and gain a significant edge in the market.

Step A: Placing a limit order(or manual)

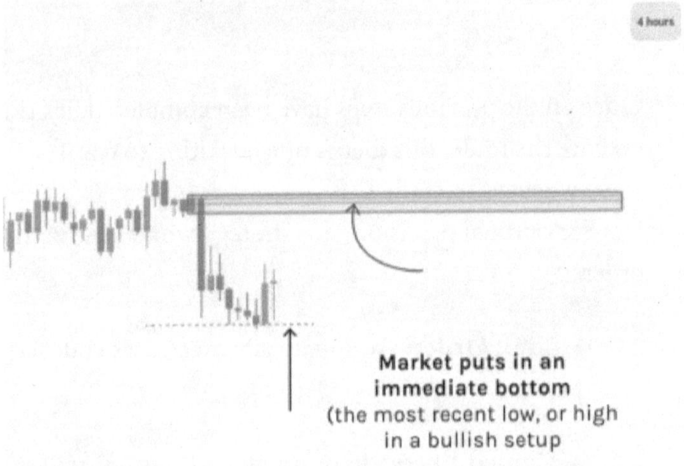

Once previous parameters are confirmed, place your limit order as soon as a new immediate bottom (or top) forms on the 4-hour chart. Place your order at:

- top of a bullish OB

- bottom of bearish OB

Step B: Precise Entry/Exit

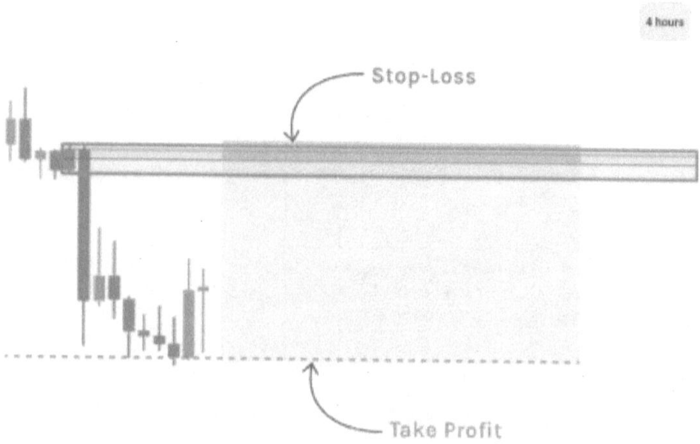

Proper stop-loss(SL) placement ensures risk is limited to a safe zone just beyond typical institutional reversals:

- **Bearish Trades:** Set your SL 5-10 pips above the 1-hour order block's top.

- **Bullish Trades:** Set your SL 5-10 pips below the 1-hour order block's bottom.

Take Profit Targets:

Aim for the most recent immediate low or high (structure depending on the setup) where retail traders are likely to be targeted by institutions.

Trade Complete!

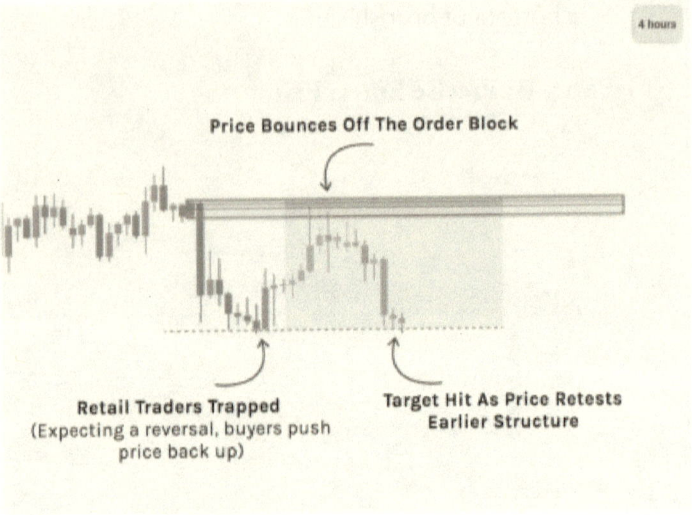

If you've followed all the steps correctly, your trade is positioned for success.

Mastering this strategy can give you a powerful edge in markets dominated by institutional activity:

- **Forex:** High liquidity and heavy participation from central banks, hedge funds, and corporations make it ideal.

- **Crypto:** Though volatile, institutional players like whales and funds leave clear footprints in BTC and ETH.

- **Stocks:** Large-cap stocks show consistent institutional patterns due to accumulation and distribution by major players.

- **Commodities:** Assets like gold and oil reveal institutional moves tied to global economic trends and large-scale positioning.

Whether you practice in our simulator or a demo account, stay disciplined and manage risk. Good luck and let's continue your learning journey.

Chapter 12: Guide To Trading Platforms

Lesson 1: Dirty Truth About Brokers

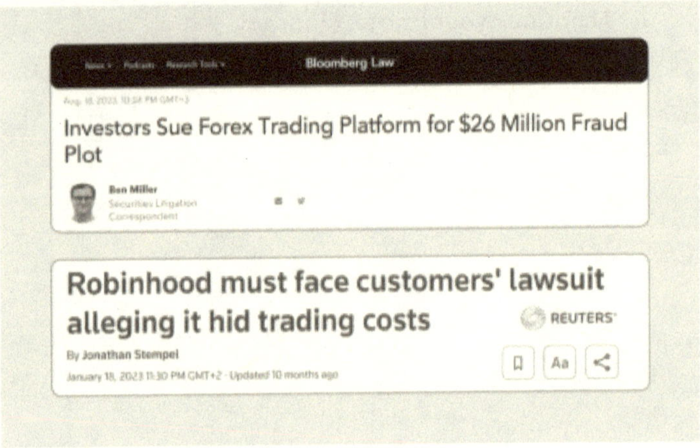

For new traders, finding a suitable trading platform that ticks all the boxes: safe, trustworthy and easy to use, is almost impossible.

Many well-known platforms are regularily marred by legal issues for unlawful practices and price manipulation.

As trading is complex enough, the last thing you need is to worry about the safety of your money and decisions.

Navigating this landscape

Finding the right trading platform is likely meeting the perfect partner. Often you have a few bad experiences before meeting the right one. But in the finance world, these experiences can be financially damaging and our goal is to protect you from it.

Over the last decade, based on consumer reviews of over 2,000 global brokers. Here's what I learned.

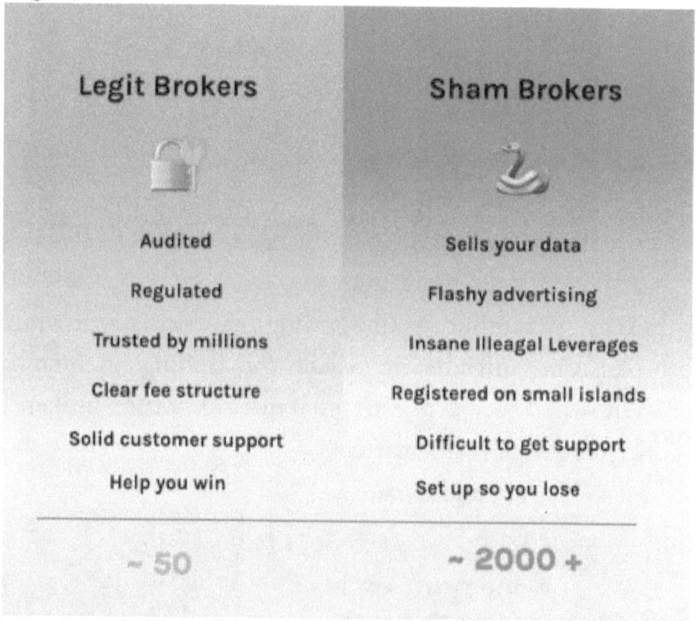

The reality is that you can trade without experience, a strategy and even without much money, but it's impossible to trade without a broker. In the next lessons, I'll guide you on what to look for to help you trade confidently and securely.

Lesson 2: 5 Key Points To Look For

A broker does more than just connect buyers and sellers. They streamline your trading experience, providing a platform and diverse assets for trading. Remember, a renowned name doesn't guarantee a secure broker. Let's explore what really matters.

1. Safety and trust

Would you choose the cheapest car seat for your kids or the cheapest door lock for your house? Likely not. Similarly, you should not go for the first trading platform you see, even if the fees are low.

Safety and trust are paramount, but don't get swayed by online reviews praising one platform over another, these are often paid promotions. In addition, a disgruntled trader might unjustly blame their broker, instead of taking accountability for their mistakes.

You should steer clear from such biases when searching for recommendations, and look at facts only.

2. Financial stability

You have to think long-term. While you may start trading and investing with a small sum, in 20 years it might turn in to half a million.

Ask yourself: would I trust this broker with a million bucks? If the answer's yes, that's a good sign. A broker that has weathered market crashes and maintained stability during them is another positive indicator.

3. Fees

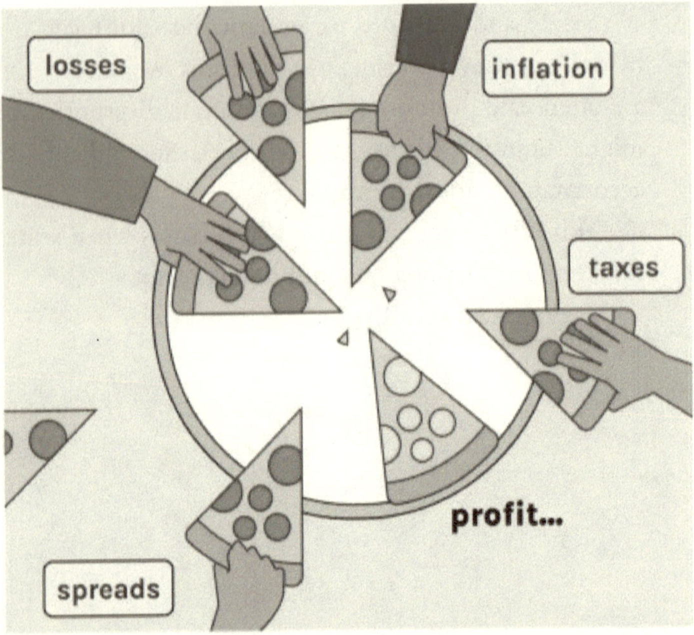

If you're aiming to trade full-time, fees can eat into your profits. Whether it's trading fees such as the spread, withdrawal charges, or currency conversion, every penny counts. Why? Every dollar spent on fees is money that you can't spend on your dream retirement on a yacht. So your focus should be to find ways to spend less.

4. Asset selection

What assets you plan on trading is equally important. Look for a broker that offers the 'full package'. Stocks, Forex, ETFs, crypto - you name it.

Additionally, consider extra features such as copy trading, which is only available with a few top-tier brokers. The right brokerage for you should align with your strategy and needs.

5. Taxes

Stay on the right side of the law when it comes to taxes. Ensure your broker provides clear reporting structures for tax purposes.

There is no point in paying back all your gains in fines, or possibly face criminal charges for tax evasion. We'll delve deeper into this in a lesson dedicated to trading taxes.

Lesson 3: Where To Start?

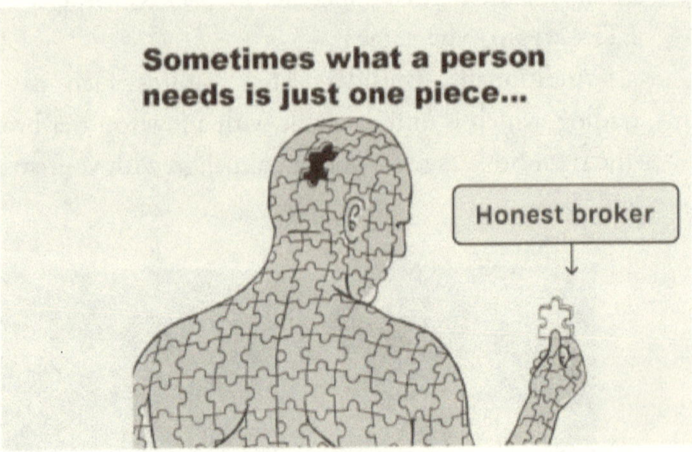

Picking a trading platform is your decision, but it is my responsibility to share my experience and help you make your decision wisely. The brokers listed are two of the most used among newbie traders, chosen based on specific criteria.

Best overall for beginners: eToro

- **Top-tier regulation globally:** including FCA in the UK, SEC in the US, and ASIC in Australia.

- **Founded in 2007.**

- no major regulatory incidents or fines.

- **The original pioneer of copy trading.**

Besides these key factors, eToro is an excellent choice due to low trading fees, high asset variety (3000+), and arguably the easiest to use trading platform on both desktop and mobile devices.

In fact, eToro can be likened to a social network, with the added functionality of trading and investing. It's one of the main reasons, along with the safety, that makes beginners start and stay with eToro for a long time.

Limitation: Limited options for U.S. citizens (only crypto trading) for now.

Best for US citizens: Oanda

- **Top-tier regulation globally:** FCA in the UK, CIRO in Canada, and ASIC in Australia.

- **Founded in 1996.**

- **Main focus:** Forex Trading.

Oanda is perhaps the best choice for US citizens looking to trade a wide variety of assets in a relatively easy to use and simple trading platform. While the broker places stronger emphasis on currency trading, there are thousands of other assets available as well. A great mix between safety and easy of use for US citizens.

When should you open a broker account?

This choice is entirely up to you - open an account when you feel confident to try real trading. For some, this moment arrives after 20 simulated trades; for others, it takes months to feel confidence.

There is one pro-tip which might come in handy at the right moment.

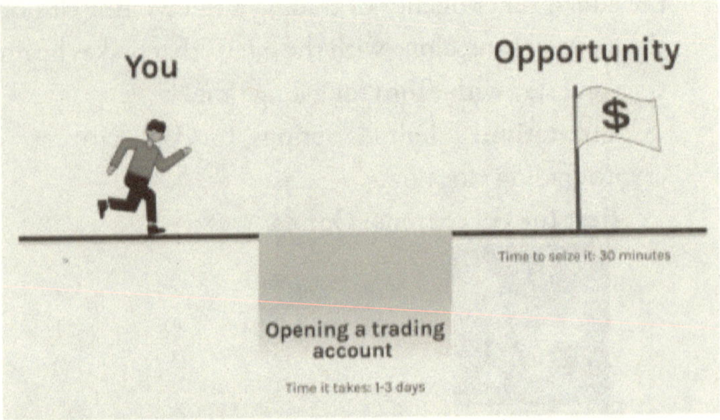

Ancient Roman philosopher Seneca once said:

"Luck is when preparation meets opportunity"

Lottery winners, on average, buy tickets for 8 years before hitting the jackpot. Foolish, and unproductive, but still. You can't deny the preparation.

Opening a broker account today and practicing with a free demo account is an effective strategy to be prepared when the lucky trading opportunity comes. Consider it like putting fuel in your car beforehand, so that whenever you need to drive, it's ready.

Exam: Guide To Trading Platforms

1. Which are more common?

- Safe, regulated and trustworthy brokers

- Questionable, shady, unverified brokers

- Awesome, but complicated brokers

1. What is the benefit of opening a broker account early-on?

- To check if a broker is safe

- To pass the time while you're learning

- To make sure you are prepared to trade when you're ready

1. What is the key role of brokers?

- To predict market trends.

- To offer a platform and a range of assets to trade safely

- To provide legal advice on trading

Answer:

1. Questionable, shady, unverified brokers

1. To make sure you are prepared to trade when you're ready

1. To offer a platform and a range of assets to trade safely

Chapter 13: Stocks 101

Lesson 1: The Stock Market Explained

Most companies start out small, with a couple of enthusiasts and a dream.

The early investors are usually the founders, family members and bank loans. When a business gets bigger and more successful, it needs more money to continue growing, that's when a company can go public.

From Private To Public

1. Companies want to raise more money.

1. They decide to sell parts of themselves (Shares)

through an IPO (Initial Public Offering).

1. These shares are sold on the stock market.

1. Members of the public (investors) buy these shares.

1. The company receives the money it needs to grow.

And that's how a private company becomes a public one, trading on the stock market.

It's also a big step up in responsiblity as it is now the shareholders that dictate how much the company is worth.

If the company consistently makes money and becomes popular for the right reasons, its share price will invariably rise. Investors will make huge profits and demand for the stock will be high, the opposite is true for false promises and questionable business practices.

Stocks are the best way to support your favorite companies and make $$$ at the same time.

- Love the iPhone? Become a part owner of Apple which returned over 350% in the past 5 years, let them earn you a new one.

- Drink Starbucks? Skip a few lattes and grab a share that will pay for your coffee later on.

- Dreaming of driving a Tesla? Start working for it by investing in a fractional share today.

What is a fractional share?

The best modern brokers can help you build the portfolio you want but couldn't previously afford.

For example, if a stock trades for $3,000 per share — which isn't unheard of — you'd need at least $3,000 just to add it to your portfolio.

Want to buy more than one share? You'll have to purchase in increments of $3,000 ($6,000 for two shares, $9,000 for three shares and so on). If you don't have that much set aside, you'll need to find another investment.

But this isn't the case with fractional shares. Fractional trading lets you buy the amount of stock you can afford, whether that's $5, $50, $500 or $5,000.

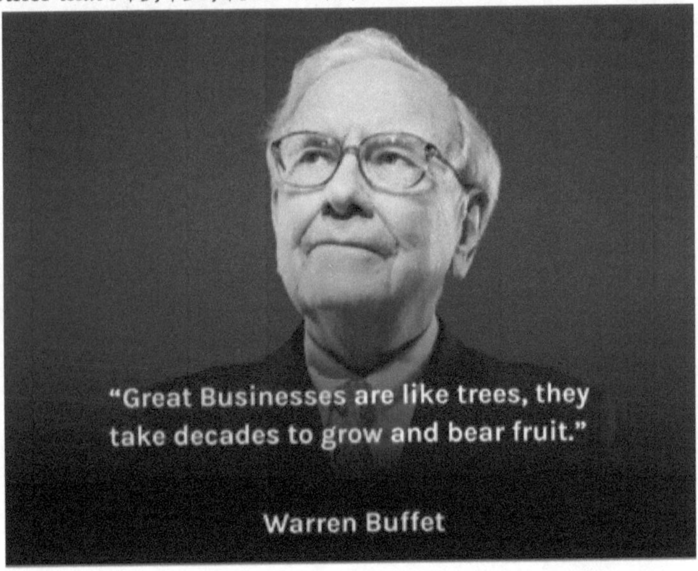

Warren Buffet says "**investing is the process of laying out money now to receive more money in the future.**"

When you buy a stock with a long-term investing mindset, you're planting a seed with the hopes that you will get to pick some fruit as it grows.

Just like trees, companies are different in how they operate, how they grow, and how they benefit the investor and that's what you'll learn in the next lesson.

Lesson 2: Diversification

The more diversified your stock portfolio the better!

A growth stock will bring you tremendous returns during a bull market, but a defensive stock will give you a stream of income even when markets are down and everybody is fearful.

Instead of trying to memorize and categorize each company, think of them in terms of how they follow the economic trend of expansion and contraction - periods of good and bad times.

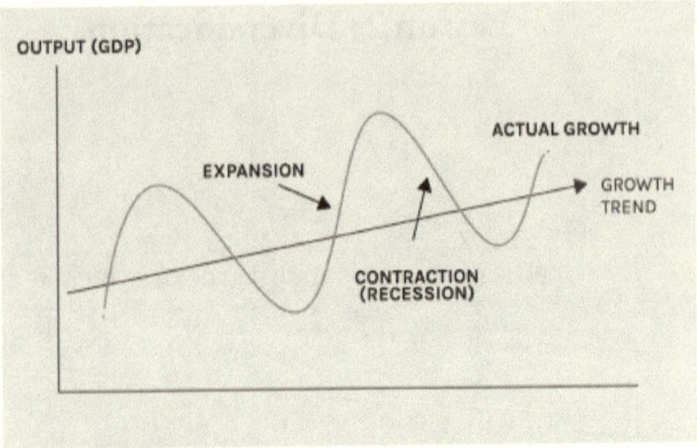

Cyclical stocks are found in manufacturing, travel, and luxury goods; a period of bad times can take away customers' ability to make major unnecessary purchases quickly. Thus these stocks may suffer. In a strong economy, however, these stocks can rebound sharply!

On the other hand, **defensive stocks** do not experience big swings in demand. No matter how bad the economy is, people still need to eat, people still need to drink water and have electricity.

These usually have a steady performance through bad times, while cyclical stocks can outperform these stocks during strong economic rebounds.

Good diversification between different types of stocks and stock market sectors is the best way to maximize your returns and minimize losses in all market situations.

Stock Market Sectors

More Sectors - Less Risk

If you're buying shares in 5 different companies, it's best to pick them from different stock market sectors.

This way an unexpected event in one sector will not affect your other investments.

Communication Services - telephone, internet, media, and entertainment companies.

Consumer Discretionary - retailers, automakers, and hotel and restaurant companies.

Consumer Staples - food, beverage, tobacco, household and personal products companies.

Energy - oil and gas exploration and production companies, pipeline providers, and gas station operators.

Financial - banks, mortgage finance specialists, and insurance and brokerage companies.

Healthcare - health insurers, drug and biotech companies, and medical device makers.

Industrial - airline, aerospace and defense, construction, logistics, machinery, and railroad companies.

Materials - mining, forest products, construction materials, packaging, and chemical companies.

Real Estate - real estate investment trusts and real estate management and development companies.

Technology - hardware, software, semiconductor, communications equipment, and IT services companies.

Utilities - electric, natural gas, water, renewable energy, and multi-product utility companies.

The total worth of all the shares of a company is called **market capitalization.**

Category	Market Capitalisation Range
Mega-cap	More Than $200 Billion
Large Cap	$10 Billion - 200 Billion
Mid-cap	$2 Billion - $10 Billion
Small-cap	$300 Million - $2 Billion
Micro-cap	$50 Million - $300 Million
Nano-cap	Less Than $50 Million

It can help you differentiate between up-and-coming businesses, which might generate great returns down the line, and huge well-established players, which could be a safer investment right now.

Lesson 3: Most Profitable Time To Trade Stocks

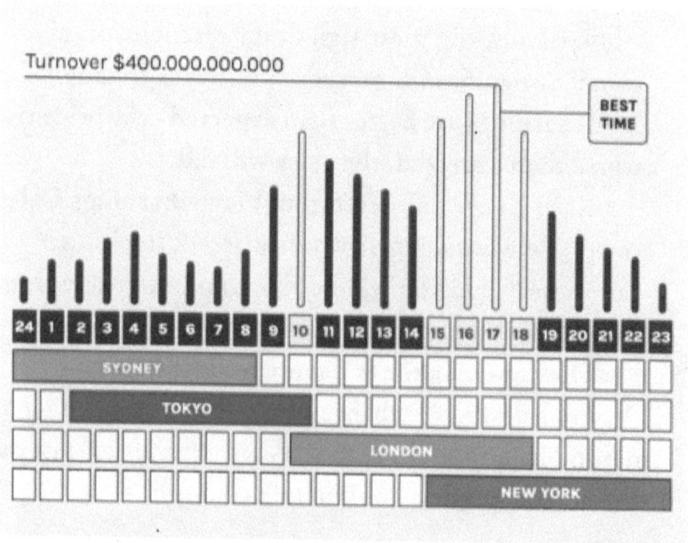

Without a doubt the biggest trigger that impacts the supply and demand of a stock is the **earnings season.**

For stock traders, the earnings season is like Christmas, except it's 4 times per year.

It usually begins one or two weeks at the end of each quarter.

- **Jan, Feb, Mar = Q1**
- **Apr, May, Jun = Q2**
- **Jul, Aug, Sep = Q3**
- **Oct, Nov, Dec = Q4**

The release is a big deal because investors don't know how well companies are doing in real-time, so they rely on these reports.

Typically, the most significant reactions occur when a company significantly exceeds or misses expectations.

If earnings are better than expected - the price rises, if worse than expected, the price will fall.

Keep an eye on the **TradingView's Earnings Calendar** (https://www.tradingview.com/markets/stocks-usa/earnings/ [1]) and you will be able to profit greatly from the initial reaction to positive or negative news.

How opening times dictate traders' behavior

Global stock exchanges have different opening times depending on your time zone. Generally they operate during the normal business hours in that country.

1. https://www.tradingview.com/markets/stocks-usa/earnings/

SYDNEY

The Australian stock exchange (ASX) operates normal trading hours between 10am-4pm Australian eastern standard time.

TOKYO

The Tokyo Stock Exchange - 9 a.m. to 11:30 a.m. and 12:30 p.m. to 3 p.m. Japan Standard Time (JST)

LONDON

London Stock Exchange 3 am to 11:30 am (EST)

NEW YORK

New York Stock Exchange (NYSE) and Nasdaq 9:30 am to 4 pm (EST)

A trading day is called a session and it can be split in to three parts:

The opening hour

This is when the market factors in all of the events and news releases since the previous closing bell, which can cause big moves in a short period of time.

Seasoned day traders consider the first 15 minutes after the open bell to be the most important as they offer some of the biggest trades of the day.

When starting out, **it's best to avoid trading the first hour,** as those without experience often get burned first.

Middle of the day

The markets have calmed and traders are eagerly awaiting further news to determine where the market may be heading for the remainder of the day.

Because prices are relatively stable during this period, it's a good time for a beginner to place trades, as the action is slower, and the returns might be more predictable.

The closing hour

When the market nears closing, volatility and volume starts to ramp up again. Experience shows that sharp reversals and pullbacks often happen in the last hour as day traders close out their positions or join a trend with the hope of continued momentum into the next trading day.

With time and practice, predicting these behaviors will become natural.

Lesson 4: Stock Market Indices

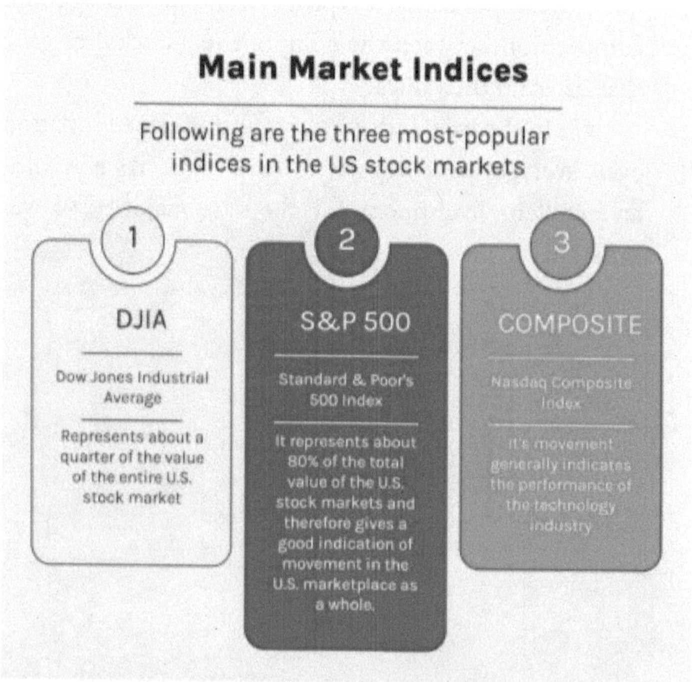

The majority of highly developed, as well as developing economies have at least one financial index.

An index is essentially a basket of the largest, most successful, and best-performing companies in a certain country or sector.

Investing in index based ETFs is a relatively secure strategy to retire wealthy. Heres why:

#1: The risks of investing in indices are always lower than the risks of investing in individual stocks or other asset classes.

Even though there have been losses in the past, in the long run, indexes almost always rise in value. This is because their components are constantly upgraded and rebalanced, but more importantly, it is progress and increasing economic competition between the components (stocks) of an index that drive up the value.

#2: In the past, indexes have outperformed inflation and even average bank deposit interest rates. As a result, it is an excellent investment for the vast majority of wealthy individuals.

#3: Unlike an individual company, an index can't go bankrupt. If a Dow Jones constituent starts performing badly or shows signs of dragging the index, it is replaced by the 31st company in the list of leading American companies. With the ever-increasing competition of modern business, there is always a competitor waiting to prove itself.

#4: Most importantly, you are putting your eggs into different baskets, which decreases the overall risk. With the

NASDAQ 100 index, you diversify into the most-prominent American high-tech companies.

#5: Choosing the DAX, you invest your money into 40 major German companies. This way, you can easily diversify your money into different markets, industries and geographies. You can benefit from both the positive and negative dynamics of the global economy. Even if one company fails, the index can still rise and shatter new records.

Lesson 5: Stock Investing Success Secret

At first glance, investing seems simple: **buy low, sell high.** Yet, beyond the surface it offers a universal opportunity for regular people anywhere in the world to build wealth. But there's a key element at play...

The power of time

Time - the one common element between the richest of the rich and the poorest of the poor. With every tick of the clock, we lose more time, and when it comes to investing, these seconds add up.

Consider Warren Buffett, known as the world's greatest investor. He earned his fortune and fame through disciplined investing principles.

But, let's not skip over the fact that he has had the benefit of time on his side.

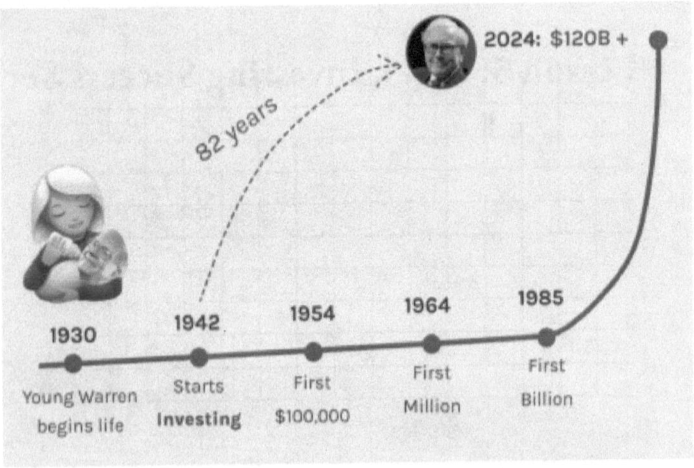

Let's draw a parallel to your work life. Your employer buys, in other words invests, in your time, hoping it yields profitable returns for the company. **But there's a catch.**

You exchange finite hours for finite pay, potentially shackled to this cycle for years until retirement. Then you're replaced.

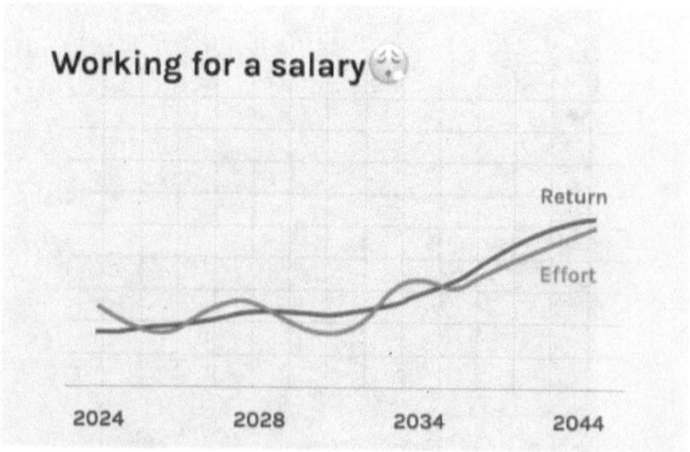

Unfortunately young people don't think so far ahead, but without meaningful savings, the quality of your life after you retire may not be of so much quality. **Remember time will pass either way,** whether you work and save, or do nothing at all.

Ray Dalio, another famous and respected billionaire investor has a famous saying.

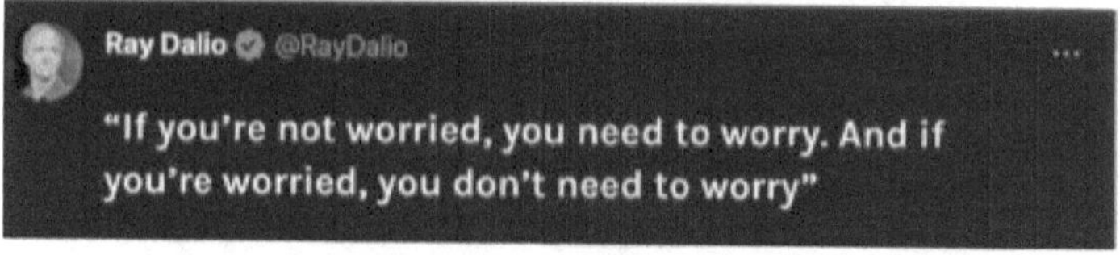

In a nutshell, it means that a healthy worry about your future will motivate you to take the necessary precautions, so you don't have to worry.

It is not worrying at all that leaves you exposed. I really don't want to worry you, but there's another factor to consider.

The thief you don't see

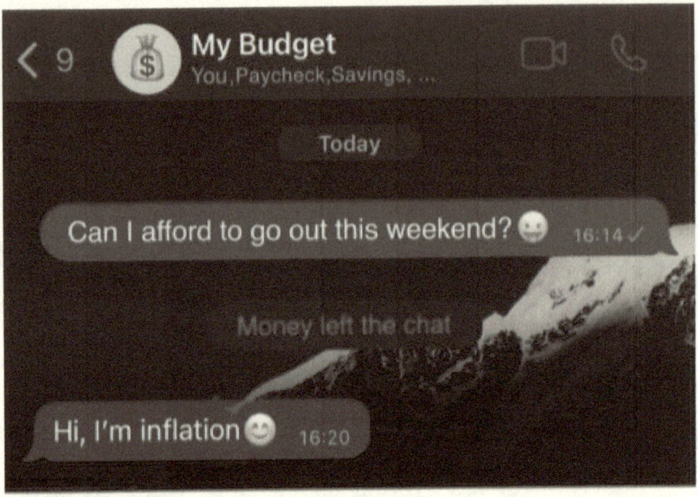

Inflation further complicates matters. Let's asumme your salary increases by 5% each year. Factor in a global inflation rate of 5%, and you are actually getting no salary increase at all. Any money you save? It's affected just the same way.

Beating the vicious cycle

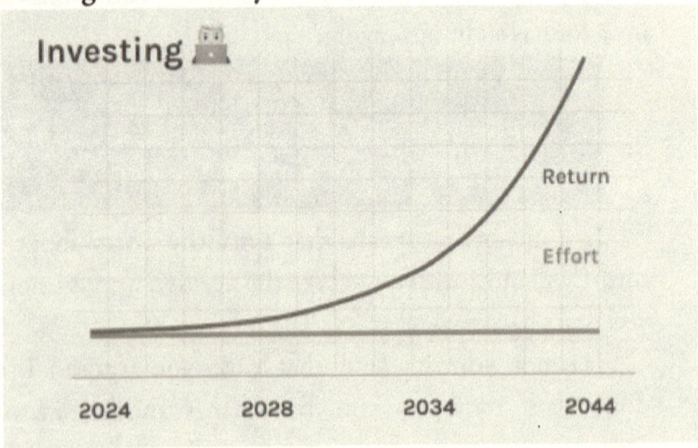

Investing wisely allows you to leverage time, which passes either way, to your advantage.

The sooner you start, the more you benefit from compound interest, which increases your wealth exponentially over time.

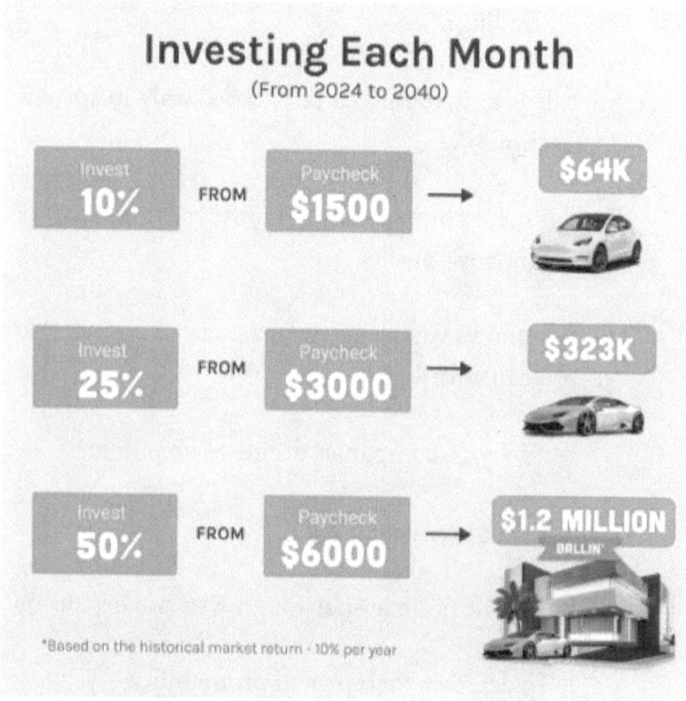

Unlike a regular job, where effort and returns are static, a simple investment strategy requires only a few hours per year but can turn small regular investments into life-changing sums over time.

With that let's explore a no nonsense investing strategy you can start today. Time invested beats investing skill. Let's begin!

Exam: Stocks 101

1. What is the concept of a fractional share in stock trading?

- It is a share that can be traded only in specific fractions

- It means buying only the most fractional part of a company's profits

- It allows you to invest in a piece of a stock that you can afford

1. Why do companies decide to go public?

- To avoid paying taxes

- To raise more money for growth and expansion

- To decrease their overall profitability

1. Why is the earnings season significant for stock traders?

- It's a holiday season when the stock market is closed

- It marks the period when stocks can't be traded

- Company earnings reports can significantly impact stock prices

Answer:

1. It allows you to invest in a piece of a stock that you can afford

1. To raise more money for growth and expansion

1. Company earnings reports can significantly impact stock prices

Chapter 14: Crypto

Lesson 1: Crypto Currencies Explained

Cryptocurrencies like Bitcoin and Ethereum have captured the world's attention, but not just because they've made some people millionaires overnight. Their true potential lies in the promise that they may revolutionize how we handle money altogether, challenging traditional banking and financial systems.

Despite some views that cryptocurrencies are a fleeting trend or a bubble bound to bust, their resilience suggests otherwise.

During the peak of the 2022 crypto bull run, the total market cap (money invested in all crypto) reached around $3 trillion.

To put that in perspective, here's that compared against the GDP of several major economies.

USA	23 T
China	16.8 T
Japan	5.1 T
Germany	4.2 T
India	3.1 T
Crypto Market Cap	3T
UK	2.9 T
France	2.8 T
Italy	2.3 T
Canada	2.1 T

This is crucial proof that critics tend to overlook. Such amounts of money simply don't vanish.

Market Dynamics and Potential

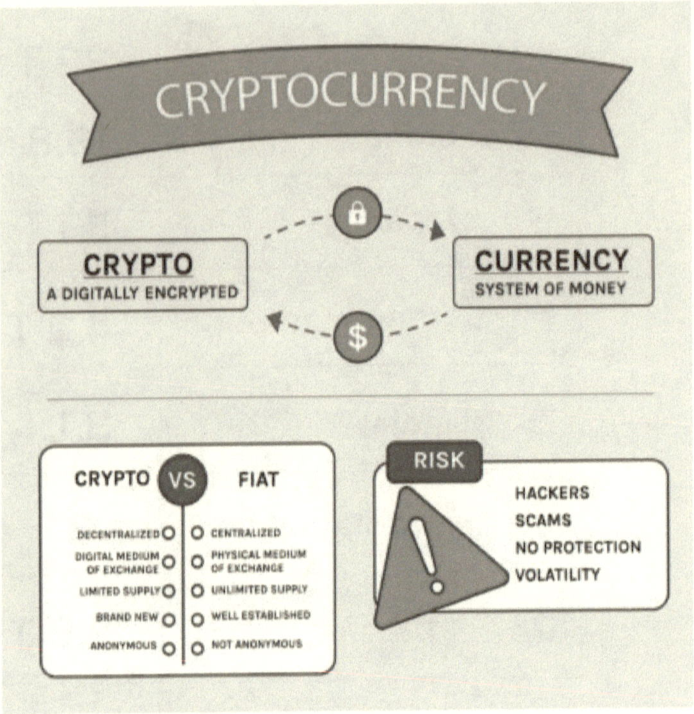

Trading in cryptocurrencies is marked by high volatility - prices can change by 5% in a single day, creating both risks and opportunities.

Also, the market never sleeps, operating 24/7, allowing traders from all over the world to participate whenever they choose.

However, we have to keep in mind that the crypto market is still a baby, which has both pros and cons.

Emerging Market: While traditional assets have decades of history, the crypto market is relatively young which means it is still evolving and subject to change.

Profit Potential: The emerging nature of the market suggests significant profit opportunities as interest and demand continue to grow.

Regulatory Challenges: As

cryptocurrencies grow, so does the likelihood of increased regulation. Governments are keen to control and oversee all financial systems.

Disruption: As disruptive technologies, cryptocurrencies often face opposition from established financial institutions, which can create barriers to widespread adoption.

Now let's look as some case studies of price fluctuations.

Lesson 2: Crypto Case Studies

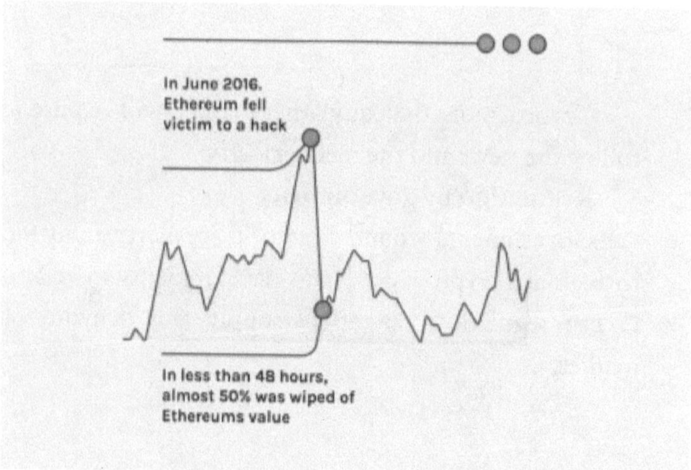

News in relation to a particular crypto asset can influence its supply and demand. Positive news, such as news that a certain crypto asset is seeing a higher level of adoption, can increase demand.

By contrast, negative news, such as news that a crypto exchange has been hacked, can reduce demand.

When a celebrity such as Elon Musk, so much as even mentions a crypto coin, it tends to experience a surge in demand and starts trending higher.

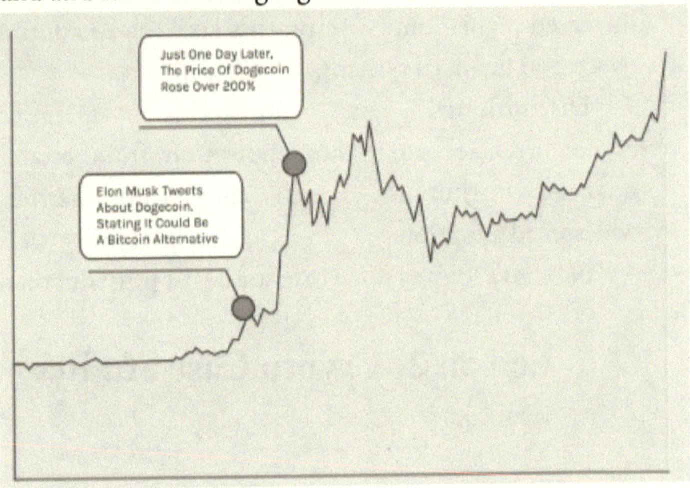

Crypto, more than any other market, will require you to follow the news and the media closely.

Regulation by governments

Governments around the world are increasingly looking to regulate crypto assets, and developments in relation to crypto regulation can affect supply and demand of the market.

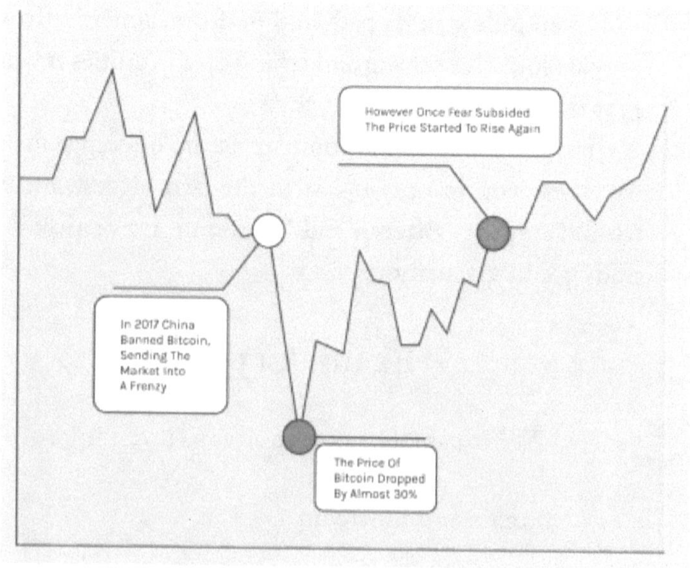

When China announced that it was blocking all websites related to cryptocurrency trading in early 2017, demand for Bitcoin and other cryptocurrencies fell significantly, pushing their prices down sharply.

The price of Bitcoin

Bitcoin (BTC) is the first, the most famous and the most valuable crypto asset and the market has a tendency to "follow the leader".

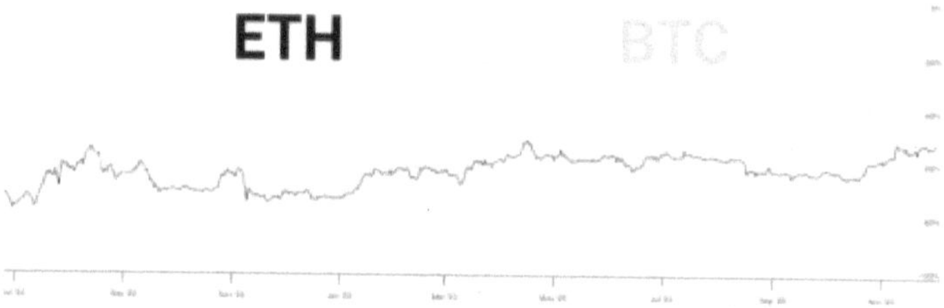

Historically, whenever **BTC** goes on a bull run or conversely crashes, **Ethereum** and **altcoins** (all other crypto)

will often follow in its path and perform similarly. This can provide lucrative buying and selling opportunities if you can spot the "followers" in advance.

However, due to the complex nature of crypto markets, we advise you to only invest in the two biggest and most trusted cryptos - **Bitcoin** and **Ethereum**. Leave **altcoins** for trading and speculation.

Exam: Crypto

1. Which are the safest choices to invest in?

- Bitcoin and Ethereum

- Altcoins

- Elon Musk coin

1. What's the key difference between cryptos and other assets?

- Cryptos can be traded in standard business hours

- Cryptos can be traded 24/7

- Crypto market has restricted trading hours

1. What tends to happen to other crypto assets as Bitcoin rises?

- Their price tends to fall
- There is no correlation
- Their price also tends to rise

Answer:

1. Bitcoin and Ethereum

1. Cryptos can be traded 24/7

1. Their price also tends to rise

Chapter 15: Forex

Lesson 1: Forex Explained

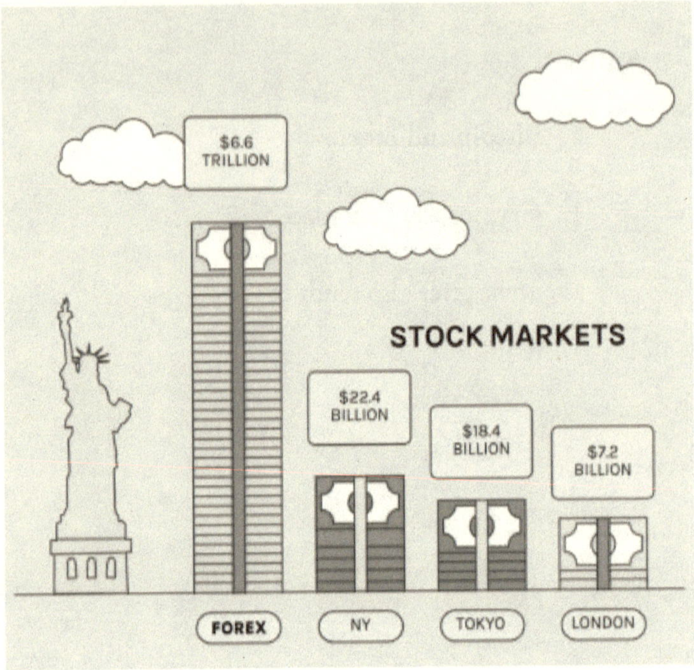

The greatest advantage Forex has over other assets is the fact that it can offer **great trading opportunities even in the most volatile times.**

When financial markets crash or the housing market recedes, or even during a health crisis such as Covid, there are always trades that can make you a profit because currencies are always traded in pairs. **When one falls, another rises.**

Currency Pairs

Currencies are always traded in pairs because you are always buying one currency and selling the other one. The pair quotes may seem confusing at first, but reading them is actually pretty straightforward.

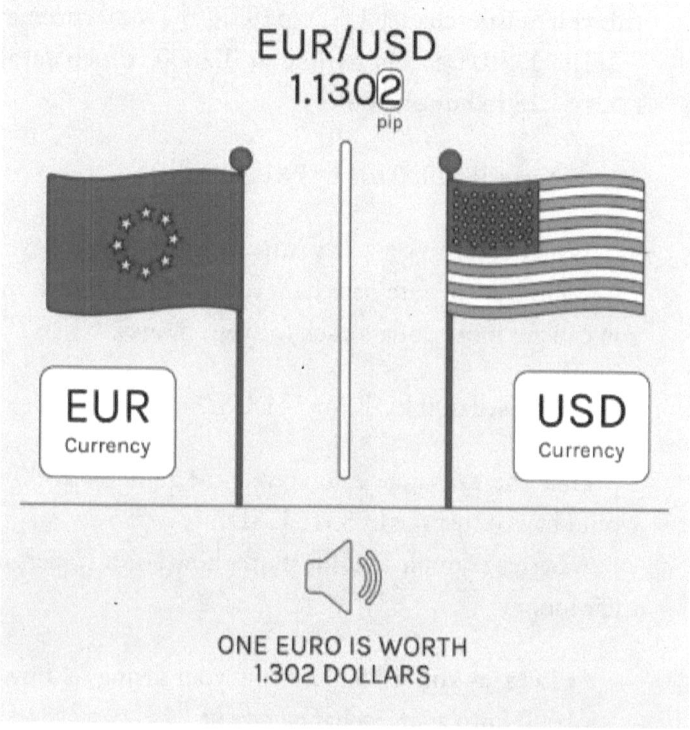

For example, the EUR/USD quote of 1.1302 shows how much one euro (EUR) is worth in US dollars (USD). This means that one euro is worth 1.1302 US dollars. **The base currency is always the first one listed in the pairing.**

Price Interest Point (PIP) represents the smallest change in a currency pair. Typically, it is the fourth decimal point, although many brokers quote using the fifth decimal.

However, the fifth decimal doesn't really affect the price as it changes really quickly.

Real World Forex Trade

Say you wanted to travel from the USA to Germany, for this you must exchange USD to EUR, the local currency.

The EUR/USD is trading at 1.2800, which means it takes $1.28 to buy one Euro.

- You sell $1000 to buy 781 euros.

When returning back to the USA, you still have 400 EUR left, but the rate has changed to 1.1700, which means you can get more dollars back for your money.

- You sell 400 EUR for 341 USD.

Had the exchange rate stayed the same (1.2800) you would have only bought $312 USD.

A better example that illustrates how Forex traders make their money:

- Let's say you sell $2000 from your savings to buy 1600 Euro at an exchange rate of 1.25.

- You hold the Euro for a month, and now the exchange rate has climbed to 1.35 after bullish data from the ECB.

- You sell 1600 Euro to buy $2160.

You profited $160 by just holding the currency while the exchange rate fluctuated.

In currency pairs that include the U.S. dollar, a pip is 1/10,000 of a dollar, whereas when the currency pair consists of the yen, a pip is 1/100 of a yen because the yen is closer in value to 1/100 of other major currencies.

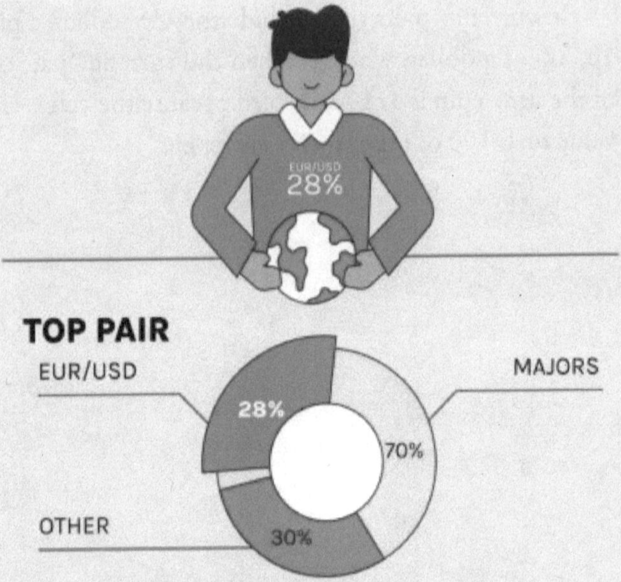

MAJORS

EUR/USD USD/CHF
GPB/USD EUR/JPY
USD/JPY USD/CAD

CROSSES

GBP/JPY AUD/CAD
EUR/GBP EUR/AUD
CAD/JPY NZD/JPY

EXOTICS

USD/TRY USD/MXN

The main task of a forex trader is to buy a currency pair when exchange rates are expected to rise in the future, then sell a currency pair when its exchange rate is expected to fall.

The next lesson will help you understand very important economic metrics that can predict these rises and falls.

Lesson 2: What Makes Currencies Fluctuate?

Fundamental news events drive nearly all price moves in the Forex market, but they're only reactions to them - not the cause. In other words, news alone doesn't change prices, **supply and demand does.**

Employment reports, manufacturing sales reports, and retail sales figures are some of the main points of attention for Forex traders. When these figures get released into the news cycle, the market reacts.

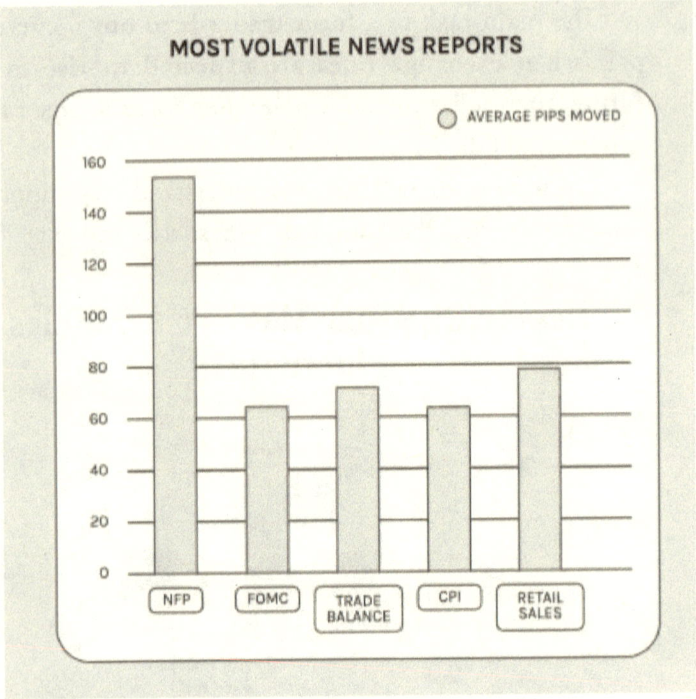

The basic formula for predicting trades

If a report comes out:

- very high (expectations< actual figure) - **BUY**
- very low (expectations>actual figure) - **SELL**

The exceptions being certain negative reports like jobless claims where the reverse is true. It's better that they're lower than expected.

The currency rates often start moving because of expectations and forecasts before the actual data comes out or the event occurs.

When it comes to determining which reports are the most important, the Economic Calendar is an invaluable tool, as it can also help you investigate the potential outcomes beforehand and better prepare yourself when it's time to buy or sell.

Here's what matters for FX traders

Interest Rates

Interest rates are controlled by the central bank (a government-appointed independent agency) that aims to maintain a healthy economy by controlling inflation (advanced economies like the US, UK, and Europe, target a 2% inflation rate, while emerging markets target a 4% - 6% inflation rate) levels. To achieve such objectives, central banks frequently adjust their interest rates.

Central Bank's Announcements

World Central Bank's Announcement Frequency

1. Reserve Bank of New Zealand (RBNZ) - NZD (New Zealand Dollar) - 8 times a year.

1. US Federal Reserve System (The Fed) - USD (U.S. Dollar) - 8 times a year.

1. Reserve Bank of Australia (RBA) - AUD (Australian Dollar) - 11 times a year.

1. Bank of Canada (BoC) - CAD (Canadian Dollar) - 8 times a year.

1. Bank of Japan (BoJ) - JPY (Japanese Yen) - 8 times a year.

1. Swiss National Bank (SNB) - CHF (Swiss Franc) - Quarterly.

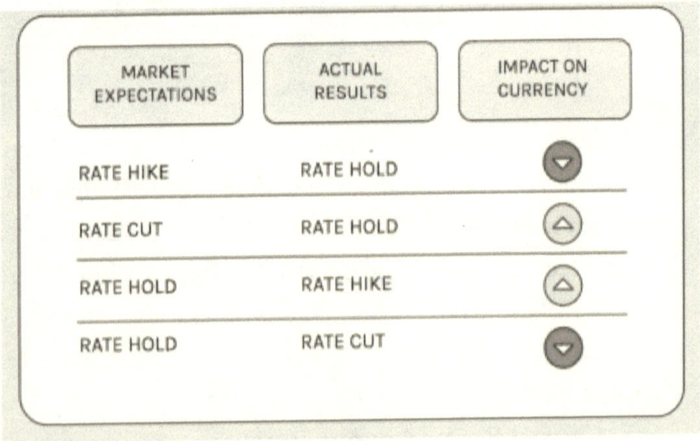

When interest rates are cut, it means that central banks want to warm the economy by urging people to spend money on loans rather than saving. Popular effects of interest rate cuts are:

- Increases inflation, decreases currency exchange rate.
- Cheaper cost of borrowing (ex: lower cost of mortgages or loans).
- Real estate prices rise due to increase in cheap credit.
- Exports become more competitive due to the lower currency exchange rate.

Obviously, if interest rates are increased, all effects are opposite.

Quantitative Easing (QE)

During and after recessions, such as the financial crisis of 2008-2009 and the Covid-19 recession, interest rate cuts alone weren't powerful enough to recover an economy. This was when central banks announced Quantitative Easing, supplying commercial banks with ultra-cheap funds, which they can pass on (lend) to businesses, homeowners and individuals to stimulate economic growth.

In other words, with QE programs central banks print new money, thus increasing its supply out of thin air. Historically, forecasts of QE have sent currency values down.

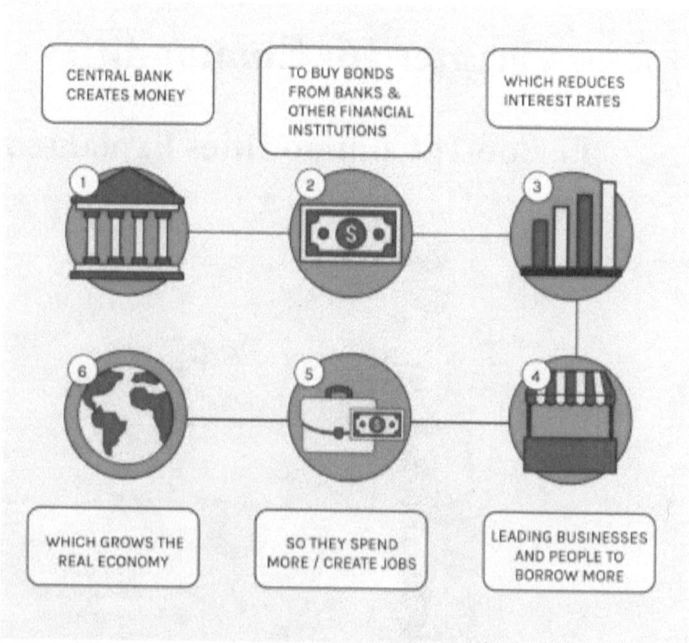

If you become a proficient Forex trader, it will give you an advantage in all other markets as well. You will have a better understanding of economics, politics and the dynamic between buyers and sellers that ultimately makes trading profitable.

Chapter 16: Commodities

Lesson 1: Commodities Explained

The commodity is the oldest financial instrument. Almost as old as human civilization itself.

Historical evidence suggests that rice might have been the 1st traded commodity, around 6,000 years ago.

A commodity is either grown or produced naturally in the environment. Examples of commodities include gold, cotton, wheat, cattle, lumber, oil, natural gas and sugar. The most traded, thus having the highest liquidity, are oil, gold and silver.

Metal prices are not only important to manufacturers and end-users but have long been used as a tool for monitoring economic and market conditions.

The uncertainty benchmark

If the economic future is uncertain, the price of gold tends to rise. The opposite is true if the economic outlook is bright and stable.

It happens because gold retains its physical value even in times of economic uncertainty and market turmoil. Therefore it is considered a **safe-haven** asset.

There will always be a need for commodities

Large businesses and companies need commodities to operate - clothing manufacturers require cotton, supermarkets and restaurants need cattle and construction companies need lumber. And the trucks transporting them will need fuel, largely made from oil.

Hence there will always be a demand for raw materials.

Trading commodities trough stocks

It is possible for you to participate in the global commodity trade by investing in a stock that works within the industry. For example, you could buy an oil drilling company. In theory, should oil prices go up, the company should be more profitable, and that would be reflected as an increase in its share price.

If forecasts predict a stellar season for growing crops, you could invest in an agriculture business to profit from increased wheat production. The added bonus of trading commodities indirectly is that you aren't just betting on the underlying commodity. Should it be a year of drought and less grain produced the company could have a great management that figures out ways to make money otherwise.

Naturally, this goes both ways - a great performing commodity doesn't necessarily mean the business is running successfully and profits consistently. Although it's arguably simpler to buy, hold and trade commodity stocks instead of commodities, careful research should be done before each and every trade.

Forex and commodity correlation

By now you should understand that the financial markets are intertwined in many ways, especially Forex pairs and the price of certain commodities.

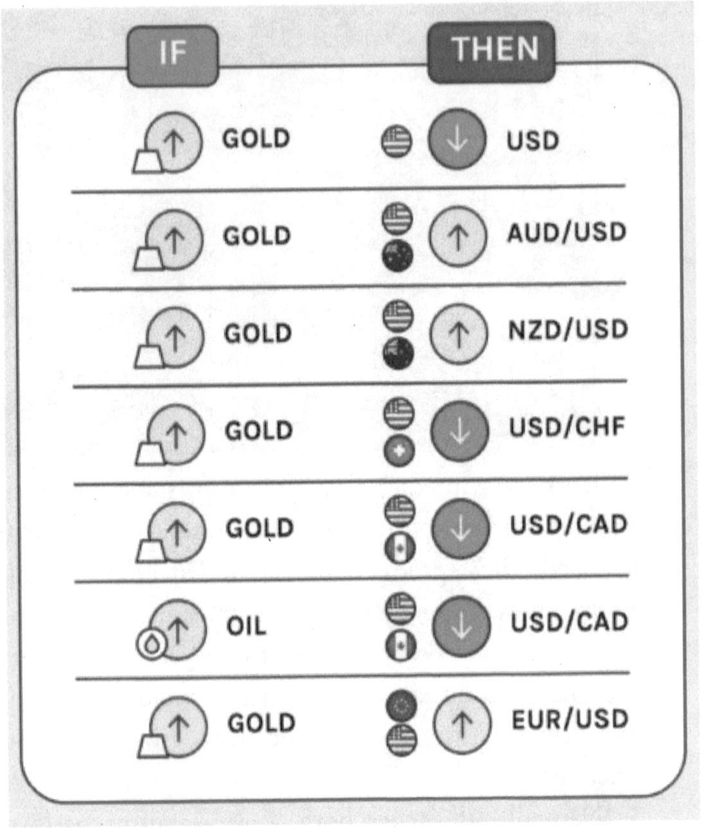

Be aware that this is just a rough guideline and there may be exceptions depending on other market conditions. The next lesson will teach you the most important triggers for commodity prices.

Lesson 2: Commodity Price Fluctuations

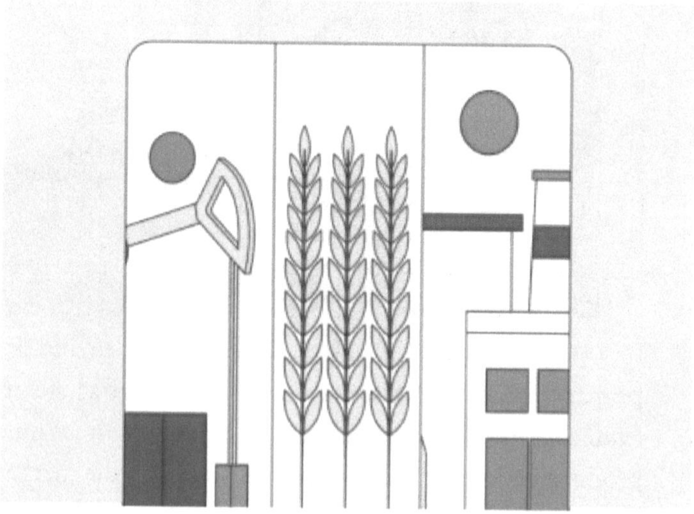

Commodities are known to be a riskier investment because their market supply and demand is impacted by uncertainties that are difficult or impossible to predict.

However, once these uncertainties happen, you can be almost sure of where the price will go. Here are some factors to consider.

Physical supply and demand

As with all asset classes, supply and demand is the primary force that moves the price, and nowhere it's as evident as is with commodities. A balance of how much is produced and how much is needed stabilizes the markets. A lack of balance sends the price on a trend.

Knowing the production data from major producing nations is the bread and butter for a commodity trader. For example, Chile for Copper, Russia for Nickel and the OPEC+ Group for oil.

The global output of a raw material cannot immediately meet a sudden surge in demand. Coal mines cannot merely increase production levels overnight, and consumers are incapable of always replacing one metal with another based on price fluctuations.

Mother Nature

Weather and natural disasters around the world often affect the prices in all related markets.

- Chile suffered a large earthquake in 2010 that wrecked the copper mining industry by shutting down approximately 20% of production capacity, raising global copper prices bv 3.45%.

- The 2005 Hurricane Katrina swept across the southern United States, shutting down about 24% of annual oil production. Oil prices rose to a twenty-year high, and US gas prices shot up by 45 cents and stayed elevated for two months.

Stay up to date with critical natural events and you will find many profitable trading opportunities.

Geopolitics

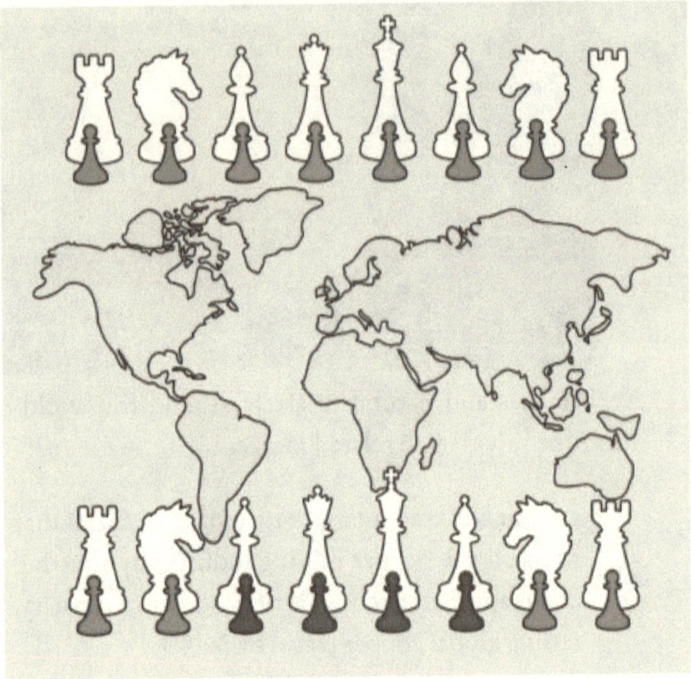

Politics in specific regions can impact the price of commodities extracted or produced in those regions.

- When extremist affiliates attacked Saudi Arabia's oil processing facilities in September 2019, the country's oil production was cut in half from 9.8 to about 4.1 million barrels of oil a day. Losing about 5% of global production meant a 20% price rise for oil, one of the largest increases in history.

Copper production is concentrated over a few regions, with the top mines providing 40% of global supply. Workers striking against copper-producing mines can be common from time to time. This has a considerable impact on copper prices.

Sanctions on Russia, and tarrifs on Chinese imports and exports, two commodity superpowers, have caused increased volatility for not just every commodity but global trade as a whole.

Pay attention to localized events and geopolitics as a whole when speculating on commodity prices.

Before heading to commodity charts, let's take a test!

Exam: Commodities

1. How to trade the commodity market indirectly?

- Buying stocks of companies in the commodity industry

- Trading in foreign exchange markets

- Investing in combine harvester

1. Which description best fits a commodity?

- A company which harvests grain

- Natural earth resources

- Services used to transport oil

1. Which factor is a major influence on the price of commodities?

- The season in which the commodity is processed

- Supply and demand imbalances

- The popularity of the commodity in media

Answer:

1. Buying stocks of companies in the commodity industry

1. Natural earth resources

1. Supply and demand imbalances

Chapter 17: Taxes

Lesson: Stay Rich, Stay Legal

Making money in the markets is fun and exciting. So much so, that most new traders tend to overlook an important aspect that comes with all the fun - paying taxes.

What a bummer

Trading and taxes go hand in hand, but don't let that bring you down! Here are some positive points to help you navigate the world of trading taxes:

- **Progressive tax systems are often used, meaning that small traders are not taxed excessively, and sometimes not at all.**

- Being sure that your earnings are legally yours is the ultimate goal of trading for autonomy and freedom.

- Tax types and amounts vary by country and income level, but generally are based on net profit after expenses.

Remember, paying taxes means you are contributing to society. Stay positive and stay legal! Now let's get into some details for certain countries.

USA:

- Traders need to report their gains and losses on their tax returns, using IRS Form 8949 and Schedule D.

- Short-term capital gains (assets held for less than one year are taxed at ordinary income tax rates, which range from 10% to 37% depending on income level.

- Long-term capital gains (assets held for more than one year) are taxed at lower rates, ranging from 0% to 20% depending on income level.

- **Traders can also deduct certain trading expenses, such as brokerage fees and software subscriptions, as business expenses on Schedule C.**

- Traders who trade frequently and with large amounts may be considered "**trader tax status**" and may be able to deduct additional expenses, such as home office expenses and education expenses.

Remember that each trader has unique circumstances and the rules might change over time. It's best to contact the **Internal Revenue Service (IRS)**, to be 100% sure.

United Kingdom:

Trading taxes are regulated by the Income Tax Act, which states that you need to pay taxes on your profits from trading activities.

Tax returns must be filed on or before January 31st of each year.

The tax you pay depends on the type of trading you do and your overall earnings.

There are three taxes that might apply to you if you're a regular trader (i.e., you make more than 4 trades in 5 days).

Income tax

This is a tax on your overall income, which includes your trading profits.

The rate varies based on how much you earn, with the basic rate at 20% and the higher rate at 40%.

National Insurance Contributions

These are mandatory for self-employed individuals, like professional traders. If you're self-employed and your profits are £12,570 or more a year, you usually pay Class 2 and Class 4 National Insurance rates.

- Class 2 - £3.45 a week.

- Class 4 - 9% on profits between £12,570 and £50,270.

- 2% on profits over £50,270.

Capital gains tax (CGT)

This applies when you sell an asset (like a stock) and make a profit above £6,000. The capital gains tax rates are 10% (basic rate) and 20% (higher rate). Your overall earnings determine which rate is used.

Remember that each trader has unique circumstances and the rules might change over time. It's best to contact the **HM Revenue and Customs,** to be 100% sure.

Germany:

In Germany, when you make money from selling financial investments like stocks, you have to pay a flat tax rate of 25%, plus an extra 5.5% solidarity surcharge.

This means you'll pay a total of 26.375% tax from your profits. Essentially, if you make €100 in profit, €26.37 will be paid as tax. But there's good news for beginner traders, you get a tax-free allowance of €1000 per year for all your financial investment income. Even better if you're married, then the allowance is doubled.

The same tax rate applies to stock dividends.

Remember that each trader has unique circumstances and the rules might change over time. It's best to contact the **Federal Central Tax Office (Bundeszentralamt für Steuern)**, to be 100% sure.

Australia:

Aussie traders are subject to **capital gains tax (CGT).** Here are some key points to keep in mind:

- CGT is calculated on the profit you make only when you sell an asset.

- The CGT rate depends on your income and the length of time you've held the asset. If it's less than 12 months, you'll be taxed at your marginal income tax rate. If you've held the asset for more than 12 months, you'll be taxed at a discounted rate - 50% of your marginal income tax rate.

- There is a tax-free limit of $10,000 for CGT. This means if your total gains for the year are under $10,000, you don't have to pay any CGT.

- If you lose money, the losses can offset any capital gains you've made in the same financial year. Which means you have to pay less tax on your gains.

Since each trader has unique circumstances, and the rules might change with time, it's best to contact the **Australian Taxation Office (ATO)** to be 100% sure.

France:

The French have made it simple: Unless you're using some specific account types (which you wouldn't do for regular trading), all gains are subjected to the "**Prélèvement Forfaitaire Unique" (PFU).**

It's a 30% flat tax on every gain. Say in a year, you make €6000, but lose €2000. You'd have a €4000 gain which would be taxed 30%.

(€4000 * 0.3) = €1200 to the government.

Remember that each trader has unique circumstances and the rules might change over time. It's best to contact the **France - Tax Adminstration** (impouts.gouv.fr), to be 100% sure.

Italy:

Traders in Italy are subject to a capital gains tax on the profits made from the sale of financial instruments such as stocks, bonds, and derivatives. The tax rate is 26% and is applied to the difference between the purchase price and the selling price. However, if the financial instruments are held for more than 12 months, the tax rate drops to 12.5%.

Additionally, traders must pay a financial transaction tax on purchases of certain financial instruments, including stocks and derivatives.

The rate of this tax varies depending on the type of instrument and can range from 0.1% to 0.2%.

Remember that each trader has unique circumstances and the rules might change over time. It's best to contact the **Agenzia delle Entrate,** to be 100% sure.

Afterword

As you turn the final pages of Win More, Trade Better – A Practical Guide to Trading and Investing, I hope this book has given you not only a deeper understanding of the markets but also the confidence to approach trading and investing with a disciplined and strategic mindset.

The financial markets are ever-evolving, shaped by economic forces, technological advancements, and shifting investor sentiment. While strategies and techniques will adapt over time, the fundamental principles of risk management, patience, and continuous learning will always remain relevant.

Success in trading and investing is not about chasing quick profits or following the latest trends blindly - it's about developing a structured approach, maintaining emotional discipline, and refining your skills with each trade. The greatest traders and investors are lifelong students of the market, constantly learning from their successes and, more importantly, from their setbacks.

As you apply the lessons from this book, remember that consistency and adaptability are key. No single strategy works forever, and no investor wins every trade. The goal is to make informed decisions, manage risk effectively, and steadily grow your capital over time.

Thank you for allowing me to be part of your trading and investing journey. I encourage you to keep learning, stay disciplined, and embrace the process. The markets will always present opportunities - your success will depend on how well you prepare and execute.

Wishing you prosperity and wisdom in your trading and investing endeavors.

Andy Hai Dinh

Don't miss out!

Visit the website below and you can sign up to receive emails whenever Andy Hai Dinh publishes a new book. There's no charge and no obligation.

https://books2read.com/r/B-A-YYJBB-RDHCG

Did you love *WIN MORE, TRADE BETTER - A Practical Guide to Trading and Investing*? Then you should read *A Beginner's Guide to Trading - Stock and Forex Technical Analysis*[1] by Andy Hai Dinh!

[2]

Welcome to "A Beginner's Guide to Trading - Stock and Forex Technical Analysis". Whether you're looking to build a new income stream, grow your wealth, or simply gain a deeper understanding of financial markets, this book is designed to help you navigate the world of trading with confidence.

---

1. https://books2read.com/u/mKk7AE

2. https://books2read.com/u/mKk7AE

The stock and forex markets offer incredible opportunities, but they can also be overwhelming for beginners. With countless strategies, indicators, and data points to consider, knowing where to start is often the biggest challenge. That is where technical analysis comes in. By learning how to read price charts, recognize patterns, and interpret market trends, you'll be able to make informed trading decisions without getting lost in the noise of economic reports and news headlines.

This guide is structured to take you step by step through the fundamentals of technical analysis. You'll learn about key concepts like support and resistance, trendlines, candlestick patterns, and popular indicators such as moving averages and RSI. More importantly, you will discover how to apply these tools to both stock and forex markets, helping you develop a practical approach to trading.

No matter your experience level, this book will equip you with the essential knowledge to begin your trading journey. The goal isn't just to teach you theory but to help you develop a trader's mindset - one that balances analysis, risk management, and discipline.

By the time you finish reading this book, you will have a solid foundation in technical analysis and a clear path forward in your trading journey. Let's get started!

Read more at https://pensight.com/x/lona.

Also by Andy Hai Dinh

ACRYLIC AND DIPPING POWDER - Product Knowledge and Applications
The Nail technician's Career Guide
A Beginner's Guide to Trading - Stock and Forex Technical Analysis
WIN MORE, TRADE BETTER - A Practical Guide to Trading and Investing

Watch for more at https://pensight.com/x/lona.

www.ingramcontent.com/pod-product-compliance
Lightning Source LLC
LaVergne TN
LVHW090303210926
848480LV00001B/115
9798230501367